AF521786

Algerian Imprints

Ethical Space in the Work of
ASSIA DJEBAR and HÉLÈNE CIXOUS

Brigitte Weltman-Aron

Columbia University Press *New York*

Columbia University Press
Publishers Since 1893
New York Chichester, West Sussex
cup.columbia.edu

Library of Congress Cataloging-in-Publication Data
Weltman-Aron, Brigitte, 1961–
Algerian imprints: ethical space in the work of Assia Djebar and Hélène Cixous / Brigitte Weltman-Aron.
pages cm
Includes bibliographical references and index.
ISBN 978-0-231-17256-1 (cloth: alk. paper) — ISBN 978-0-231-53987-6 (e-book)
1. Djebar, Assia, 1936—Criticism and interpretation. 2. Cixous, Hélène, 1937—Criticism and interpretation. 3. Women and literature—Algeria. 4. Politics and literature—Algeria. I. Title.

PQ3989.2.D57Z94 2015
843'.914—dc23

2014042955

Columbia University Press books are printed on permanent and durable acid-free paper.
This book is printed on paper with recycled content.
Printed in the United States of America

c 10 9 8 7 6 5 4 3 2 1

COVER DESIGN: Milenda Nan Ok Lee

For Dragan

In memory of Ghislaine

Contents

Acknowledgments

This book could not have been written without the generous help of many colleagues and friends. I am profoundly grateful to Deborah Amberson and Alioune Sow for their invaluable comments and lucid suggestions for revisions and their unfailing support at various stages of writing this book. I am also indebted to those who invited me to present my work about Hélène Cixous or Assia Djebar and to the editors who included me in their projects: Ralph Albanese and M. Martin Guiney, Isabelle Cata, Michael Du Plessis, Florence Fix, Bernadette Fort, Catherine Jones, Jonathan Judaken, Peggy Kamuf, Laurence Le Diagon-Jacquin, Eric Prenowitz, Najib Redouane, Frédéric Regard, Martine Reid, Anna Rocca, Marta Segarra, Georges Van den Abbeele, Samuel Weber, and David Wills. Grateful acknowledgment is made to the University of Memphis and the University of Florida for awarding me internal grants that helped me complete this book. I particularly wish to thank the Department of Languages, Literatures and Cultures at the University of Florida and Mary Watt for their support of this project. In preparing the manuscript for publication, I benefited from the experience and guidance of Wendy Lochner, Christine Dunbar, and Susan Pensak, and I thank the three of them for their kindness and their patience. It is my pleasure to thank the friends and family members who were dedicated to my work: Dragan Kujundžić, who provided constant feedback and encouragement, as well as Shifra Armon, Tace Hedrick, Anna Klobucka, William Little, Sarra Tlili, Bénédicte and Marcel Weltman-Aron. I am particularly grateful to Réda Bensmaïa, Verena

Conley, Hafid Gafaïti, and Mildred Mortimer, for their kindness to me, as well as their resourcefulness and expertise. Doris Kadish, Jennifer Wagner-Lawlor, and Leonard Lawlor have been for many years friends and colleagues of extraordinary generosity and assistance to me.

The writings of Hélène Cixous and Assia Djebar have accompanied me closely for many years. I am deeply grateful to Hélène Cixous for her invariable kindness and generosity. The last stages of this book's production were saddened by news of the death of Assia Djebar. I never had the opportunity to meet her but I am thankful to have had the chance to read her.

Material for three chapters of *Algerian Imprints* was previously published and appears here in revised and expanded form. Chapter 2 appeared as "The Pedagogy of Colonial Algeria: Djebar, Cixous, Derrida," in "French Education Fifty Years Later," ed. Mortimer Martin Guiney and Ralph Albanese, *Yale French Studies* 113 (2008): 132–46. Chapter 3 appeared as "Assia Djebar's *qalam*: The Poetics of the Trace in Postcolonial Algeria," in "Naming Race, Naming Racisms," ed. Jonathan Judaken, *Patterns of Prejudice* 42, nos. 4/5 (September/December 2008): 489–507, reprinted in Jonathan Judaken, ed., *Naming Race, Naming Racisms*, 155–73 (New York: Routledge, 2009). Chapter 5 appeared as "La Sirène résiste: Figures d'Ulysse chez Assia Djebar," in "Ulysse1/2," ed. Laurence Le Diagon-Jacquin, *Le Paon d'Héra* 9 (December 2012): 175–85. I thank the journals and editors for granting me permission to reprint the essays.

Introduction

Dissensus; or The Political in the Writings of Djebar and Cixous

On July 5, 1962, following on 132 years of French colonization, Algeria became independent after a long war. Relations between France and Algeria remain fraught to this day, in particular because of conflicting interpretations regarding their common history and its legacy. Throughout their diverse, but mostly literary works about Algeria, Assia Djebar and Hélène Cixous, two writers who were born respectively in 1936 and 1937 and grew up in French Algeria, locate and represent signs of conflict and enmity; *Algerian Imprints* argues that Djebar and Cixous evoke or inscribe discordant histories within their works so as to reappraise the political on the very basis of dissensus, a term that designates antagonism within a discourse or indicates dissent, nonconformity with predominant views in a community. Incidentally, the use of this word, according to the *Merriam-Webster's Dictionary,* is first attested in 1962, the year of Algerian independence. In *Experimental Nations,* Réda Bensmaïa rightly objects to political interpretations that avoid the examination of the literariness of writings from the Maghreb and ignore the diversity of their literary strategies.[1] Thus, while focusing on the elaboration of an ethical/political space in Djebar's and Cixous's works, I also perform a close reading and analyze the poetics of their major works about Algeria, paying attention to the singularity of each author's project. In that respect, while I agree with critics who point out that some transformations are discernible over time in these prolific writers' corpuses, I generally emphasize instead the remarkable political coherence of each oeuvre, calling on several texts to bring to light the evidence of profound continuities.[2] Writing about Cixous's first book, Jacques Derrida remarked that "there was already everything in *Prénom de Dieu.*" Coherence has been less often attributed to Djebar's work; the interpretation of those who divide Djebar's writings into periods being sometimes linked to a supposed distinction between works that would be fictional and others that would be autobiographical, a position I will dispute in the next chapter.[3]

Most works by Assia Djebar and Hélène Cixous have been translated into English, and they have long attracted critical attention in the United States, in particular because of their original poetics but also because of their groundbreaking discussion of sexual difference (especially in the case of Cixous), as well as for their examination of contemporary political issues inside and outside of Algeria. I have gratefully relied on and referred to existing translations when they are available, and my occasional silent modifications are intended to render the motifs I analyze in their texts as closely as possible to the original French. There are several monographs entirely devoted to each, and other studies analyzing two or more francophone writers may include among them a discussion of either Djebar or Cixous. Yet bringing these two writers together in one study, as is done in this book, has rarely, if ever, been undertaken by critics. Alison Rice is a notable exception, but she encompasses her analyses of their works within a larger group of Maghrebian authors, while Mireille Calle-Gruber's separate publications about Cixous or Djebar may point to the recognition of a proximity between the oeuvre of the two writers, which, to my knowledge, she has not explicitly brought up; thus Liana Babayan may well have been the first author to have focused exclusively on Djebar and Cixous in her dissertation.[4]

It should also be noted that Cixous and Djebar generally do not refer to each other's works.[5] Even critics who analyze both authors in the same study shed light on their divergences, which is legitimate when discussing the specific poetics of each. However, without minimizing stylistic differences between Djebar and Cixous, *Algerian Imprints* insists on a congruence between them that has not been noted and studied previously in such detail. Cixous's inquiry is steeped in her formative encounter with exclusion or grudging integration while growing up Jewish in French Algeria; Djebar reflects on the separation colonization effected between "French" and "Arabs," self and other, but she consistently shows that the self does not simply apprehend itself along one side of that divisive limit, but is rather traversed by differences. *Algerian Imprints* contends that Cixous's and Djebar's writings consistently reclaim, for ethical/political purposes, imposed demarcations and unconscious disjunctions that are first experienced existentially, or rather textually, by the narrators or protagonists of their fictions. Such a position stems from these writers' analysis of ascribed partitions within colonized Algeria, triggering in each a dual defiance of the limit in general, as that which excludes and separates, on the one hand, and as the problematic fusion of a community of insiders, on the other. Thus, with a suspicion of what is construed as the intrinsic and the foreign, a demarcation that commands several other oppositions, including spatial divisions, Djebar and Cixous foreground multiple internal borders (Djebar talks, for instance, of the permanence of several territories in Algerian memory), or, conversely, nullify the boundary between inside and outside through a spatial interrogation of difference (Cixous writes for example that to be inside is also to be outside, in the sense that a community may foster other forms of marginalization or be divided from within along lines it ignores or represses). This reappraisal is mostly staged through fictional scenes that do not simply reproduce or mimic preexisting familial or sociopolitical conditions, but significantly imagine and alter them. In the first part of the book and in the conclusion, I discuss Djebar and Cixous together within the same chapter and bring to the fore their proximity in thinking through the political through the examination of similar motifs or identical thematic scenes of apprenticeship in both authors. In contrast, in parts 2 and 3 one chapter is devoted to each writer in turn, and the comparison between the two authors rests on the different paths their reflection takes in approaching the same issue (language and writing in part 2 and women and war in part 3). Yet each chapter exposes sequentially as well what turns out to be converging assessments of the political. In sum, my demonstration of Djebar's and Cixous's political and ethical proximity is coupled with a sustained engagement with each author's poetics and texts about Algeria; but my general purpose is to determine the ways in which their configuration of and response to the political are comparable in spite of and through their different textual strategies. This, I claim, is the novelty of my book, which teases out, through differences, the common mapping out of the political in their "Algerian imprints."

While critical studies devoted to Djebar or Cixous have mostly focused on each writer's poetics, which is understandable given the scope of their respective fictional corpus, others have also examined these writers' denunciation of the persistence of inequities and their poetical/political elaboration of resistance as well as of conditions for bringing about the possibility of reparation and justice.[6] The former interpreters of Djebar and Cixous I have most capitalized on are those who analyze each writer's reflection on language and gender as a reconceptualization of the political, and I agree with their conclusions that for both authors the issue is to reframe the Algerian space so as to bring out disregarded cultural and political potentialities. But *Algerian Imprints* also differs from these earlier studies by focusing on a recurring gesture on the part of Cixous and Djebar, which consists *not in deploring but in affirming* the chance for thinking afforded by marginalization, exclusion, expropriation. I argue here that on that affirmation is built their reappraisal of the political. The title of Djebar's last book, *Nulle part dans la maison de mon père* (Nowhere in my father's house) and Cixous's claim in her essay "My Algeriance" of being "perfectly at home, nowhere" provide a good example of the stance that I analyze in *Algerian Imprints*.[7] Such statements do not denote regret, nostalgia, and suffering, but already perform an ethical mode of inhabitation of Algeria against which these writers' political strategy is deployed. In that respect, Djebar's works challenge the viability of returning to a point of origin—whether it is construed as home, language, self—while being disentangled from the pathos of exile; but they also ask the question of *where* to be, focusing on dislocation or fleeting points of contact as a way out of illusory identifications. As for Cixous, who refers to scenes of expulsion as "the very form . . . of our relationship to the world," she consistently writes about departing "so as not to arrive," anchoring responsibility in the figure of the *arrivante de toujours*, her phrase for a position of nonappropriation of and nonbelonging in a place. That figure retains the ethical dimension of uprootedness, claims only to visit or pass through the land or home of others, and puts into question the stance of the privileged insider.[8]

Some critics point out the lack of a concretely exposed political program by each writer; I argue on the contrary that the elusiveness of the political delineation, which I insist is nevertheless discernible, corresponds to an ethical motive. Likewise, studies on postcolonial Algerian writers often emphasize the ways in which colonialism still haunts political participants today and establish that such traumas are reflected in contemporary fiction.[9] The specificity of my approach consists in focusing on the ways in which the reflection about colonized Algeria on the part of Djebar and Cixous leads each to elaborate strategies other than the confirming or aesthetizing of victimization, which does not mean denying the inequalities of colonization. *Algerian Imprints* insists on an affirmative thinking in Djebar and Cixous, whose delineation of the political aims to preserve a space for difference informed by an experience of marginalization and nonbelonging. In that respect at least, there is a definite coincidence between the two writers, which is by no means widespread in that generation of writers born in French Algeria.

This book thus investigates Cixous's and Djebar's writings as exemplary of a philosophical interrogation of the political that takes into account the complicity between the political and the symbolic, a conjunction that is both oppressive and enabling. Their works do not merely operate outside a historical context but respond to it explicitly. I locate the specificity of their assessment of the political within a network of other evaluations with which they engage at times openly in dialogue. Philosophers who are juxtaposed to and contribute to this thinking in *Algerian Imprints* are, among others, Jacques Derrida, also born in Algeria, who wrote several essays on Cixous (among them *H.C. for Life . . .* , and *Geneses, Genealogies, Genres, and Genius*), and whose thinking of difference and of the racialized other's exclusion from the properness and property of language is crucial to both Cixous and Djebar; Jean-François Lyotard, whose elaboration of "phrases in dispute" in *The Differend* is related to Djebar's reflection on language; and Emmanuel Levinas, whose thought on hospitality (for example in *Totality and Infinity*) is linked to Cixous's own reflection on invitation and visitation. Albdelkebir Khatibi and Kateb Yacine have extensively discussed the situation of the Maghrebian writer impacted by French colonization, which informs their reflection on the legitimacy of their own writing project. *Algerian Imprints* also puts Djebar's and Cixous's works in dialogue with colonial and postcolonial historians of Algeria, such as Benjamin Stora, Pierre Nora, and Mohammed Harbi, as well as with militant critics, such as Frantz Fanon and Djamila Amrane-Minne, among others, whose polemical writings provide the background for Djebar's and Cixous's own provocative positions about Algeria. My purpose is to shed light on the ways in which the issue under examination in each chapter has been framed by authors other than Cixous and Djebar, and not to recall a national history, which would be insufficient to explain why both writers call for existential and political relations that do not simply reflect or contradict preexisting social polities. Recalling other thinkers' take on the issue Djebar and Cixous write about helps me isolate the consistency of their responses by opposing them to other critical and artistic positions.

Each part of *Algerian Imprints* consists of two chapters. The first opens with a chapter that explores Djebar's and Cixous's approaches to rethinking spatiality by examining scenes in which the body's ascription to a place becomes untenable. Both invest in a writing of the body, not only in the sense theorized by Cixous, which endows writing with shedding light on and performing alternatives to what has been politically and sexually repressed. Dislocation of the body and of the site is shown to be ascertained and taken up by Djebar and Cixous, that is to say, not only denounced but upheld as a paradoxical model of spatial inscription with positive political virtualities envisioned similarly by both authors. After they represent a form of interdiction for a girl to ride a bicycle (an example of a scene of apprenticeship found in both), their ensuing reflection on the female body is linked to a reassessment of its ties with the site and, by extension, with the political body. This chapter also addresses the issue of the genre of Djebar's and Cixous's works, which deliberately resist classification by straddling several, thus invalidating the solidity of their separation.

Chapter 2 first contextualizes access to education in French Algeria. The narratives written by Cixous and Djebar reopen the archive of colonial education and investigate its legacy. In a world posited as cut in two ("Arabs" and "French"), other differentiations tend to be silenced. Cixous emphasizes both the minimal admission of Muslims *and* the contested inclusion of Jews in colonial school. Yet she argues that it was the very exclusionary school that provided openings and fostered resistance. Exposure to the profound contradictions experienced at school as they stood for the inequalities of French Algeria anchors the political/ethical interpretation of Algerian scenes in Cixous. Djebar, who was one of a small number of Algerian girls attending school, has also remarked that colonial partitions were reiterated within the school; yet school was at the same time one of the few places in which Algerians and Europeans could share and contest a territory. Djebar's writings are especially mobilized by instances in which imposed separations and attachments do not quite succeed in strictly opposing one group to the other. Each author responds to the partitions enacted by colonial school and pedagogy: while its inequities are underscored, colonial school appears as a contradictory space that provides partial openings and enhances different competing memories. For both Djebar and Cixous, the literary space they started approaching at school exemplifies the calling into question of cultural and linguistic boundaries because of its distance from the reproduction of the real or the given, thus affirming and imagining possibilities of other political configurations.

I investigate the implication of that conclusion in part 2, which focuses on the relation of Djebar (in chapter 3) and of Cixous (in chapter 4) to a politics and a poetics of language that enact this position. In these two chapters each writer is shown to assess the issue of language and writing, not through the lens of a national language or a mother tongue but as a cluster of languages that advances the evaluation of Algeria as heterogeneous plurality and asserts the political benefits of suspending allegiance and identification. Djebar formulates a number of contradictions inherent in writing in French, but she also assesses Algeria as a locus in which multilingualism has had a long history. Former examples in the Maghreb of an at least dual but mostly multiple mode of relation to language enact for Djebar a felicitous cultural possibility of linguistic plurality. Examining Derrida's notion of "ex-appropriation" (rather than "alienation"), Lyotard's elaboration of the *differend* (a tool for comprehending injustice caused by the lack of a common idiom), and the Moroccan writer Khatibi's investigation of bilingualism helps distinguish Djebar's own position with respect to language. Through her use of the term *qalam,* an Arabic word that can be relatively understood in French as *calame* (a quill or writing instrument), I argue that Djebar brings together Arabic and French so as to promote a paradoxical recognition at the time when the foreign is encountered or the recognition of the self in the location of the other. She writes about what remains elusive and radically defies presentation by focusing on vanishing multilingual inscriptions as a model for the Algerian writer, who is not asked to restitute or reconstruct the past before and during colonization, but to explain why it is challenging or impossible to recall or present it. From that model are derived the political benefits of suspending identification.

In chapter 4 Cixous is shown recalling the gradual deprivation of the Algerian Jews' mother tongue (Judeo-Arabic) during French colonization and displacing the consideration of speaking a so-called maternal language onto that of writing in another tongue resonating with more than one language (including Arabic). One of her approaches to the issue of the mother tongue consists in confronting it with the position of the mother, which she defines as that which resists separation, the relation to the mother being also linked in her view to her relation to Algeria. Emphasizing disappearance and loss, she characteristically reflects on the ways in which to maintain in writing a memory of disconnections and ruptures that could be upheld differently through ethical models of respect, distance, and separation. What she calls the language of the poets is Cixous's response to the lack of an authorized mother tongue. On the one hand, she attributes to poets the faculty of writing the unthought of the political; on the other hand, fiction exemplifies untenable inhabitation. For Cixous, fiction is endowed with the potential of altering the political because of its deconstitution of and radical break with too familiar topographies or, on the contrary, because it shows the ways in which so-called demarcations gather rather than separate. While distrusting the imperative to fuse with a community or a nationality, she nevertheless acknowledges the boundless hospitality of language.

Part 3 puts that conclusion to the test: in chapter 5 I show that Djebar's writings and films about the Algerian war of independence assess the ways in which women's testimonies ought to be heard so as to complicate the history of the war and of Algeria today, and radically transform the conditions of its reception, while in chapter 6 I argue that Cixous analyzes the possibility of hospitality, or what she prefers to call visitation, against the background of Algeria at war. Their interpretation of Algerian space clearly entails no irenic view of Algeria; on the contrary, Djebar and Cixous have not only reflected on economies of war (and in particular the Algerian war of independence) but also on the relation such economies have entertained with the polity they ushered in, and have obliquely proposed alternative outcomes. Djebar's main objective is arguably to shed light on some of the motives or forces at work behind the occlusion or distortion of historical figures or acts of resistance by women. But for her, none of that distortion can be explained without first considering collective patterns impacting both men and women and without addressing the ways in which individual, or what she likes to call "improvised," acts are socially received and interpreted. This approach frames Djebar's examination of women resisters in film and fiction. Agreeing that the testimony of Algerian women's participation in the war was double-edged, and could result in women's self-censorship or silence, Djebar looks for testimonial alternatives that would both recount and respect a wish for silence and secrecy. She promotes a verbal exchange and deemphasizes the visual within the testimonial act between the survivor who speaks and the listener. The geographical location of her films and fictions is allusive and her representation of the war is stylized, just as, in testimony, she stresses the meandering ruses of memory over the factual accuracy of the narrative. Through her reading of the encounter between Odysseus and the Sirens in *La Femme sans sépulture* (Woman without a tomb), a book that documents and imagines at the same time the life of the resister Zoulikha Oudai, I examine Djebar's argument in favor of "hearing another history" (a plea by Kateb Yacine) that would be told by a woman. The Roman mosaic from Cherchell that is the focus of her analysis is interpreted as an allegory of the lesson to be retained from Algerian women's resistance, one that still remains to be understood in itself and in its relation to memory and to the possibilities for political participation today.

Chapter 6 argues that, when examining instances of unrequited love, denied hospitality, and noninvitation in Algeria, Cixous elaborates an account of violence that requires another configuration than the opposition of war to peace, hate to love, activity to passivity. In that respect, her writing is driven by the ethical question of politics or of responsibility. I examine the impact in Cixous's work of what she terms a "togetherness in hostility," experienced in Algeria, on which is built a symmetrical proposal, love as a force of disruption, infinite distance, and separation. That position is related to Levinas's rethinking of subjectivity and justice. Like Levinas, who addresses the pitfalls of understanding dwelling as implantation in a place, or rootedness in his elaboration of hospitality, Cixous's analysis of the body politic as nonreciprocal asymmetries leads her to endorse a relationship of the self to the other founded on the transcendence of the other. The impossibility of being credited for the desire of being on the side of the colonized gives rise in Cixous to another consideration of the self, not this time *with*, but *for* the other, irrespective of the self's position. In that respect, Zohra Drif, a former classmate and well-known participant in the 1957 Battle of Algiers, has deeply informed Cixous's ethical reflection on Algeria. By displacing her focus from invitation, explored at length in her oeuvre, to the notion of visitation, Cixous performs an affirmative acquiescence to the other's unpredictable call.

The conclusion of *Algerian Imprints* brings Djebar and Cixous together again, examining their respective reflection on the culture of the veil, within which one arguably finds oneself inscribed one way or another. The chapter investigates what can be epistemologically gained from their examination of the motif and relates their examination of the veil as spatial marker or interval to the general focus in *Algerian Imprints*, which is to take note in Cixous and Djebar of the sites through which they contest both the nexus of injustice *and* the reduction to the same. Through the figure of the veil, associated with truth, vision, or luminosity and, conversely, with blindness, invisibility, or anonymity, they converge in an analysis that puts into question the asserted continuity between seeing (*voir*), having (*avoir*), and knowing (*savoir*). Both address the issue of cognition by seemingly adopting a strategy of unveiling; yet they also derail the epistemological objective of disclosure of a hidden truth and prefer to posit the veil as a figure or a threshold that is neither predicted in all its effects nor appropriated, its lesson being not so much received as deferred, suspending the order of knowledge. I start by contextualizing Djebar's texts with respect to canonical essays about the veil in Algeria such as Fanon's "Algeria Unveiled." Unlike Fanon, she does not merely interpret the veil as the last bastion of resistance to the colonizer but also ascribes the requirement of women's "invisibility" to a perceived risk attending woman's unconstrained sight. On the one hand, Djebar counteracts the drama she diagnoses in the dynamics of watching and being watched by referring to some extant cultural artifacts (songs, poems), which attest to the ability to experience the other's gaze less traumatically. On the other hand, Djebar consistently advocates for the benefits of invisibility and supports what she perceives to be a general aspiration for it. Cixous's attention to the effects of eye surgery invokes the veil through some major philosophical scenes, such as Plato's allegory of the cave, in which education occurs as unveiling, or through a passage from relative blindness to seeing. The interest in the passage from blindness to vision stems for her from what can be learned about nonseeing as much as seeing. Her inquiry concentrates on the interval, which is known only belatedly, an untenable position that she strives to keep intact, thus distancing truth from unveiling, since it was unforeseeable and is unlocatable. The passage is not merely an access to vision, but keeps enfolded the trace or the promise of blindness. It is another example of the ethical investment in intermittence, (resistance to) separation, and dissensus, which will be examined throughout *Algerian Imprints*. Algeria's troubled colonial history left an imprint on the formation of two of its most important women writers, but their oeuvres also provide a transformative imprint *on* Algeria by proposing a positive construct of political ability that rests for both writers on evaluating dispossession and discontinuity in unexpected ways.

PART ONE

Colonial Demarcations

CHAPTER ONE

The Gravity of the Body

Djebar's and Cixous's Textuality

ALGERIA IN CIXOUS AND DJEBAR: THINKING DISLOCATION

The first question asked by this book about the writings of Assia Djebar and of Hélène Cixous revolves around what "Algeria" stands for in their respective oeuvres. Algeria is written in quotation marks, because both writers develop a critical, political, and ethical reflection that takes its point of departure from that site but is not circumscribed by its borders. Hélène Cixous has said that "writing was born for [her] in [her] early childhood. That is to say in Algeria, in the tension between what was beautiful and noble, and which was founded on the truly upright spirit in my family . . . and what I saw was foul as soon as I crossed the threshold of the door."[1] The French Algeria where Cixous was born and grew up, then, was an awakening to constitutive dissonance, to the evidence of profound contradictions that required interpretation, which in turn informed her poetics, inseparably linked to a political and ethical stance in response to such Algerian scenes. Likewise, Djebar consistently reflects on patterns of exclusion in colonial and postcolonial Algeria. However, just as Cixous thinks through tensions rather than clear-cut oppositions in order to side with and affirm neglected outcomes, so is Djebar attentive to partial openings and overlaps that can be read as chances and even promises of other political potentialities.

When Cixous famously asked women to write their selves, she added the urgency of writing (through) the body, and called that writing "feminine" because historically woman had been less able to inscribe her own libidinal economy, her body and her *jouissance.*[2] Writing such an economy, she argued, would be a leverage allowing for the advent of another history, to the extent that libidinal economies are political (879). The spatialization of desire as "cosmic" allowed Cixous to defy assumptions about the body and to oppose a conception of desire she denounced as centralized, indeed "regionalized" (889). Woman's body is said to defy contours and borders; it is "a whole composed of parts that are wholes, not simple partial objects but a moving, changing ensemble, unlimited cosmos" (889). Recommending writing the body was all the more necessary since, as she noted in another contemporary essay, woman "has not been able to live in her 'own' house, her very body."[3] At stake, then, was a preliminary reflection concerning the delineation and the inhabitation of the body so as to rethink the organization of sociopolitical systems on the basis of this new spatiality. For, as Cixous argues in "The Laugh of the Medusa," along lines that Djebar agrees with and promotes in her own texts, woman carries out a dislocation of the body and of place, the effect of which is to transform the way in which to address the political body: "As subject for history, woman always occurs simultaneously in several places. Woman un-thinks [*dépense*] the unifying regulating history that homogenizes and channels forces and herds contradictions into a single battlefield."[4] It is this consistent erosion of a homogeneous discourse that paradoxically functions as a common trait linking woman's personal history to the collective history of women (882). Clarisse Zimra has pointed out the extent to which the inscription of the female body in Djebar's oeuvre is conceived at times as "a subversion of, and alternative to, the socius"; while, on other occasions, "the text is polarized by two visions of the female body," one in which it is obsessively and impotently being watched and another in which "the flesh has its own language," that of the caress and the affectionate touch.[5] Djebar's and Cixous's narrators often tell stories about diverse constraints faced by someone (or, more precisely, some*body*) who is thus led to put into question and challenge the limits of the body that is generally inhabited without reflection, as well as its inscription within a given location and a specific time. These restraints can cruelly maim, tear apart and dislocate the body, for example in ailing and in death throes (Cixous) or under torture and other wartime atrocities (Djebar). But there are also other scenes in Cixous and Djebar in which violence is not simply inflicted, but where the body, escaping the confining presumption of integrality, becomes explosive and exploring at the assumed risk of disintegration. Christa

Stevens has drawn attention to Cixous's "surgical writing," scenes of "autopsies" and portraits of the author as "écorché," or flayed anatomical model; likewise, Djebar often lays bare what the outermost epidermis protectively covers, "under the slow scalpel of autopsy of living flesh, showing more than one's skin."[6] If the figure of flight, in the sense of flying away, not to mention that of robbing, which Cixous has made much of, has always been prevalent in the texts of the two writers, it does not contradict the evidence in their works of a body anchored or attached in, which also means, by the same token, detachable and removable from a given place.[7] I will argue in this chapter that rethinking the body and its limits occurs within a spatiality, the imposed partitions or perceived divisions of which are themselves interrogated as a preliminary step to a different potential positioning within the political and social landscape. Specifically, Djebar and Cixous examine ways in which dislocation (of the body and of the site) may be ascertained and taken up, that is to say, not only contested and deplored but addressed as an ethical and political chance. This chapter will also examine the difficulty faced by several critics when attempting to classify each writer's oeuvre, particularly as far as the distinction between fiction and autobiography is concerned, an opposition their works consistently complicate or collapse. This two-pronged approach frames in advance the focus of *Algerian Imprints*, which argues that Cixous's and Djebar's Algerian writings are a consistent invitation to de-limit the body in order to reframe its potentialities in an Algerian space that is manifold or heterogeneous. The project of rethinking the body or entities that are taken to be self-enclosed is inseparable from the denunciation of false dualities that restrict the possibilities or deny the actuality of a plural political body. In this chapter, I start with their reflection on the de-limitation of the body, but I contend that this initial demonstration of the articulations between body and space posited by Djebar and Cixous is confirmed in different forms in every chapter of this book.

TWO WHEELS, TWO CYCLISTS, TWO CIRCLES: WRITING THE BODY IN SPACE

Djebar's Cycles

The figure of the circle is used massively as a means by which Djebar and Cixous respectively address and reconceive spatiality. In Djebar's writings the figure of the circle is fundamental; it shapes her texts as well as it structures forms of sociability. In the first instance, her works are often declared to be cyclical or circular: the last section of *Nulle part dans la maison de mon père* starts, for instance, with the remark that "the circle that this text unfolds is the first step of the undertaking."[8] Socially, "the circle of women" implies, first, the hospitality of visits paid and of conversational exchanges between relatives and friends.[9] This circle is associated with the inside or "domestic interiors" (21). Secondly, the forms taken by sociability familiarize the body with a given spatiality. The circle of women gathered inside teaches the young girl in its midst, or, perhaps more accurately, at its margin, to think of space as circular. Inside is yet another circle, "the circle that whispering elders traced around me and within me"; the question then may become how to "blow the space within me to pieces" (4). Djebar often reflects on dislocation and its effects on the body and the understanding of one's inscription within a place. But her writings demonstrate that sidestepping the circle is only a partial break or liberation from circular spatiality. *Fantasia, an Algerian Cavalcade* examines that predicament through the destination of written words. On the one hand, the beginning of *Fantasia*, which displays several sorts of epistolary exchanges, official or private, sent out at different periods of Algerian history, reflects on the gesture and on the varying success of sending a letter out (44), of construing words as mobile and detachable, traveling (3) in defiance of circularity. On the other hand, circularity is not only deemed to be the devalued automaticity of cyclical repetition; when words come back to haunt or shed light on the sender, the familiar/familial circle takes up the letter and appraises it so as to criticize it, but also be touched, transformed, or altered by it as a result. This is true of the colonizer's archive that Djebar has contributed to "rewrite" by extracting from and reacting to it, or by returning it to the site of its inscription and responding in French to French words that were not intended to be read by an Algerian. It is even true of the father's tender postcard to the mother commented upon by the astonished circle of women because it was addressed directly to her in contradiction to custom (37–38). In such instances the return of the "mobile" words to the circle is not a return to the same.[10] Djebar often makes the point that projecting one's body or one's words out can be figured by circularity as well as linearity, since one does not merely go around in circles with circular spatiality. The Algerian novelist and playwright Kateb Yacine explained in that respect why the circle was fundamental in his view: it figures "man's freedom always in motion, his freedom in space and time."[11] Instead of unfolding the events in his works chronologically, Kateb proposed to read them as "a rotation in time which makes them ceaselessly return to the origins and go on carrying new forces along each time" (41). His fascination with the circle was, in short, a way of delineating "my condition as a man situated on an earth in perpetual rotation. He who places himself on a single straight line never goes very far" (42).

Cixous's Circles

Cixous, for whom "the encirclement, the Circle, the siege, are primitive figures of my Algerian scene," also shares with Kateb and with Djebar the notion that "the time of an oeuvre is not linear, but circular or spherical."[12] Her early fiction *Inside* formalizes the structure of encirclement, in which inside is both a refuge and a prison: "MY HOUSE IS SURROUNDED. IT IS ENCIRCLED BY THE IRON GRATING. INSIDE, we live. Outside, they are fifty thousand, they surround us. Inside, all the same, I'm home."[13] At the same time, the outsiders' hostility is predicated on the fragility of the tie that insiders are perceived to hold to the interiority of and familiarity with the land that they tread: "the entire land outside was the temple of the others. . . . We would have had to have wings to be at home outside."[14] This realization gives rise to several questions as to the motives and the legitimacy of spatial division (32–34), since the narrator acknowledges a persecution conducted by the very persecuted, an encirclement by those already imprisoned within their own land. Cixous's first book, *Le Prénom de Dieu,* also reconfigures topography by emphasizing the relentless separation between inside and outside (its first sentence also records that "I am inside"), while investigating its motives and the effects of the boundary on the I.[15] The narrator derives encirclement from hostility, but its premises are ascribed to a "fault" that precedes and encompasses the I:

> Never, as a child, did I go out of the protected garden without immediately being harassed by a gang of spectral children. . . . We all waited to be grown so that bread and spitting would be replaced by life and death and for war to begin at last. Then they would kill me and eat me, at last I would taste the peace of the victim, everything

> would be just, I would be rewarded, I would not have any more to open the gate of the garden every day on my fault of being in the garden while they were outside.
> (195–96)

Inside and *Le Prénom de Dieu* do not directly name Algeria, but both install paradigmatic scenes of encirclement that are more explicitly linked with Algeria in later fictions, such as *Reveries of the Wild Woman.* One far-reaching interrogation consists in putting into question the actual location and the efficiency of the limit separating inside from outside: "Who neglected to tell me that there's an outside and an inside?"[16] Thus the figure of encirclement expands and prevents the stable location of an inside opposed to outside. Moreover, the father's death, which is the main motif in *Inside* taken up in many writings of Cixous's, induces a receptivity to the porosity of the borders between life and death—"the passage from life to death was not a door that opened and shut" (8)—which triggers in turn a radical interrogation of limits, including that between humanity and animality, which often redoubles that between being and nothingness: "I began by dismissing God, whose uselessness was only too apparent, and replaced him with my father. Then I abolished the distinction between man and woman, which seemed to me to be an excuse for every kind of sloth. Finally I pushed aside the limit of life on both sides of the present" (11–12). In another recurrent formulation of the figure of encirclement, Cixous writes about the situation of Jews in Algeria, asking for admission in a circle that apparently granted it while perpetuating several forms of exclusion: "The circles intersected. To be inside was also to be outside."[17] Encirclement proliferates, pushing out the boundaries that were supposed to hold insiders enclosed and clearly demarcated from outsiders. The marginalization that is depicted in the last instance is insidious, since it does not correspond to a peripheral expulsion, but rejects as it claims to incorporate. This assessment of the circle leads both Cixous and Djebar to reflect on the modes of inhabitation afforded by such spatiality.

I will examine their response to this inquiry throughout this book, but will start addressing it here by focusing on a similar sequence in Djebar's *Nulle part* and Cixous's *Reveries of the Wild Woman,* which narrates a young girl's first attempt to ride a bicycle.[18] In both cases, Djebar and Cixous start from the premise that riding a bicycle would be tantamount to conquering space autonomously (Djebar), or to "knowing Algeria"

(Cixous).[19] In that view, the exploration out and forward that the bicycle indicates—in spite of its rotating circular wheels—could be an invitation to break away from the cycle of circularity or encirclement. In both texts, though for different reasons, bicycling abruptly stops short and the disruption inaugurates another thinking of the link between body and space as well as of the relation of inside to outside. My point is not merely to address thematic convergences between the two writers by referring to a paradigmatic scene of apprenticeship that several authors besides Djebar and Cixous have also written about. Instead, I argue that both draw ethical/political consequences from this existential scene, which is the convergence I aim to bring to the fore.

Disarticulation in Djebar

The metaphor of lameness or limping is frequent in Djebar's work when bringing up the risk of disorientation, and even paralysis. In an interview with Marguerite Le Clézio, Djebar explains thus her complex relationship to French as well as to Arabic: "my bilingualism limped with both legs."[20] In the foreword to one of her early fictions, *Les Alouettes naïves*, lameness stands for the process of decolonization: "because we are constantly torn between the past paralyzed in the present and the present giving birth to the future, we, Africans, Arabs, and doubtless others elsewhere, walk with a limp. . . . This is why we wonder at times whether we move forward."[21] What the figure of limping engages in such instances is the question of the orientation of the body as well as of thinking, as well as the consideration of how to persevere painfully in proceeding or in moving forward.[22] In *Nulle part* and other texts, Djebar reflects on the female body, such as it inscribes itself in a specific location and period in a way that is both expected and unpredictable. In the scene in which the little girl of *Nulle part* learns how to ride a bicycle, her legs become the synecdoche of the female body, deemed immodest by her father who pronounces "these two words in Arabic: *her legs*."[23] Between the forbidden two wheels of the bicycle and the two legs of the grown young woman pacing towns up and down, there will have been "two words in Arabic" that are then immediately given in French ("ses jambes"/"her legs"), a linguistic discrepancy or limp that Djebar recounts and comments on throughout her oeuvre. Riding a bicycle, with which the little girl hoped to conquer not only the machine, but also balance and space (47), being strictly forbidden to her by the father, the daughter respects the interdict (52), the paralyzing effect of which is emphasized (51), and claims imbalance for herself. But later the teenager somewhat circumvents the interdict without invalidating it, for instance by practicing track and field or by taking long solitary walks. Constrained, the body is first detached from the machine in order to obey the father who takes exception to an association body-machine that obsesses him: "I do not want my daughter to show her legs by riding a bicycle" (49). But the body itself becomes a performing machine, which is a way of getting round the interdiction, when the repetitive, mechanical imperative of the training of the athletic body is achieved: "Secretly, my body . . . will take its revenge . . . by prolonged practice in basketball and track and field" (52). All the same, the little girl induced from her father's reaction a restriction in the use of her legs: "this pair of legs . . . I was to use only for walking" (52). The adult's exhilarating, solitary, silent, and anonymous walks will not contradict that initial verdict. Furthermore, the narrator insists on several occasions on the activity of legs, which are examined as if they were distinct and removed from the rest of the body and from thinking. For instance, at the boarding school, "I remember the joyful energy of my legs when I jumped on the tables in the preparation room" (169).

This confirmation of the body as body part needs to be elucidated, for Djebar does also criticize the fact that the body, and in particular the female body, is too often comprehended as disarticulated and in pieces ("her legs"). In the bicycle scene after the father's reproach, "I was offended to feel that he had thus delimited my person. . . . Having separated them from my person in that way was, I realized, insulting, but why?" (51). Instead of that outcome, the narrator imagines racing on a bicycle and being welcomed with affection by her father: "He, transformed, he, not talking any more of 'my legs,' but simply, of me" (58). Reading that scene, Henri Sanson underscores the implications of such a cutting up of the female body: "how could the girl, and later the young woman, belong to herself in her entirety, possess herself, if she is at the origin already broken up, fragmented, symbolically amputated from a part of herself?"[24] He also shows that this passage can be linked to other scenes of "paternal diktat" in Djebar, which are also charged with setting up a relation to the female body in pieces (321). While I agree with Sanson's reading, what must also be understood is the motive behind proffering the reduction of the girl to her legs or other body parts, not only as an instance of (paternal) misogyny that is denounced but also as a deliberate strategy on Djebar's part. In that view the disarticulated female body is the synecdoche of a whole that remains to be claimed or recognized in itself.

For, on other occasions, Djebar relates differently to the assumption or reconstruction of the wholeness of the body. If Djebar subscribes to the feminist recommendation of writing the body and its story so as to thwart the "blotting-out" of women's bodies, she often handles it by taking up negative disarticulation in her writings and by affirming it in at least two ways.[25] The reduction of the girl to her legs, to remain a little longer with that example, and therefore that of the self to a broken up body, may acquire positive significance elsewhere. For instance in *Les Alouettes naïves*, when the little girl Nfissa shares a bed with her sisters and grandmother, "her legs fidget to defend their space" or, as a grown-up, Nfissa's legs are lovingly intertwined with those of her husband.[26] In such benign examples, the self is not endangered by such parceling out of the body, which is, on the contrary, energized by this atomization and unmistakably conveys Nfissa's own will and desire. In a second approach, Djebar accelerates at times the impact of disarticulation and interprets it as a strategically incalculable multiplication, a complication of the body that makes it difficult to situate it since it defies integrality and self-sameness. She does so, for instance, as we shall see at greater length in the last chapter, in her interpretation of the reception of a woman's gaze in a space construed as predominantly masculine. Reflecting on the unsettling force of woman's gaze in *Women of Algiers in Their Apartment*, Djebar links its disturbance to a body that is figured as hyperscopic, for which everything becomes visible in that it is made of proliferating eyes that are themselves more or less hidden from view, "as if all of a sudden the whole body began to look around."[27] In that fantasized construct, woman's body is decomposed into parts that do not add up to a single, recognizably unified body. Likewise, Djebar interprets Picasso's painting taking up Delacroix's motif of women of Algiers in their apartment as "bursting out" both the space of the apartment and the very body of women, as happened at times to the bomb carriers and other women resisters of the Battle of Algiers (149–50). Remarkably, the body thus exploded and disintegrated is the sign for Djebar of "women's rebirth to their own bodies" (150). In these last examples, there is more potential in refusing the attempt or the temptation to present a harmonious and reassuringly whole body. On the contrary, confronting fragmentation so as to engage it in another direction is the genuine first step forward. Reversing the perceived atomization, leading at times to the effacement of the body, is certainly the objective, but leaping too hastily to the reliance on its plenitude and integrity risks being ineffectual. Moreover, Djebar distrusts the idealization and condescending protection of woman's body. In order to circumvent paralysis, it may then be necessary, through a seeming paradox that is not one, to assume imbalance and division and provide oneself with a strategic limp, which is a first step to figure the body otherwise in the corpus.

The Weight of the Body in Cixous

In Cixous's *Reveries of the Wild Woman*, riding the bicycle is also an attempt of short duration for the girl. It is not interrupted as the result of a parental interdiction, but because the bicycle fails to function for the girl as the hoped-for opening to the outside when encountering the hostility of outsiders: "Falling off the bike doesn't leave a scar but it takes the outside back."[28] For the girl and her brother, the imagined Bike passionately longed for allowed for an opening, represented "a door with wheels" (30) to Algeria itself, to the land or to the ground. But when they receive an actual bicycle, which is a girl's bike (13) to be shared by the two children, two different positions start to emerge, one being assigned to the brother, the other to the sister, regarding the sense of that opening and, more profoundly, the construction of outside. Incidentally, one may note that the arrival of the Bike, as maternal preference for the daughter or at least the determination that the daughter should be a biker (13), or as the mother's disavowal of the boy's sex, or the boy's existence (18), starts dividing the single spatial unit that brother and sister had been (30). The division is not due to sexual difference, but is also attributable to nothing else (a girl's bike that a boy ends up riding exclusively), sexual difference being another boundary or limit that Cixous consistently complicates with greater differentiations. For the brother, the bicycle is endowed with the capacity to "know Algeria" (12) in the sense of exploring it, as well as with the possibility of evading the constraining incarceration of being inside: "this Bike which would set us free, give us space height and therefore Algeria" (11). The sister's avoidance of the bicycle is taken to be an indifference to, and detachment from Algeria: "You refused the Bike and therefore Algeria" (11).

The position assigned to the sister puts into question what could be understood by "knowing" in that sense: "But what does it mean to know—I say—Algeria. . . . Not-to-know Algeria is also to know it" (51). First it is not possible to know Algeria in the brother's sense, because one has not yet arrived there; not being inside it, one cannot detach oneself from it. The beginning of *Reveries* allegorizes the impossibility of entering Algeria in a scene in which the opening pages of the manuscript—starting with "The whole time I was living in Algeria I would dream of one day arriving in Algeria" (3)—get irremediably lost: "now this is exactly what used to happen with Algeria, when I was living there: I had it, I'd got a grip on it—I didn't have it any longer, I'd never have it, I'd never held it in my arms" (5). Precisely, that impossibility of owning, but also of being truly in Algeria while inside, leads Cixous in a second step to think a radical dispossession or mode of non-relation to "the country of our birth and not ours at all" (32). In that respect, reading enables both an "absence from the world" (29) and a reconfiguration of inside as inner life, solitary thinking. *Reveries* pursues Cixous's reflection on the spatiality depicted in other texts, such as *Inside*, whereby exclusion is not simply peripheral but also concentric, interiority divides itself anew or harbors another inside fostering marginalization. The bicycle inaugurates a new turn, a new cycle: reading provides more than escape, it becomes a means of rethinking spatiality and one's positioning. While the brother absconds with the bicycle from "our common and respective chains" (12), the sister delves into the depth of the house, and inside becomes another name for reading: "I saw you retreat even further into the house into the depths of your room, which you almost never came out of, digging yourself a burrow or a den if you prefer in your handful of books" (12). The madness of spatiality, which is also due in Cixous's analysis to the fact that one finds oneself ascribed within it to a position that is not of one's own choosing, is thwarted by the book. Absorption in the book prevents sinking in the abyss. The book is solid, material; it anchors the body while allowing it to be transported elsewhere: "it sufficed that there be a rectangular volume with the dimension of my foot on which to land to cross the abyss" (47). Instead of crossing the gate to reach an impossibly receding outside, the position of being inside is explored, which inaugurates other passages according to the expanding propensities of interiority indicated earlier, for example passages from one book to the next. This is why pedaling and reading can become equated as a way out in an untranslatable portmanteau word ("nous pédalisions"), rendered as "we pedaled with all our strength" (47).

However, precisely because the way out can be equally achieved inwardly, through an investigation and complication of the inside as valid as an exploring venture outside, Cixous is wary of addressing the limit solely through the metaphor of soaring or laterally breaking chains, which is what the bicycle essentially stands for in the brother's position: "I from the vantage point of the Bike I knew I was soaring over the Clos-Salembier and our common and respective chains" (12). The release provided by the book happens instead through a certain confirmation of the chain, because the body is never left behind, or with the understanding of what inseparably ties the body to the ground. In *Reveries* the foot touches on the book, or the book is also corporeal, having for instance a back in contact with the girl's body: "I slip from one back to the next" (47).

Another scene in *Inside* (24–26) also brings together a brother and a sister, wondering whether it is possible to liberate the body from fetters, to be one's own master, free and unchained. In order to prove that she is free, the sister starts running and gathering speed, until she "takes off" (25). We have mentioned the recurrence of the figure of flight in Cixous as well as in Djebar, emblematic of the daring ascending gesture associated with the advent of a new thought, detached from the unimaginative daily grind. However, the scene in *Inside* ends with a turn that is equally frequent and characteristic of Cixous and Djebar: "I was going up. I went just high enough to learn my first lesson: no sooner had I broken loose that I felt the leash" (25). This position indicates the risk involved in every flight, in every thought taking off. But the "first lesson" is far from being negative. The scene recalls that the body is grounded, that it is anchored to the earth: "I felt the leash, each of my limbs, and even every hair was tied to the ground by what must have been millions of invisible fetters" (25). Without an accurate measure of such ties, no writing of the body would gather any momentum. Furthermore, they are not unwelcome servitude. Freedom is not opposed to what holds the body to the earth: "I fell free. While I was falling, my fetters fell away. . . . The earth was waiting for me" (25). An optimistic reading of that scene will stress that "only the body keeps us back" (26), which means that all other fetters can be relinquished once the body is given its due. But even if that conclusion is provisional, the consideration of the weight of the body, not only as a consequence of gravity but also in deliberating grave issues such as liberty, will endure. The scene of *Inside* just evoked could be compared to the recurring depiction of a young woman's suicide attempt in Djebar's writings (for instance in *Fantasia, So Vast the prison, Nulle part*). In *Nulle part* the woman's desire to throw herself into the sea is modified into a project of disarticulation on the ground: "At the ultimate second, I imagined my body, that of a young girl cut . . . in three!"[29] Taking off, the body falls back to earth, and is awakened in the process to another understanding of corporeality: the body remains, attached to earth or to the land. This position is tied to Djebar's investment in the figure of the body in pieces, which enables her to reorient the reflection on the female body, which should not be impossibly idealized, protected from itself and its immodest attractions, but grounded to the earth and to the articulation of a will and a desire. The implication is that the ways in which the political body construes itself depends on prior assumptions about the body and/in a site. The outlook on both must be revised simultaneously for other modes of inhabitation and coexistence to be invented.

MULTIPLE I'S, OTHER-BIOGRAPHY

The question of the genre of the works expounding Djebar's and Cixous's Algerian scenes is one that critics often find necessary to raise, particularly the extent to which they are autobiographical. As Paul de Man's essay on autobiography has shown, much in the answer to this question depends on prior assumptions about autobiographical discourse. Among such assumptions, de Man mentions the "distinction between autobiography and fiction," in spite of the acknowledged difficulty of relying on that distinction, including among self-declared authors of autobiographies and confessions.[30] Jean-Jacques Rousseau, sometimes called the first autobiographer in French, listed at the beginning of his *Confessions* fictional elements that did not compromise, in his view, the autobiographical project of "unveiling [his] interior."[31] Indeed, as several critics have rightly pointed out, authenticity trumps veridicity for Rousseau. Philippe Lejeune, who is considered by most critics as one of the foremost theoreticians of Francophone autobiography, recognizes, for instance, that the narrator of an autobiography may be mistaken, lie, forget, or distort and may even provide an entirely *invented* story.[32] But unlike de Man, who after his own examination of the issue is not disturbed to have to conclude that "the distinction between fiction and autobiography is not an either/or polarity but that it is undecidable," Lejeune insists on finding criteria to differentiate between the two.[33] Essentially, autobiography ends up being characterized in Lejeune's theory by the author's recognizably avowed intention to write an autobiography, and, conversely, fictitiousness must also be affirmed in the fictional pact.[34] The affirmation of fictitiousness is supposed to be guaranteed on the cover of the book, by the generic subtitle *novel* for instance (15), while the pact entailed by autobiography is referential in the sense that the names in the text (author-narrator-protagonist) unquestionably refer to the name of the author (14). If identity is for Lejeune the formal trait grounding autobiography, if it does not matter for the autobiographer to be true to what was or is, but to declare that he or she aims to be true, and if the task of the reader is to recognize that identity and that intention, the necessity to exclude fiction from autobiography becomes all the less motivated. Yet that necessity is repeated in several passages of Lejeune's *Autobiographical Pact*. It is the mimetic ability of fiction, not only to resemble but also, through its verisimilitude, to be a substitute to the referent while claiming to be distant from it. In other words, it is fiction's ability to make reference undecidable that Lejeune attempts to avert when using such demarcations, either through denial (resemblance does not matter), or through the notion of reading as a contract (author or publisher must clearly tell the reader what to expect without lying). However, it should be added that, with his notion of contract commanding a mode of reading (29), Lejeune also anticipates breaches in the contract (26) that could be provocations to all sorts of textualities.

Lejeune's positions are predicated, as de Man has shown, on unquestioned assumptions regarding readability on the part of "a single subject whose identity is defined by the uncontested readability of his proper name" and, furthermore, on the part of the reader.[35] For de Man, as is well known, affirming such readability or, more generally, the possibility of referring the text to meaning or truth, is far from evident. Even if the assumption of the readability of the proper name were to go unchallenged, its impact should then be generalized, and in that view autobiography should be taken as "a figure of reading or of understanding that occurs, to some degree, in all texts" (70). Or, conversely, all texts are fictional in the sense that even the specular structure at once differentiating and uniting at the same time the name(s) of the author occurs in a language that is cognitively problematic because it is also figural, indefinitely substitutive with no assurance that its meaning can be arrested: the interest of autobiography is precisely "that it demonstrates the impossibility of closure and of totalization . . . of all textual systems" (71). This position explains de Man's greatest objection to Lejeune's theory, concerning his notion of "pact" in which "the reader becomes the judge, the policing power in charge of verifying the authenticity of the signature and the consistency of the signer's behavior" (71). As Rachel Gabara writes, in her discussion of what she calls Francophone autobiographies in the third person, investigating, on the contrary, "what happens when we do *not* inherently recognize autobiography" thoroughly transforms the act of reading such narratives.[36] Several critics have noted that Cixous's and Djebar's texts are constitutively hybrid and unclassifiable as either fictions or autobiographies. It may be added that such a distinction, if it were to be attempted (or when it is), would preclude a condition in which the reader, while not being left entirely without a contract, is exposed throughout the texts to the need to tread the line of attachment between and detachment from the two (fiction/autobiography).

Cixous has consistently collapsed the distinction between fiction and autobiography: on the one hand, she claims to "have always been autobiographical, no more nor less than Montaigne or any other writer," while on the other hand she consistently writes "not an autobiography, but an other-biography [*autre-biographie*]."[37] At times, that other-biography takes the form of books written in dialogue with others, such as *Rencontre terrestre* with Frédéric-Yves Jeannet or *Rootprints* with Mireille Calle-Gruber, which includes "captions" by Cixous of some photographs/roots. *Rootprints* calls attention to the fact that autobiography is a textual trope substituting the other for the author or revolving around the auto-other: "All biographies like all autobiographies like all narratives tell one story in place of another story."[38] As she puts it in "Coming to Writing," "Hélène Cixous isn't me"; within each of her texts, Cixous thinks "the non-adherence between me and myself" or a subject that is split.[39] This singularly alters the autobiographical project, its relevance, and its possibility: in *Rencontre terrestre*, she shows that "the 'auto' is always already other, translation has always already started" (31). Likewise, for Cixous the task of the writer does not consist in exposing the eventfulness of existence but in bringing to the fore "what would prevent us from existing, from continuing our ordinary, domestic lives."[40] This investigation explains why the writer can both be said to be "looking at what must not be looked at" (61) and claim to "proceed in a constituent blindness" (32). The way this process can shore up as much as ruin autobiography is exemplified in one of Cixous's references to writing as "the self-portrait of a blind painter" (32). As we shall see in another chapter, blindness is not simply opposed to lucidity, but this condition and its effects always call for elucidation. *Fiction* is a middle-ground word generally accepted by Cixous to designate her writings, but it is a compromise that does not accurately reflect the interplay within her narratives of the first- and third- person pronouns *I* and *she* that interfere with the applicability of commonly tracked generic categories. "I dread the word 'novelist'," Cixous writes; when applied to her early works, such as *Inside*, the generic determination "novel," inscribed on the cover, is itself called "a fiction."[41] Cixous invites us to read without codes or conditions. Readers of her "transgenic work," in Derrida's words, are asked to reflect on narrative, modal, generic combinations which structurally install a de-limiting, bridging syntax along with a reflection on demarcations, borders, passages.[42] As Derrida remarks with respect to Cixous's characteristic multiplicity of narrative stances within a single text, neither "I" nor "she" are *with* or *without her*, which raises questions "between literature and its other, fiction, the possible, the real, and the impossible" (27). Cixous weaves a poetics that Derrida calls "fictional hyperrealism" (29) so as to underscore the challenge it poses to classification as well as the direction Cixous takes, working at and against the borderline between generic opposites: "This very nullification of the border . . . is the very work of her writing, its operation and its opus, which, although literary through and through, also goes beyond literature, just as it goes beyond autobiography" (12).[43]

Djebar's positions on autobiography may not appear to be as coherently thought through as Cixous's; yet, her complex textual practices evince great sophistication as well as recurring questions of method. In an interview with Clarisse Zimra, she explains that she addresses "the relationship between writing and autobiography," that is to say, not merely the question of the opposition or link between fiction and the writing of the self but also the place of autobiography with respect to writing in general.[44] As the Moroccan writer Abdelkebir Khatibi once wrote, "Maghrebian literature is a radical experience and experiment of autobiography. Yes, the Maghrebian writer tells of the self in telling the tales of languages."[45] Khatibi's remarkable formulation contests several assumptions. First, many critics have asserted that saying "I" or writing the self is a taboo in "the Islamic tradition," or at least transgresses cultural rules of politeness. Djebar has herself spoken of those rules of decorum: "The upbringing that I received . . . had two absolute rules: one, never talk about yourself; and, two, if you must, always do it 'anonymously,'" the latter meaning "one must never use the first person pronoun."[46] She explicitly ties that polite rule to the issue of autobiography in *Fantasia*: "How to say 'I.' . . . Only speak of conformity, my grandmother might reprove me."[47] Yet, it is made abundantly clear throughout *Fantasia* that, far from disappearing, difference is, on the contrary, irrepressible regardless of cultural expectations, and not only as far as the narrator is concerned. In the passage just quoted, the grandmother's recalled objection precisely arose after an uncontrolled outburst of singular affective display on the part of a female relative. In other words, thought, will, and sensibility, when expressed (and they are), should avoid being channeled through the personal. Djebar's lexis in this passage is generally negative—she talks of "collective resignation" or of "mortification" (156)—but she also recognizes that even though personal grievances are shared through "hackneyed formulas," in which "the 'I' of the first person will never be used," this does not prevent "every woman, raw inside, [from having] found appeasement in collective listening" (154). As even the most superficial reading of *Fantasia* and her other writings demonstrates, the goal for Djebar is never simply to say "I," but to undertake a writing of the self that does not leave others behind.

When reading Djebar's multifaceted response to questions such as "How to say 'I,'" the issue of obedience to, or transgression of a so-called interdict must not be overstated. At any rate, as soon as the question of knowing who is authorized or who feels entitled to write an autobiography, then several oppositions ("Islamic"/"Christian," "Maghrebian"/"non-Maghrebian," "male"/"female") become irrelevant: any autobiography may be deemed illegitimate or self-indulgent; indeed the justification of their undertaking is itself a hackneyed formula on the part of autobiographers, at least in the Francophone tradition. Montaigne, whose *Essays* are often thought to foreshadow autobiography, and Rousseau feel compelled to define the merit of their experiment, which lies, in their view, in the depiction of someone unlike others and not someone socially or morally exemplary.[48] Such well-worn defensive arguments have not lost their currency and are found in proponents of autofiction, such as Serge Doubrovsky, who argue that autobiography is a daunting privilege that few are entitled to. Cixous makes the same point, "'I am': who would dare to speak like God?"; but she argues, as we shall see in another chapter, for the impertinence of writing in general, a discrepancy that puts into question political operations of legitimation: "You wantto Write?. . . . With what right?"[49] Precisely, Khatibi describes such a displacement when he explains that Maghrebian literature radically experiments with autobiography, to the extent that, while still putting the self on display, it does so in a specific way: "the

Maghrebian writer tells of the self in telling the tales of languages." With a detour through the language of the other, the self is inhabited by languages and occupied with telling their story, and not with the writing of a life. Some critics have also contested the view that Maghrebian Francophone writers have only had at their disposal a French or a Christian tradition of autobiography (such as Augustine's *Confessions*). Instead, they point out that the practice of the writing of the self in another language was already available, for instance in the works of Ibn Khaldun and Sufi writers.[50] Instead of focusing so insistently on the so-called cultural paradoxes of the exposure of the self in Maghrebian literature, as many critics do, it is more promising to explore the inventive ways with which it represents, but also avoids, "the dissolution of the self in the other," in Beïda Chikhi's words, or plays at its limit.[51] In that respect, Djebar evokes the violence involved in exposing the self in the language of the former colonizer, which reflects that of the colonizing conquest. It is characteristically represented as impacting the body and threatening to disarticulate it: "Laying myself bare in this language permanently threatens me with the danger of deflagration."[52] In addition to demonstrating with this image her usual reluctance to refer too soon and naively to the wholeness of the body, Djebar indicates here that the writing of the self is intricately woven with another's intervention. Indeed, Khatibi's remark sheds light on the fact that if writing on language in the language of the other is tantamount to speaking of the self, the *autos* of autobiography is already affected by the other than the self as well as the presentation and even the justification of the self or the living already implicit in autobiography, as Derrida has shown.[53] The pain or the chance of the autobiographer consists in coming to terms with the fact that "the autonomy of the 'I' can be neither pure nor rigorous" (95).

On the one hand, Djebar notes that "writing always brings one back to oneself," therefore that any writing exposes the self, and, on the other hand, that there is a way of writing that can dissimulate even as it exposes.[54] Thus the purpose is not simply to reveal or to unveil a secret interiority but to frame the conditions of intimate display. Furthermore, Djebar particularly focuses on the potentiality of writing the body in autobiography. To all the difficulties of the task mentioned so far, Djebar adds that of the representation of a body that was either experienced or imagined as voiceless ("bereft of voice") or, conversely, as an invisible body of which only "sounds remain."[55] Writing is charged with conveying that interruption between body and voice, which explains as well why the autobiographical assertion of the "I" is not conceived as the transcription of a seamless recollection of the body but as the "fiction" of the self (216), gathering in writing what was experienced as discrete and detached. Finally, Djebar is known for the singularity of her autobiographical project, in which there is an ethical connection between the self and others, to the extent that the self is constituted by and writes in response to the damages borne by others. Recalling the atrocities of the conquest, for instance, Djebar writes, "I was born in *eighteen hundred and forty-two*, when General Saint-Arnaud arrives to burn down the *zaouia* of the Beni Menacer. . . . Before I hear my own voice, I perceive the death rattles. . . . They summon me, they support me, so that at the given signal my solitary song takes off" (217). As she phrased it in an interview, the I is understood as "not always the I, or it is an 'I-we' or a multiplied 'I.'"[56] Privileging discontinuity, she has consistently demonstrated that the plurality of sites, narrators, temporalities, or the juxtaposition of historical and collective memory to intimate memory, are approaches that best exemplify the intervention of the other in the I, or their co-location. This dual approach is not an oscillation between autobiography and other modes (such as history or fiction) but rather, in Gabara's words, Djebar's "hybrid textual form mirrors the construction of an autobiographical self that is itself hybrid, made up of self and others."[57] Hybridity goes beyond the inapplicability of generic markers and is evinced in Djebar's structuring of life stories not merely as biological/existential but as profoundly historical and linguistic. It is perhaps so as to obtain a version of the autonomous self that would "really" tell its story without dissimulation that some critics of Djebar's writings are eager to pinpoint the beginnings of her autobiographical project. Anne Guillot, for instance, writes about Djebar's last book: "*Nulle part dans la maison de mon père* is claimed by Assia Djebar as her first really autobiographical work."[58] The adverb *really* seems to indicate that all the other so-called autobiographical writings by Djebar were not, or were not exactly, what they were deemed to be. What must be done then about *Fantasia*, a work about which Djebar clearly said that it was also and already "a first autobiographical text"?[59] And what must be concluded from the fact that both *Fantasia* and *Nulle part* are books referred to as "novels" on the cover and by the press in which they appeared? The difficulty is clearly due to Djebar's construction of the I (including the multiplied I) and to the announcement through the genre of the novel of a neutralized self, unless precisely it is exposed otherwise through its disguise. On the one hand, Djebar has said: "You know that

I wrote *Fantasia* when I was over forty. It is at that time only that I decided to write an autobiography" (90). Did that decision produce an autobiography? Not quite, but rather a book that was "partly auto-biographical, or I would say in a prism" (90). In other words, autobiography is not quite possible, or autobiography is the mode of partition, of partly achieved, "not really" autobiographical works. On the other hand, she has declared that she feared having exposed her self in works that were far from being claimed as autobiographical, much before writing *Fantasia*. This is the case for instance of *Les Alouettes naïves*: "Once that novel was finished, I stopped writing because, at the heart of the novel, in forty pages perhaps, for the first time in that trajectory, I had a writing at the limit of autobiography."[60] What should be retained from these formulations is the notion of Djebar's writing "at the limit of autobiography" and always "for the first time." As Gabara shows, Djebar "puts something of herself" in all her works without exception.[61] Which is also a way of saying that her writings cut themselves from the self or, conversely, that the autonomy of the self is put into question or incorporated in a book.

In "The Laugh of the Medusa" Cixous explained that reclaiming one's body starts with remembering childhood: "Women return from afar, from always, from 'without' [*dehors*] . . . *from their childhood* which men have been trying desperately to make them forget."[62] Because of a "brainless education," women "have wandered around in circles" (877). Heeding that remark, the next chapter will focus on one central aspect of childhood, consisting in going to school in French Algeria, for that experience was key to perceiving and navigating zones of belonging and exclusion. In contradiction to that model, each writer's poetics and investigation of layers of language(s) as variegated spaces of affiliation and marginalization pave the way for a politically and ethically promising configuration of discontinuous plurality.

CHAPTER TWO

Going to School in French Algeria

The Archive of Colonial Education

HISTORY AND MEMORY

An intricate debate has unfolded in France within the last decade regarding the function of history in relation to memory and legislation. The debate, which has characteristically focused on historical research and education, involves the issue of French colonization, both the way in which it is collectively remembered and how it is taught and studied by specialists. Critics have documented the place of history in French students' curriculum, second only to the instruction of and in the French language. This bears keeping in mind if one wants to understand the ramifications of the ongoing discussion about the place of history within society. In that respect, the historian Pierre Nora, well-known for having proposed the concept of *lieux de mémoire* (sites of memory) as material or ideal units that have become symbolic elements of a community, or, in the case of France, significant entities allowing a representation of Frenchness, has shown the crucial importance of the discipline of history in French schooling in the nineteenth and at the turn of the twentieth centuries, when it was taught from primary school onward.[1] By extension, because it was often argued at the time that there was a privileged link between the knowledge of history and patriotism, the study of French history was considered by many educators "as especially vital to colonial populations."[2] In the aftermath of independence, the Algerian authorities symmetrically promoted education in Arabic and controlled the writing and teaching of history; following the coup of 1965 against Ben Bella, the teaching of history was "nationalized," in Benjamin Stora's words, so as to reinforce the legitimacy of the takeover.[3] Whether through admiration, resignation, or through a mixture of both, which significantly contributed to the sense of alienation analyzed powerfully by authors such as Frantz Fanon and Albert Memmi, the colonized were expected to recognize French supremacy and to accept French domination. Jacques Derrida, who went to school in French Algeria, has these words about "what was taught in school under the name of the 'history of France': an incredible discipline, a fable and bible, yet a doctrine of indoctrination almost uneffaceable for children of my generation. Without speaking of geography: not a word about Algeria, not a single one concerning its history and its geography, whereas we could draw the coast of Brittany and the Gironde estuary with our eyes closed."[4] Likewise, Hélène Cixous wrote that in her *lycée* in Algiers "a cult to France reigned and was not questioned. We learned France."[5] In her oeuvre, Assia Djebar, who specialized in history at the university level, sheds light on conflicting histories within the Algerian space, giving place in the process to a country ignored or bracketed in colonial education. Like Derrida, she recalls, in that respect, the spectral effect of negating children's closest surroundings in the words and images of textbooks, evoking instead unknown, distant signs eluding everyday experience. This effect may be widespread in schooling experience, but it is particularly acute among the colonized:

> I learn the names of birds I've never seen, trees I shall take ten years or more to identify, glossaries of flowers and plants that I shall never smell until I travel north of the Mediterranean. . . . Settings and episodes in children's books are nothing to me but sheer scenarios; in the French family the mother comes to fetch her daughter or son from school; in the French street, the parents walk quite naturally side by side. . . . So, the world of the school is expunged from the daily life of my native city, as it is from the life of my family. The latter is denied any referential role.[6]

The French state has officially acknowledged past crimes or injustices committed against minority groups through a series of laws often referred to as *lois mémorielles* (memorial laws), such as the Taubira law (May 21, 2001) that recognizes slavery and the slave trade as crimes against humanity and recommends that school and research programs in history and human sciences emphasize their study (article 2). Several historians have been concerned about the impact of such laws on the independence of historical research, worrying that they might promote the teaching of a normative history. The 2005 petition Liberté pour l'histoire (Freedom for history), first signed by nineteen historians and endorsed since by some six hundred, was written as a protest against a perceived political and juridical encroachment on the field of history: "In a free State, it is not up to Parliament or the judiciary authority to define historical truth."[7]

The debate on the connections between memory and history was sparked by two cases that appear at odds with respect to the legacy of French colonization in collective memory. In the first instance, the February 25, 2005 law about repatriated Europeans and *harkis* (Algerians belonging to the French Army or who fought on its side during the Algerian war of independence) to France after the Algerian independence, included in its article 4 the stipulation that school programs particularly recognize the positive role of the French presence overseas, especially in North Africa. This amendment on the "positive role" of colonization had been originated and supported by a lobby, Groupe d'études sur les rapatriés, considered by some commentators to be nostalgic for French Algeria. The article went relatively unnoticed at first, before triggering a vast campaign of demonstrations and petitions, which led President Jacques Chirac to take the unusual step of suppressing the controversial passage of article 4 by decree. The second case, which led to the petition, exemplified a growing concern on the part of historians that the dispositions in many *lois mémorielles* authorizing penal sanctions threatened much more than unhampered historical investigation, namely, the very personal freedom of historians. This worry was due to the predicament of a historian, Olivier Pétré-Grenouilleau, who, after he wrote an acclaimed history of the slave trade, was sued by a group, Le Collectif des Antillais, Guyanais et Réunionnais, accusing the author of revisionism and of minimizing the nature of slavery. This legal procedure was made possible by the Taubira law. On February 3, 2006, the president of the collective group withdrew his suit, largely because of the attention Liberté pour l'histoire was given in the French press and media.

Liberté pour l'histoire brought to light the perhaps unintended extent of the penal consequences of recent French legislation. It also defined the task of historians and assigned specific roles to history as distinct from memory. In the wording of the petition, "History takes memory into account, it is not reduced to it." On the one hand, the signatories of the petition refused to be instrumentalized in the service of the politics of the State, and on the other hand, they were wary of representing the interests of private groups who would attempt to raise their memories to the status of collective history. This distrust of memory has itself a long history, for on it rests the foundation of history as a science.[8] Memory is often taken to task by historians for its tendency to sacralize the past and to exclude from it information that does not conform to its own code of interpretation. In his discussion of the French collective memory of Algeria in *La gangrène et l'oubli*, for example, Benjamin Stora writes about the memoirs of *pieds-noirs* that "it is a sort of 'religious memory,' a ritualized memory, so that each event takes its meaning in relation to the legendary organization of the past. This form of writing entails a sterilization of historiography, the deluge of historical details provoking the decline of real memory."[9] In contrast, scientific historiography is indirectly defined by Stora as the assessment of political, economic, or cultural "actions," the "real origins" and "thus the outcome" of which are exposed (247). The implication is that historians maintain a critical distance in their evaluation, in the sense that they do not privilege specific memories and that they have appropriate methods to select amidst the material at their disposal so as to provide an overarching narrative. Likewise, the petition Liberté pour l'histoire asserts that, "in a scientific approach, the historian collects the memories of men, compares them with one another, confronts them to documents, to objects, to traces, and establishes facts." Yet Stora's work has widely contributed to demonstrating the entanglement of historians with the historiography they produce. An example of this can be found in *La gangrène et l'oubli* where he recounts the diverse and, at times, contradictory ways in which Algerian and French historiographies addressed the same events. Precisely, another signatory of Liberté pour l'histoire, the historian Pierre Vidal-Naquet, whose works on Ancient Greece, the Algerian War and torture, and revisionism have made him particularly attuned to the question of memory, makes an assessment of the issue that gives its due to particular memories and to indirection. In a 1994 interview with Elisabeth Weber, Vidal-Naquet tends to agree with Nora's position that memory has become "tyrannical" by pointing to "the obsession with remembering [*obsession mémorielle*]"; but he adds that the historian "also has to be responsible for individual memories."[10] For Vidal-Naquet, the task of the historian is to go against the grain, "in relation to all doctrines, ideologies, and previous standpoints"; a historian worthy of the name should be a "traitor" to the unity and homogeneity of the grand narrative (27) and emphasize what is discordant. The distrust of memory may then lose some of its pertinence, all the more so since Vidal-Naquet points out that memory is itself "a highly socialized phenomenon," and therefore in no way natural, but a construct elaborated in, and depending on a specific place and time (26).

It should also be noted that a number of historians wrote against some of the positions of Liberté pour l'histoire. For them, the assessment of *lois mémorielles* in the petition was not comprehensive enough, singling out as it did a few of them while omitting others, such as the 1999 law rightly substituting the words "Algerian war" to the phrase "operations in North Africa." They were also not convinced that the autonomy of historical scholarship was seriously endangered and targeted by the laws. Above all, they reacted differently to the evidence of concurring memories. They agreed that the writing of history should not be dictated, but argued that it could be enriched by disregarded memories, even when expressed confusedly. In that respect, they stressed that the awakening of memory "is often but the consequence of the lacunae or the weaknesses of scientific history and of the absence of a public position on the troubled pages of the past." Furthermore, it seemed legitimate to the authors of that article for the institutions of the French republic to have a say on those "essential repressed pages that come back in the present," and they pointed out that historians have no monopoly on collective memory.[11] The wording of this last sentence with its psychoanalytic lexis of repression, that is, of a memory that was registered and archived, though its way of returning to public consciousness may sound confused and distressing, may be related to another consideration, that *lois mémorielles,* for all their faults, attempt to provide. It consists, in Jacques Derrida's words pronounced in another context, at the Freud Museum in London, "in situating justice, the justice which exceeds but also requires the law, in the direction of the act of memory, of resistance to forgetting."[12] In his reflection on archivization with relation to memory and to history or return to the origin, still remaining within the classical paradigm of the archive, namely, that "*there is no archive without a place of consignation, without a technique of repetition, and without a certain exteriority,*" which "assures the possibility of memorization, of repetition, of reproduction" (11), Derrida opens up the concept by emphasizing that "the injunction [of memory], even when it summons . . . the safeguard of the archive, turns incontestably toward the future to come" (79). Derrida calls here for another function of memory, one that would not serve to put in reserve or reconstitute facts. Instead, memory would point to an occultation or nonrepresentation that would be addressed and directed toward the possibility of a future justice. Thus, the archive is not configured as a closed heritage, but "calls into question the coming of the future [*avenir*]" (33–34). While relying at times on archives, Djebar analyzes their potential for capturing, unbeknownst to them, an oblique truth of the event, to be differentiated from the "imprint of reality," and she also focuses on the disappearance of traces, including in the archive.[13] We will address in this chapter the numerous fictional narratives by Cixous and Djebar that reopen the archive of colonial education and investigate its legacy in consideration of justice.

ALGERIAN COLONIAL EDUCATION

The ideological role attributed to education in a colonial model that claimed it intended to achieve the "assimilation" of the native population cannot be overemphasized. The French authorities could have undertaken a program of assimilation in the sense of aligning the rights of the colonized to education with those of the citizens of France, however problematic that might have been. In fact, the rhetoric of assimilation was used as an alibi that covered "a deliberate enterprise of destructuration of Muslim society" or, in Pierre Bourdieu's more brutal words, a "social vivisection," especially through the introduction of French law in Algeria.[14] Several laws, however, including those related to education, were specific to indigenous Algerians and offered fewer guarantees than French legislation.[15] In an article published in 1939 about Kabylia, which exposes economic and social disenfranchisement, Albert Camus noted this discrepancy between the official discourse of assimilation and the lack of education the children were actually receiving in the villages he visited: "The number of children deprived of education in the region is reportedly 80%."[16] He also deplored the lack of schools for girls and the inept distribution of funds leading to an unequal geographical repartition of classrooms. By all accounts, the overall participation of Algerian children in the colonial school system, or in any schooling at all, was very low.

Jonathan K. Gosnell writes that between 1882 and 1892 there were special schools for natives. "Skeptics of colonial education" feared that it would encourage unwanted aspirations among the colonized, and even when the number of schooled children increased, for instance after World War II, Gosnell shows that throughout French colonization it was the settler opposition that "limited the level of Muslim participation in colonial schools."[17] This should not be taken as a criticism of the dedication of many French teachers in Algeria, who in some cases, as Stora has pointed out, succeeded in eliciting sympathy from local populations, especially when they shared their difficult living conditions in the country.[18] As for literacy for girls, it was extremely limited, even though, as Gosnell remarks, "educators and administrators claimed to prioritize instruction for girls."[19] In his study of populations in Algeria during French colonization, Kamel Kateb shows that, "until 1954, [Muslim] female presence in schools remains relatively low"; at that time "schoolgirls represented 8.4% of the female population age 6 to 14. In 1948 and in 1954, schoolchildren of both sexes represented 9.3 and 15.5% of children."[20] Stora's figures for the same period, slightly higher (from 11.5 percent in 1945 to 18 percent in 1954), also indicate a great discrepancy between cities and the country. In the countryside the proportion of Muslim schooled children abruptly dropped during this same period.[21] Assia Djebar was therefore an exception, doubly so because of her sex and because she received a university degree. She has said that "up until my *bac*, and even after my *bac* . . . I always was the only Arab girl among the French students."[22] By the time a far-reaching educational reform in Algeria was truly contemplated by the French government, with the view once again (or at last) of fostering an integrative community, the Algerian war of independence had already started. Djebar emphasizes the correlation between reform and the Algerian insurrection: "The progression occurred between 1954 and 1962. As soon as the uprising started, France tried schooling massively."[23] James D. Le Sueur has shown that as late as August 1958, late to the extent that Algeria became independent four years later, Charles de Gaulle presented an eight-year plan of reform of public education in Algeria with the aim of increasing "the pace and number of those to be educated." Even the Algerians who participated in these last efforts at rapprochement, such as the writer Mouloud Feraoun, incidentally a fellow student of Djebar's father who was assassinated by the OAS (Organisation Armée Secrète) in 1962, were aware that it was too late to rectify what had been a deliberate policy of exclusion on the part of French colonists. In the words of Feraoun quoted by Le Sueur, "In the beginning, there was a choice to be made, and they made it. Why talk about mistakes at this point?"[24]

The French republican principle of equality was not respected as far as the admission of children in colonial schools was concerned. Likewise, Algerians' access to French citizenship was strongly inegalitarian and in contradiction with the laws of the republic. Laws granting citizenship varied over time in colonial Algeria, and a difference of access was also established in 1870 between two indigenous populations, the Muslims and the Jews. There again, the official claim of assimilation acutely showed its limits. Because Algerian natives were juridically placed under a Muslim status (personal status), which was posited as incompatible with French citizenship, a distinction between nationality and citizenship was in fact introduced in an unusual legislation. Since naturalization implied relinquishing their legal status as Muslims, the acquisition of French citizenship by Muslims was interpreted by their coreligionists as apostasy and was not broadly requested.[25] As Stora points out, hurdles to citizenship were predicated on the perceived "inassimilable" character of the autochthonous population, while the restricted possibilities of access to French citizenship that were left to Algerians gave them the choice between "radical assimilation or rejection."[26] This French policy, along with other contradictions between the official claim of assimilation and the actual social and political dispossession of the majority had the ultimate consequence of accelerating the emergence of a national sentiment among Algerians. The harsh repression of demonstrations in Sétif and other Algerian towns in May 1945 confirmed the vacuity of purported assimilation. Yet a few years earlier, between the two world wars, Algerian intellectuals such as Ferhat Abbas, while denouncing the injustices of the colonial system, still thought it was possible to fight them in the name of "French values" (126) or to reconcile peacefully nationalists' theses and those of assimilationists: it is only as the ill will of the French authorities and their inability to achieve reforms became manifest that independence, and later on, armed insurrection, appeared to them to be the only possible course of action (128).

At the beginning of French colonization, there were about thirty thousand Jews in Algeria.[27] Up to 1870, when they were granted citizenship, Algerian Jews were also under personal status laws. Cixous has pointed out that "the Jews [in Algeria] were not asking to be French. . . . In spite of themselves, the Jews had become a political card."[28] When the Crémieux decree of 1870 naturalized Jews collectively, one of the results was to separate the two indigenous populations and, at least in principle, to integrate the Jewish population of the Maghreb into France. It also entailed, as Jacques Derrida points out, cutting the Jews off from their culture and their language.[29] However, the collective attribution of French citizenship was almost immediately restricted in 1871, while some Jews (for example, in the South) never benefited from the Crémieux decree.[30] Furthermore, the decree was abrogated under the Vichy regime in 1940, which, as Derrida noted, implied for Jews not only being deprived of French citizenship but also not gaining any other.[31] The abrogation of the decree severely limited as well the participation of Jews in many professions (including teachers, but also doctors, such as Cixous's father) and their attendance in schools, as was the case for Derrida, who was expelled from his school under the *numerus clausus* regulating the proportion of Jewish children in schools (first 14 percent, then 7 percent in primary and secondary schools and 3 percent in institutions of higher learning).[32] As for Cixous, she started "school" in 1941 in Oran in one of the improvised schools organized by Jewish leaders and parents as a substitute for public institutions.[33] Colette Zytnicki notes that a great number of settlers never accepted the Crémieux decree and that "anti-Semitism was a permanent given in Algerian political life." The *numerus clausus* targeted professors and university students at first, but the measure was later applied to primary and secondary schoolchildren, despite the fact that such application was not required by any legislative text.[34] Likewise, anti-Jewish laws were unilaterally imposed (and promptly executed) in Algeria by the French authorities, since Algeria was never occupied by Germany—in fact, according to the historians Michael R. Marrus and Robert O. Paxton, Vichy was put under pressure by Algiers and not the other way round; even after the Allied forces landed in November 1942, the *numerus clausus* was not completely abolished until March 1943, while the whole anti-Jewish legislation was only dismantled and the Crémieux decree reestablished in October 1943, illustrating well an anti-Semitic climate that was not solely due to the Vichy regime.[35]

The measure of discrimination excluding some but not all Jewish schoolchildren made it particularly incomprehensible to them, while bringing few advantages to those who were kept as students, whom Cixous names "alibi and hostage Jews."[36] She even claims that some schools, such as the Lycée Fromentin that she attended in Algiers, seemed to perpetuate secretly a form of *numerus clausus* well after the war (85). Just as Djebar wrote that she was the only Arab girl in her class, so too Cixous recalls, "I was a student in a school where the Jews could be counted on the fingers of one hand. I was almost always the only Jew in my class" (85). In a film devoted to him, Derrida attests to the prevalent anti-Semitism in Algeria and confides to his interviewer, "But what was most painful wasn't simply the administrative decision to expel us from school. It was what took place in the streets—the insults, the children calling us 'dirty Jews.' This violence that was continually expressed towards us. This was our daily experience. The persecution of children towards other children."[37] In addition, while parallel schools were improvised by the Consistory as of the end of 1940 with the help of dismissed Jewish teachers, the Jewish students of such schools termed private were not allowed to take examinations above the level of "certificat d'études" (a degree obtained at the end of primary school).[38] The intention was then clearly to limit the access of most Jews to higher education by curtailing their rights to attend schools and to receive degrees. Stora writes that, in general, the Muslim elites did not rejoice over the abolition of the Crémieux decree, seeing instead in the reversal of the statute of the Jews the evidence that amelioration of their own political rights was not forthcoming (105–7).[39] In *Nulle part dans la maison de mon père*, Djebar also recalls the reactions of republican and socialist Algerian teachers to the pro-Vichy measures taken by the authorities. In one scene the teacher's daughter receives a biography of Pétain as a prize for excellence, a provocation to her father whose Gaullist positions are resented by his school principal.[40]

CIXOUS AND COLONIAL PEDAGOGY: THE INVISIBILITY OF THE COLONIZED

Both Djebar and Cixous show that colonialism relied on dividing society in two and compartmentalizing communities, and, when detailing these barriers, they are often led to reflect on processes of nonreciprocal exchanges across so-called communities. For Djebar the issue is to recognize the intended organization of the colonial system while problematizing its operation and, at times, its success. Cixous, who evokes on several occasions a relative's store in Oran called Aux Deux Mondes (The Two Worlds), remarks that it was possible to take for granted that "the world was two," while at the same time never understanding "in a clear, explicit or decisive way which the two were."[41] Just as for Djebar, this uncertainty is one of Cixous's ways of contesting the colonial partition as much as its efficacy and ethical validity; but, unlike Djebar, undecidability as to the essence of the two worlds is also informed by her inscription of the Jews as an element that destabilizes the solidity of the opposition posited between two groups, namely "Arabs" and "French." The Jews' position in that equation is complex, since thanks to the Crémieux decree they are no longer Arabs; but because of anti-Semites, they are never quite French either. This is an effect that Cixous sums up at times as that of the *numerus clausus*: a small number that is "first admitted *so as* to be rejected."[42] In effect, for Cixous, inclusion remains an unfulfilled promise at best and at worst a cruel hoax. "Entering gave on to exclusion. This is the logic of the *Numerus Clausus*."[43] In general, Algerian writers do not approach the colonial world through that analytical angle, especially but not merely when they deal with the perspective of the colonized child. In "Encounters," for instance, Mohammed Dib refers to foreigners, French or Europeans, as external to the Algerian child's group: "a whole other world used to live next to mine but, throughout my early childhood, I had hardly noticed it."[44] School gradually alters the child's sense that foreigners are frightening (108), and even "extraterrestrial" (106). But it is mostly in adolescence that the division between French and Arabs becomes insufficient to account for other demarcations, which must at least be superimposed on it, such as the opposition between the city and the country and especially divisions produced by social inequalities among Algerians (112–13). Therefore Dib complicates the initial understanding of homogeneous groups. In that account, David the Jew with his pastry stand does not frighten the child because of the felt closeness to him (112). Likewise, Djebar, who rarely includes the situation of the Algerian Jews in her narratives, often shares with Dib's approach the characteristic of presenting at first an apparently impenetrable separation between two worlds, in which the Jews differ from but are related to the Arab community; then she shows that boundaries are both less absolute and more complex, but without Jews being a factor in accounting for that complexity. In *So Vast the Prison*, for instance, a passage that ends with the realization that "these 'French from France' did not seem to me (how strange this is) completely foreign," starts with the assertion of a world cut up in two: "It should be recalled that the foreigner, during this period of collective servitude, did not merely seem different. No, if not always seen as 'the enemy,' he was still at all times the *roumi*."[45] The name *roumi,* which was given to Christians or Europeans by Muslims, triggers the following parenthetical reflection regarding the status of Jews in that configuration: "(The native Jews were excluded from this category in our eyes, especially when the women, the old people, had kept 'our' language, which was of course theirs as well, that they spoke in a 'broken' accent that was their own.)" (263). What is "strange" and needs to be elucidated is the way in which the relation Arab/French or us/them becomes unsatisfactory, from a perception of absolute difference to that of relative foreignness. As far as Jews are concerned, just as in Dib's story, Djebar presents them as familiar, and not on the side of the foreigner or of the other group; their relative proximity to Muslims is not shown as a potential for enmity. It is true that Djebar qualifies this statement by writing "especially when, etc.," with the implication that a non-native Jew, and above all an assimilated native Jew who would not "have kept" a competence in Arabic, might be considered a roumi. This interpretation of Jews by Muslims is precisely what Cixous, whose father was Algerian and whose mother was German, and who never learned Arabic like the vast majority of Jewish children of her generation, asserts happened practically all the time, and caused hostility, including at school: "The Cixous children those not really Jewish false French odd inadequate people who loved the Algerians who spurned us as enemy Francaouis, Roumis and Jews."[46] Cixous's narratives about Algeria consistently return to the double wound of being excluded by the (anti-Semitic) French and of being rejected as "French" by Algerians. At the very least, this would induce what Derrida has called a "disorder of identity (*trouble d'identité*)."[47] Cixous shows that colonialism throve on setting up opposed camps that were somehow inescapable even though they were felt to be contrived: "one was forcibly played in the play, with a false identity."[48] Remembering being "assailed in the Clos-Salembier" by Algerian children, "by those whom we wanted to love, with whom we were lamentably in love, to whom we were attached we thought by kinship and communities of origin," is perhaps more painful than the recognition of anti-Semitism on the part of the French, because responsibility and even structural fault are felt when confronting Algerian oppression: "There is a fault. And it is my fault, somehow."[49] This is the outcome of being "forcibly played in the play," the consequences of which are confronted by Cixous in a way that forbids innocence and good conscience. On the contrary, the grudging acceptance of the Jews by the French brings the paradoxical hope that Jews and Muslims are equally despised by the French, a situation that Cixous welcomes as a promising factor of solidarity with Algerians. The failure of that hope and promise is also explained by the fact that French Algeria is a "construction of hostilities" (22). We will return in a subsequent chapter to Cixous's deliberate refusal of a conciliatory discourse, but it should already be clear at this point that the only community she recognizes as true to French Algeria is one revolving around conflict: "Moreover we were not separated, no, we were *together in hostility*. Gathered together in hostility by hostility."[50]

This view is reflected in Cixous's analysis of the colonial school. Both Cixous and Derrida have noted the small number or the lack of Algerians in their classes. Derrida mentions "the cartography of the primary-school classrooms where there were still little Algerians, Arabs, and Kabyles, who were about to vanish at the door of the lycée."[51] School constituted an "Algeria without Algerians" in Cixous's words.[52] The colonial "plan to efface the Algerian being" was partly mirrored by "the effacement of the Jewish being," with the difference that, apart from the Vichy period, Jews could attend school, a possibility that was much more restricted in the case of Muslims.[53] Cixous recognizes that difference by stating both the partial, contested belonging of Jews and the lack or minimal admittance of Muslims. On the one hand, as a Jew, "in those days in the Lycée, when I entered and I was inside, I was in an exacerbated outside" (71); on the other hand, Algerians remain outside of the school without even the luxury of such an acrobatic positioning: "The first thing I saw when I arrived each morning was that I could no longer discern a trace not a single trace of malgeria, I saw the excised enormity of all I had seen just before I walked through the guarded gate, my passport showing that I belonged to the gate's elect, I saw the glaring absence of the country proper which from this side of the border was improper" (71).[54] We will return in the last chapter to the elaboration of vision in Cixous, in which seeing (*voir*) becomes dissociated from having (*avoir*) and knowing (*savoir*); much of that thinking has to do with the early recognition of a deliberate blindness that the colonial student was unable to share: "I could obviously not not see what there was to see, those big holes, those blanks or black spots" (70). Seeing that there is nothing to see opens up a "critical space" within the adolescent (70), requiring that blindness or invisibility be read and interpreted. Childhood is a state of hyperlucidity in the narrators of Cixous's oeuvre: "In truth, I was never a child; I'd imitate the other children out of caution and by guile. . . . I hid the fact that I was a growing and ancient force."[55] A question haunts the politically aware student: "How can one make people see the invisible?"[56] In the vein of Ralph Ellison emphasizing invisibility as fundamental to oppression, Cixous underscores the "substitution, excision, and phantomization" of Algerians in the school.[57] A remarkable scene depicts a counterattack in which schoolteachers, standing for French Algeria, are poetically transformed into phantoms, photographed out of existence. Using a broken camera, the young student "made it into a tool for fabricating ghosts. . . . With the vacant camera I snapped pictures of the teachers. . . . So I inexisted them" (84). Not only does this undertaking, intended to mimic and turn upside down the "plan of effacement" of Algerians through a spectralization of the masters of the rules of deception, bring to the fore the necessity of fighting the injustice done to Algerians, it also exposes the means—political annihilation through invisibility—with which it is effected. The colonial system is built on what is called a "semantic slippage" in which "untruth is in command" (80).[58] Instead of attacking the system frontally, the student deliberately reiterates the strategy of deception and disavowal that is denounced with a technical apparatus of reproducibility—feigning to take images with a defective camera—as an ironic response to untruth. Thus she demonstrates the fallacy of the apprehension of the world, a radical cut from referentiality, or, conversely, she shows that in colonial Algeria, the only option left is to affirm "make-believe, pretense, masks" (84). The "fullness of . . . solitude" (85), which such measures entail for the lone activist whose project is deemed akin to a "terrorist plot" (84), can only be borne as a springboard for other means of escape.

Openings are said to have come mainly from two sides. The first opening is made possible by the school itself, once it is perceived that it is a contradictory space. Although it is exclusionary, there is at the same time "a delightful Lycée in one part of the Lycée in disguise" (83). Some of the teachers are just and honest (83), especially "the French teachers from France who brought the fresh air of a foreigner."[59] At the surface, the space of the lycée is enthralling, "it was a femininity, modern, sumptuous . . ." (85). One of the reasons why Cixous consistently distrusts the perception of Algeria and, here, Lycée Fromentin as "edenic" (85) is that such enchantment can be distracting and blinding or make one turn a blind eye to what beauty harbors or dissimulates. But what is especially productive for thinking is the juxtaposition of that physical external enticement with the other attraction of the school's labyrinthine underground passages, the entrance to which always remains elusive. The appeal of going underground and discovering a secret passage is akin to the student's subversive reading of the school as a machine to produce racism and colonialism. The spatial configuration of the school can then give an insight into the methods of colonial pedagogy and the social and racial lessons it provides, out in the open as much as secretly, for "everything is *trompe l'oeil*" (84). In that respect, the astute decoder is exposed to the challenge of interpreting what the school often promotes only obliquely or through antiphrasis. Her ability to interpret is stimulated by that very opacity: "Note that there was no explicit discourse. . . . But everything was sign and symptom. So I did my political reading alone, and with no one in whom to confide my suspicions, young, not yet trained, but having always been on alert" (85). That political reading is sustained by and could perhaps not have existed without the perception of tensions that constitute Algeria in and out of the school: "Each scene always had other contradictory sides."[60]

It is then possible to retrace Cixous's path, starting from the "cardboard school" that the Jewish school in Oran resembled in the Vichy period, at which the "first francolinguistic ecstasies" were experienced, to her condition of writing today "as a decentered, out-of-the-Hexagon mix, camping close to the gates of the City."[61] In that trajectory, books are apprehended first as a line of escape "without moving" from Algeria.[62] Likewise, learning English (or "languelait"), studying in England, and reading English literature are ways of rejecting "French" Algeria.[63] Cixous, who became the youngest university professor in France to earn a doctorate (Doctorat d'Etat) in English literature in 1968, has written about her difficult relation to a certain classical French literature—"Even the Enlightenment was too French for me"—and instead about her preference and kinship for "Anglo-Saxon penumbra."[64] But literature that is so highly and consistently valorized by Cixous is much more than a line of escape or a point of departure; whereas being anchored in nationality and territoriality is constantly depreciated and even disbelieved by Cixous, who disqualifies any claim to such belonging as far as she is concerned, the reverse is true for language, reading, and writing, which haunt her and which she inhabits in turn. Even then, literature is both her element and shore and not a point of arrival. Literature is given, yet always differs from itself; it cannot be owned, though it can possess the reader: "writing is never read: it always remains to be read, studied, sought, invented." Reading and writing are "everlasting" in the sense that no reading can ever wear out what literature tells. Thus there are only beginnings in reading, a condition of acquiring and losing "sites of memory" in the moment of reading, which she summed up once in the untranslatable phrase "*oublire*."[65]

A second opening took place at school. It was an anticipation of the future, the welcome irruption of Algeria itself in the premises of Lycée Fromentin, the promise of "Algeria for the Algerians," thus "a glimmer of history," history not only in the making, but already made.[66] Cixous has recounted several times the arrival in her *lycée* of three Algerian girls. Two of them, Zohra Drif and Samia Lakhdari, were to become celebrated resisters and take part in the 1957 Battle of Algiers. The realization that her former classmates were part of the resistance movement in Algeria was at the same time another confirmation for Cixous of her contradictory position with respect to Algerians, based on a closeness that could not be mutually felt. That position was stated in "Letter to Zohra Drif," in which she testifies to a necessary reserve on her part, an admiration that had to remain silent, "in the image of my fatality of Algeria."[67] Such asymmetry had already happened in and out of school in Algeria; it was in fact constitutive of everyday life: "They lived in me, I did not inhabit them" (87). By invoking her classmates' indifference as the catalyst for leaving Algeria, the ethical paradigm repeated throughout Cixous's work, consisting in departing rather than arriving, gets enacted for new purposes.[68] This time, noncoincidence with the self may be assumed deliberately and with other strategies in mind. Whereas, for the three Algerian classmates, "surely I was what I was not: a French girl," once not quite arrived in France, the young woman with a French passport "was the foreigner that I was," without having "to carry the sins of France."[69] Cixous's vigilance about various forms of expulsions, literal or figurative, will lead her to take note of another interdiction, against which she will famously rebel with as much tenacity and perhaps much more impact than she did against colonialism in Algeria: "In France, what fell from me first was the obligation of the Jewish identity. On one hand, the anti-Semitism was incomparably weaker in Paris than in Algiers. On the other hand, I abruptly learned that my unacceptable truth in this world was my being a woman. Right away, it was war."[70]

DJEBAR AND COLONIAL PEDAGOGY: TREADING THE DIVIDING LINE

Djebar's relative isolation in the predominantly European classes she attended in her French school in Blida confirms Cixous's narratives. The school reflects the general partition of the colonial world, the colony being shown as a world divided in two, with time fractured into two histories unfolding with different duration in the same place.[71] From the perspective of the colonized, Mohammed Harbi has written that the assertion and endorsement of traditional collective structures can be understood as a gesture of solidarity against the colonizer and could be perceived then as the only possibility of surviving culturally and socially.[72] Separations between "clans" were evident in and out of school, but although Djebar talks of a general experience of segregation, she also notes that the lines dividing two perceived groups were often shifting (not only French/Arabs, but also boys/girls, French school/Quranic school, and other such constructed opposites). The perception of a reducible difference makes Djebar reflect on the motives for exclusion; in her discussion of colonial schooling she emphasizes the instability of posited heterogeneities and points out the partial openings provided by each group she was part of.

In Djebar's narratives, the figure of the father is presented at the limit of two communities, "the only Arab teacher of French" in a French elementary school. "He had a 'native' class: During this period, at least for boys, school segregation was justified in this colonial village by the fact that little Arab boys, because they did not speak French in the family, needed 'remedial' teaching. And for native pupils—a native teacher."[73] But, working within such socio-racial constraints, the father also pushes them to the limit. On the beach "strictly reserved to Europeans," for instance, he deliberately overturns all the signs bearing the words "forbidden to Arabs."[74] Contemptuous of such tokens of racial discrimination, he is by no means successfully "assimilated" through his French training. French schooling may be "sacralized" (51), but it is in bad taste to "ape the other clan" (116). Instead, education is embraced as the means to contribute to an indigenous elite, following the model of emancipation of Egypt, Syria, and Turkey.[75] Along with a European suit, the father wears a Turkish fez in recognition of the Turkish statesman Atatürk's modernism, an inspiration to young Maghrebian Muslims in the 1930s.[76] In sum, that figure is consistently shown to be both receptive and critical; the father's interpretation of custom and culture inscribes a singular reaction to the world, often unlike that of any other. He seems to be the prototype for the solitude of Djebar's heroines (or at least, it does not contradict theirs), which is, however, serenely accepted on the whole because it is associated with the perception of a privilege.[77] From the beginning, stepping out with the father to go to school has entailed witnessing the separation between two groups, while incarnating the dividing line between both or difference itself: "The two of us, my father and I . . . walk with uncertain steps, almost at the edge of unbalance . . . between the society of 'Others' and that of the indigenous" (85).

This precarious path carves out a complex mode of belonging. Djebar's narrators' or heroines' interpretations tend to defeat expectations. In *Nulle part* the romantic confidences of her fellow boarder Jacqueline astonish the narrator, who feels, however, secure in her own positions and "values" (177–80). Yet, when she shares the story with her cousin who proceeds to berate French women, she objects to her cousin's severe judgment of her French classmate. Thus exchanges occur through a critical distance that does not preclude a certain adhesion to the interlocutor's position. Djebar always develops both motifs simultaneously—grounds for acceptance and for reticence. She insists first on the absence of communication between groups in order to denounce the colonial project and its impact on the colonized. But school, which overwhelmingly reiterates colonial presuppositions and divisions, is also one of the few places where meeting and talking to the other group is possible. *Nulle part* gives several instances of such exchanges—within tacit limits: speaking to Jacqueline at night is common, because her bed is close by in the boarding school, but it almost never happens during the day when each stays with other members of her own group. Remarking that it was rare for Algerians to share a territory other than school with their European classmates, Djebar emphasizes that it was almost out of the question to visit one another or to enter the other's house: "The two societies coexisted without coming in contact in interiors."[78] About her French friend Jacqueline, the narrator remarks, "I never entered her house, and neither did she ours."[79] But Djebar also diversifies the group gathered by the colonial school under the name "Muslim students"; they are united on some issues, but their individual trajectories vary, with different geographical or social backgrounds, and consequently they sometimes feel remote to the narrator (131). Likewise, Cixous has written about not ever being invited in by a Muslim family.[80] But, for reasons we have already mentioned, the pattern of thwarted hospitality extended also to European friends. The "French Christian" friend Françoise could visit her Jewish schoolmate, but the reverse was not true, "a great anti-Semitic complication which made impossible on her side what was possible on mine" (70). Whereas both Cixous and Derrida have evoked a "trouble of identity" in spite of their apparently greater integration to the European group in

Algeria, an integration that was contradicted, however, by the blatant or subtle forms of exclusion they were exposed to, Djebar declared once that she did not experience any such trouble and "felt naturally Algerian."[81] Thus Djebar affirms her incontestable belonging to the oppressed group. But this position does not preclude an inner complication, and her writing is especially mobilized by instances in which imposed separations and ties do not quite succeed in strictly opposing one group to another. This is the productive point at which the posited borderline and its purpose can be interrogated. Djebar has written about being "both the besieged foreigner and the native," but she did so in connection with her discussion of languages, which may be one of the instances in which difference within the self could be felt to be the most acute, as we shall examine in the next chapter.[82] Yet, even though it was caused by colonization, that internal split may have a number of positive consequences in postcolonization.

With respect to education, Djebar has explained in several texts the obstructions to learning Arabic she encountered at school. They had an impact on her command of written Arabic, which, as a child, she had started learning in the Quranic school with her mother's encouragement.[83] In *Nulle part* the request to learn Arabic in secondary school is framed by several considerations that Djebar unfolds in order to make explicit the multilayered and interwoven motives at work as far as access to languages is concerned. To begin with, Djebar emphasizes the strangeness of the request to study Arabic or the "mother tongue" as a "first foreign language."[84] This phrase strikes the narrator as absurd when uttered by Algerians with respect to Arabic. Logistics are invoked to justify the refusal: if she had been enrolled in modern literature, she could have studied Arabic along with other students. And since she chose Latin as a classical literature student, she could not take Arabic but English (105). It is doubtful that the rigidity of such administrative rules was reserved to colonial schools or is a hallmark of that period. The narrator reflects further on the difference between the two options (classical and modern) by underscoring that the first was intended to track the best students, the elite who would go on studying Greek, a language thus qualified: "I alone, however, knew the Arab saying, retailed even by illiterate relatives, namely, that 'if Arabic is God's language,' since Mohammed heard it from Gabriel in the cave, Greek is nevertheless 'the language of angels'" (105). Here is an instance in which the enrollment in classical literature that precludes the teenager from formally training in her mother tongue is a response to criteria of excellence endorsed by the two groups with which she is differently associated. Though these criteria may differ, both groups agree that Greek is a superior language, which each can claim as its own through learning: "Finally, thanks to having mastered ancient Greek, I landed in Greece, as if home at last!"[85] Secondly, the narrator wonders in retrospect why her European fellow students, "who were, however, born like me in this country, were disposed to learn all the languages of the world, including the so-called 'dead' languages . . . but . . . would by no means seek to understand the language spoken out of the school by the nine tenths of the population of the country! Even I had not asked myself the question, as if the colonial period in which we lived anesthetized in me as well the astonishment that should have been mine faced with the deafness of my fellow students to my mother tongue."[86]

The literary space, "a miraculous ether" (107), puts into question boundaries and their insistence on exclusion. In a scene recurring since her early novel *Les Alouettes naïves*, Djebar links the discovery of Baudelaire's poem "L'Invitation au voyage," strikingly recited by an admired teacher, with an open invitation to enter "another universe" (107), that of words, books, and literature. The student's first understanding of Baudelaire as "BEAU DE L'AIR" ("beautiful from the air"; 101) becomes an equation often posited by Djebar between the exhilarating power of reading (127) and the sensation of flying away like a bird (107), not unlike the experience of springing up "toward the azure" on the stadium when playing basketball at school (182), or of leaping when dancing (196), all these stances figuring liberty in Djebar's lexis. Reading, just as dancing or playing basketball, is a solitary activity that opens up another space, elsewhere, as well as a place in which the other is met. The issue is not merely the well-known escapism and identification made possible by fiction; in a scene related in several books, the little girl is so absorbed by a "first reading," Hector Malot's *Sans famille*, that she cries over the orphan's woes (19–21). The reader's intoxication (Djebar equates reading with drinking [19, 102]) is also incited by the rhythm of another's words. The reader's poetic trance reaches a climax when she becomes receptive to a dual cultural emphasis on tone and accent. An analogy is drawn between the French teacher's solemn, majestic recitation, with its rhythmical cuts and vocal contrasts, and that of the Quranic verses, which the young student was used to listening to at home: "I am shaken to feel the way in which beauty is one and multiple, to feel that even the Quranic verse has its counterpoint" (103). Likewise, the mystified mother ends up understanding her daughter's tears over the sentimental French story *Sans famille* by linking the little girl's reaction to the emotion she feels when singing or hearing classical Andalusian songs (21).

Djebar has recounted more than once the formative importance of fervent literary friendship, thanks to which, for example, two young girls discover modern literature (Rimbaud, Péguy, Gide) through the mediation of the published correspondence of Jacques Rivière and Alain-Fournier, two friends who were passionate about literature themselves (133). In an interview she also mentioned her political affinity for American literature, in particular with writers like Faulkner, whose South she felt related to Algeria, because the violence he depicted seemed a more accurate reflection of Algeria than the fiction of writers like Camus, even though he "shares my space."[87] That literature is inseparable in Djebar's case from a political stance is made clear in that interview, where she explains that, as the war of independence started, she was a history student in Paris, in fact the only Algerian woman at the Ecole Normale Supérieure. "In 1956 . . . the FLN asked all Algerian students to go on strike" (234). As a result, she did not take her examinations, and in 1958 she moved to Tunisia where she worked for the FLN weekly *El Moudjahid* among Algerian refugees (235), just as the narrator Omar in *Les Alouettes naïves*. However, in addition to thus circumventing the French educational system, she substituted taking examinations with a "wager," that of writing a novel in French in one month—*La Soif* (234). Djebar makes it clear that such an undertaking was not without political risks (236), Clarisse Zimra explaining in that respect that Djebar's first two books were at times criticized for not "advanc[ing] the cause of national liberation."[88] Djebar's gesture confirms what has been contended so far with respect to the autonomous path she traces at and indeed across the limit between two groups: while literally respecting the FLN watchword when she abstained from taking her examinations at one of the most prestigious institutions of higher learning in France, it could be argued that she disobeyed it somewhat in spirit by having *La Soif* published by a well-known Parisian press, Julliard, in 1957. Characteristically, her discussion of her first novel with Le Clézio focuses on the dissimulation that writing in French made possible, by using a comparison, "French as a veil," that she has often repeated elsewhere.[89] It may not be possible to determine without the shadow of a doubt whom or what her writing covers or hides from, a point we will return to later as

Djebar's call for the right to obscurity, silence, and secrecy. Dissimulation is predicated in the interview on colonialism, in which each side holds "a deformed image" of the other (236). Furthermore, the issue was not merely to address the counterfeit or blurred image she mentions, but to inscribe her novel within a literary tradition evoking and challenging political power. She notes that while many critics of her first book were looking for sociological keys, only two admired it when it came out for its "Racinian writing," which leads her to remark that seventeenth-century French writers, faced with censorship, "wrote through mirrors, through myths, through very ancient history, in order to speak about current events, with the means of this oblique writing that ends up being a writing of limpidity" (236). Indirection through clarity is a consistent approach discernible throughout Djebar's oeuvre.

While Cixous's and Djebar's experiences of the colonial school have much in common, it is important to recall the singularity of each memory. It is a question of justice, for as Derrida remarks, "not all exiles are equivalent."[90] And he makes that claim just after having asserted that a certain exile and nostalgia (from one's mother tongue and from one's very own culture) are general, constitutive, and universal. The point is to think a generality that is, however, re-marked in a singular way. In her analysis of schooling in French Algeria, Cixous extols time and again the paradoxical lucky chance for thinking that the syndrome of admittance-as-exclusion brought about. Her narratives insist on living up to that chance, which is therefore both repressive and liberating, though its cruelty is not denied.[91] As for Djebar, she is attentive to distinct temporalities and multilayered spaces that contest narratives of univocal autochthony, which she contests along with the injustice of colonial hierarchies. In her texts the I does not simply apprehend itself along one side of a divisive limit, being rather traversed by differences. The inferences both writers draw from the contradictory spatialization of the territory that colonial school constituted inform their propositions about the formalization of other systems and practices. The next two chapters will examine the relation of Djebar and of Cixous to a politics and a poetics of language that confirm and enact these positions.

PART TWO

Poetics of Language

CHAPTER THREE

Vanishing Inscriptions

Assia Djebar's Poetics of the Trace

THE COLONIZED AND LANGUAGE

Postcolonial francophone writers unanimously assess the imposition of the French language not merely as one example among others of colonial oppression but its very instrument, a fundamental vector whose impact still has enduring effects. The frequency of that charge and of that critical turn in the analysis of both French colonialism and racism is evident in the writings of *Negritude* authors such as Aimé Césaire and Léopold Sédar Senghor or in the essays of Frantz Fanon. Lately this critique has been stated by postcolonial novelists and essayists as different as the Caribbean authors of *In Praise of Creoleness* or Edouard Glissant and the Maghrebian writers Rachid Boudjedra and Abdelkebir Khatibi, to mention only a few. All have in common the recognition that the French politics of assimilation was preeminently enforced through the compulsory use of the French language. Since this shared position, however, comes from various geopolitical contexts, it gives rise to different processes of disalienation specific to the location and to the time of the diagnosed acculturation. Furthermore, although the emphasis on discrimination and domination through the French language recurs in postcolonial writings, each reaction shows that the evaluation of the extent and the impact of acculturation is remarkably diverse. I will first recall a few paradigmatic positions among French postcolonial theorists, ranging from the claim of an irreversible alienation to the embrace of "the construction of hybrid identities" or "cultural *metissage*."[1] In this chapter, I will delineate Assia Djebar's interrogation of the possibility of idiomaticity in a postcolonial context, more specifically in Algeria. As in all former French colonies, and perhaps more so than in others since Algeria was claimed "to be France," the French colonial administration in Algeria repressed until a late date (1947) the official use of any language but French, including in school instruction.[2] As we have seen in the second chapter, Djebar, who was schooled in French Algeria, was discouraged or prevented from studying written Arabic, which in turn had an impact on the "choice" of the language in which she could write, a condition on which she has often reflected. Fanon's discussion, which was not restricted to black Antilleans, but aimed to include "every colonized people . . . face to face with the language of the civilizing nation,"[3] sheds light on Djebar's predicament, and, conversely, Djebar's position is indebted to Fanon's and other thinkers' insight into the process of racialization and biologization of difference.

In the wake of the Negritude movement, what Fanon called in the first chapter of *Black Skin, White Masks* the issue of "the Negro and language" was particularly emphasized. Fanon demonstrated the extent to which in the Caribbean, the relation to the French language constituted a modality of alienation and domination which commanded all others: "The Negro of the Antilles will be proportionately whiter—that is, he will come closer to being a real human being—in direct ratio to his mastery of the French language" (18). Thus, speaking French became racialized, and Fanon went on to describe a process of alienation that got reinforced through what he repeatedly called "a lack of judgment" (38), perversely supporting the myth of French assimilation, even though it remained an unfulfilled promise to the majority. In effect, Fanon consistently argued that Europeans promoted assimilation as long as the colonized remained short of it, or as long as he "keep[s] [his] place" (34), and showed that the French perception of their racial and cultural dominance was endangered whenever nonwhites demonstrated their command of the French language.

Aimé Césaire made a related point when he declared that "the Antilleans live in a fiction of assimilation, and the language was an excellent carapace."[4] But whereas Fanon tactically underscored the rigidity of the givens of the colonial situation and argued that the preeminence of French was not about to be overthrown, for instance by the literary use of Creole,[5] Césaire relied on the possibilities of racializing writing positively. He famously claimed, for instance, to have used French as a "tool" in order to create a "black French."[6] In "Black Orpheus," originally written as an introduction to an anthology of Negritude poetry, Jean-Paul Sartre concurred that racializing writing was a way out of the predicament of the colonized, but he detected an inevitable ambivalence in the process: "Blacks can meet only on that trap-covered ground that the white has prepared for them. . . . And since words are ideas, when the negro declares in French that he rejects the French culture, he takes in one hand what he rejects with the other; he sets up the enemy's thinking-apparatus in himself, like a crusher."[7]

The legacy of these positions cannot be overestimated. Working in and on the French language, and thereby inscribing a poetic as well as a political response to the issues Fanon, Césaire, Senghor, Sartre, and others framed—from lament to affirmation—are crucial to Francophone writers today. The ability of making a productive mark on the French language could also be viewed from a different perspective. Instead of concentrating on the issue of the creolization of the French language, for instance, Edouard Glissant foregrounded a less discussed effect of Negritude, namely, to "put into question the normative unity of [the French] language."[8] By focusing on the difference from itself already at work within the French language, Glissant reorients the discussion of the process of disalienation, while not contesting that some normative effects may still be operating. Indeed, Césaire had remarked that surrealism, the poetic form he powerfully enriched, was a mode of liberation from the French language *for the French themselves*. It was its constitutive hybridity that made that form paradoxically foreign to the French in their own language and therefore irresistible to a practitioner of Negritude: "What scandalized the French in this form of art which is so little French was precisely what pleased us."[9]

The Negritude project strove to resist the alienating effects of French assimilation through the authentication in and revalorization of the black race. Césaire aimed to encompass a "'Negro situation' that existed in different geographical areas," a situation that Senghor defined as "the whole complex of civilised values—cultural, economic, social and political—which characterise the black peoples."[10] But those who questioned Negritude were critical of what in that discourse articulated race and universality, failing to account for the heterogeneity of blacks' historical, social, and economic conditions. Césaire and Senghor defined "the values of Negritude" as "universalizing, living values that had not been exhausted. . . . We thought that Africa could make a contribution to Europe"; "they must flow towards the meeting point of all Humanity; they must be our contribution to the Civilisation of the Universal."[11] Some critics of Negritude felt that these positions could lead to the repetition of problematic Western philosophemes that were not thought through. Glissant, for instance, takes such statements to represent markers of what he calls a "system thought" or "another thinking of Being," a project that he substitutes with another, which he names the "thinking of the trace."[12] Glissant associates a poetics of the trace with the possibility of "conceiving the unutterable of a totality" (69). Although he does not explicitly name Jacques Derrida and his reflection on the trace—for example in *Writing and Difference, Of Grammatology,* and *Margins of Philosophy*—Glissant keeps from that thinking an emphasis on a trace that *is* not, that challenges a presentation and a presencing.[13] He calls for what he remarkably names "a prophetic vision of the past" (86), where the past (for instance, slavery in the Antilles) cannot be reconstructed ("the trace does not repeat" [70]), but is legible through heterogeneous elements that are not identical to it but effect an "unpredictable realization" (29). Thus the past, of which the colonized were dispossessed, cannot be recollected but may be constructed through fragments or poetically imagined. It is not rooted in memory but, paradoxically, can be arrived at only in the future in a prophetic mode.

Assia Djebar provides several instances of this odd spatiotemporality, for instance in *Fantasia, an Algerian Calvacade,* or in *So Vast the Prison.* Djebar—who became in 2005 the first Algerian woman writer ever to have been elected to join the Académie française, an institution founded in 1635 with the mandate of defining the French language by writing its dictionary—is also one of several Maghrebian writers who have minutely analyzed the condition of writing in what she calls "the adverse language [*la langue adverse*]."[14] While generally agreeing with Fanon's insight that the ascription of race occurs through language, she also focuses on the chance afforded by a thought of the trace, which would be neither a restitution of the forbidden nor a reconstitution of the forgotten in Algeria before and during French colonization, but, not unlike Glissant's poetics, would attempt to delimit what does remain unutterable. Promoting a "writing for the trace,"[15] by paying attention, for example, to scenes of vanishing inscriptions or an alphabet under erasure, is for Djebar a way of resisting colonial expropriation as well as of avoiding well-intentioned assurances of authentic recovery that would sidestep enduring political and cultural dispossession. In that respect, Djebar aligns her work with the textual strategies elaborated by other Maghrebian writers, such as Abdelkebir Khatibi, while inscribing a difference. Likewise, Djebar's position converges with the thought of Jean-François Lyotard and Jacques Derrida in their assessment of the racialized other's exclusion from the properness and property of language. For Lyotard and Derrida, though each inflects it differently, the issue is then both to deconstruct the appropriation of language by the master or the oppressor and to point to the conditions of possibility of justice not only against that fantasized totalizing language but also through and in spite of it.

DJEBAR'S *QALAM*

The reader familiar with Assia Djebar's work and with that of her critics is aware that *qalam*, an Arabic word transliterated in a Latin alphabet, appears frequently in her idiom. It is found most memorably at the end of *Fantasia, an Algerian Cavalcade*, where Djebar examines French colonial narratives written at the time of the conquest of Algeria. Drawing on the painter Eugène Fromentin's memoir of his stay in Algeria, she recalls his witnessing of the aftermath of the battles opposing the invading French army to the resisting Algerians: "In June 1853 . . . he visits Laghouat, which has been occupied after a terrible siege. He describes one sinister detail: . . . Fromentin picks up out of the dust the severed hand of an anonymous Algerian woman. He throws it down again in his path. Later, I seize on this living hand, hand of mutilation and of memory, and I attempt to make it take the *qalam*."[16] The word *qalam*, which designates a writing instrument, is written in Djebar's text with the Latin alphabet, but without any additional translation or explanation.

Much has been written on this passage, which is often taken to allegorize Djebar's position: first, the Algerian woman's mutilation is attested in the "colonizer's" text and in his language, perhaps unbeknownst to him. A sort of *lapsus calami*, perhaps, a slip of the pen like the one Jacques Derrida mentions near the end of his reading of another scene of writing.[17] Therefore, the detour through the French corpus describing the violently severed Algerian body is necessary, at least in a first gesture, as much as it is indispensable to assert women's active involvement in all Algerian wars—for there have been more than one—a condition that explains why their bodies become privileged sites of reinscription for Djebar.[18] The narrator's "attempt" to make the hand, which is now said to be "living," "take the *qalam*" has also been interpreted as a defiant acceptance of a legacy, displacing both French and Algerian historiographies of the conquest and the war of independence. Djebar is known for the parallels she points out between the French annexation of Algeria and the Algerian war. But she also includes in her assessment of war in the region conflicts that took place before French colonization, as we shall see later in this chapter. Likewise, in texts such as *Algerian White* or *La Disparition de la langue française*, she approaches the state and terrorist violence of the 1990s following the cancellation of the 1991 legislative election in Algeria through the lens of previous conflicts. Thus she shows that wars are both the outcome of singular conditions *and* that they unfold with recurrent patterns harking back to historically prior models of constitution of community and enmity, which does not imply that she endorses the terms of this opposition. Another writing seems to be promised at the end of *Fantasia, an Algerian Cavalcade*, and the attempt to make the hand take the *qalam* is often understood as a recapitulation of the entire thrust of Djebar's project.[19]

But what are we to make of the promise of this other inscription through the Arabic word, thrown in her French text, not unlike the Algerian woman's mutilated hand in Fromentin's? That *qalam* stands for difference thrown in the way or interrupting the patterns of the "adverse language" and discourse seems obvious. By using an Arabic word in her French text, is Djebar suggesting a resisting idiomaticity that can be read or heard but not quite understood by a Francophone reader? We have already mentioned that in postindependence Algeria, the issue of idiomaticity was not only linked to the expression of discourses that had been silenced under French rule. Equally crucially, the question was to determine in what language that idiomaticity would speak or could be written. No simple answer to that question has been formulated, and no mere equation can be made between the "choice" of a language for writing and publishing and a specific political affiliation as far as language is concerned. For instance, Djebar has remarked that the Algerian intellectuals under attack in Algeria in the 1980s and 1990s were not necessarily killed because of their "Francophonie," mentioning in that respect the Arabophone poet Youssef Sebti, murdered in 1993.[20] This is a singular situation for that generation of writers, which is neither exactly that of other Maghrebian writers, who, as Abdelkebir Khatibi wrote in *Love in Two Languages*, could also write "in [their] mother tongue with great enjoyment," nor that described by Jacques Derrida in *The*

Monolingualism of the Other, and summed up in that difficult sentence: "I have only one language, yet it is not mine."[21]

Unlike Khatibi, Derrida cannot rely on bilingualism, that is, "a single mother tongue *plus* another language" (36). In *Monolingualism* Derrida explains what deprived him of an "authorized mother tongue" (31), the French language being the "language of the master" (42). This is, to be sure, the story of the colonized in general—while having monolingualism imposed on them by the master, the colonized are also denied the property of the colonizer's language. But for Derrida there is never a relation of belonging, property, and mastery to language; language is "ex-appropriation" (24), and this is the case even for the master. With the thought of a general ex-appropriation from and in language, the notion of alienation shows its limitations, for no property, no self is properly speaking "alienated" in relation to language. However, to say that there is nothing but appropriations of a language, to some extent and never entirely, is not to deny the impact of the racialization of others through language. On the contrary, since the master is such inasmuch as he "can give substance to and articulate this appropriation . . . in the course of an unnatural process of politico-phantasmatic constructions" (23), it becomes possible to contest naturalized appropriations. Derrida's essay also emphasizes that stating that monolingualism is *of* or comes from the other is not only a threat but also an opening, including the possibility for something to happen in and to language (68) or the desire to "forc[e] the language . . . to speak itself, in another way, in its language" (51).

Djebar's work resonates with this last statement. Like the Algerian Francophone writer Kateb Yacine, Djebar could not easily write in Arabic, even though she might have liked to. For her, the question of "turning to Arabic" in her writing could not be the matter of returning to the comfort of a mother tongue, which she was, however, not cut off from.[22] One way to formalize this situation is to remark, as we have seen earlier, that the dilemma that these writers inherited from colonization was not the deprivation of an authorized mother tongue, in the way that Derrida recounts, but the fact that their mother tongue was neither the "language of writing" they had acquired at school in colonized Algeria nor the national language (modern standard Arabic) taught in schools as of 1964 and promoted after independence through the policy of Arabization. Several commentators describe the linguistic situation in Algeria as violent,[23] but rethinking dispassionately the plurality of languages within Algeria is crucial to Djebar's project. Lucette Valensi writes in this regard that Assia Djebar turned for a while to television and cinema, because these forms allowed her to use vernacular Arabic rather than the modern standard Arabic she had trouble "mastering."[24] This assessment is true, but it is not the whole story. Djebar's writings and films are not merely constrained from the outside; they are also energized by this historical configuration. In his elucidation of the "complexity of the problems posed by the relation to language" in the Maghreb, Réda Bensmaïa recalls that since Algerian independence "the number of works written in French by Maghrebi authors has continued to multiply."[25] This remark leads him to propose a notion akin to Djebar's project, involving "a new geolinguistics" (14) in which "writers have had to imagine or explore as if they were territories to rediscover and stake out, step by step, countries to invent and to draw while creating one's language (8).

When reflecting about Djebar's relation to Arabic and to French, the following positions emerge: to begin with, she puts into question the definition of Arabic as "the 'national language,'" considering instead the Algerian nation as harboring a "cluster of languages," with Arabic as one of them;[26] we shall return at length to that paradigm in her writings. When discussing Arabic as the potentiality and actualization of diverse linguistic practices, Djebar notes that the experience of Arabic as diglossia is not a new occurrence in Algeria: it is not merely the consequence of the postwar policy consisting in adopting modern standard Arabic in preference to the vernacular in education and some public sectors. On the contrary, in its diglossia Arabic has been a factor of Algerian culture for fourteen centuries (18), namely, since the Arab conquest of the region in the seventh century: the vernacular language, an essentially oral discourse, converges with and differs at the same time from literary, written Arabic.[27] Within spoken Arabic there are further internal divisions, with variations in the ability to handle different registers denoting social hierarchies—the figure of the mother being consistently presented in Djebar's writings as the heir to the classical Andalusian culture, with a refined speech, elegant writing, and classical musical erudition. In a sense, then, the use of Arabic in the region, which is in principle dual and in fact multifaceted, is already exemplary of a fluid, pragmatic, but also poetic mode of relation to a language that is not identical to itself. If the question for Algerian writers, in Bensmaïa's words, is *"How can we live within several languages and write in only one?"*[28] part of Djebar's answer consists in emphasizing that the use of Arabic already illustrates the cultural possibility of linguistic plurality or of the cluster of languages that she finds felicitous.

Djebar's education in Arabic was not inexistent, but limited to years of attendance at a Quranic school during her childhood (transposed, for instance, in *Fantasia*), followed, as we have seen in chapter 2, by a hampered and discontinuous teaching that put the burden of her progress on her personal study of the language and of Arab writers. When Djebar states that she has a "dual relation" to Arabic,[29] she is within the parameters of what she indicates to be the position of Arabophones in general, though it is weighted in her case by colonization. Yet, even though she reports the challenges she faced and did not quite overcome when she contemplated writing in Arabic, her conclusion is not that she is doomed to alienation by having to write in the "adverse language," for at least two reasons. First, Djebar frequently insists on the affective charge of discourse in the mother tongue. Precisely her study of Arab writers gave Djebar the perception that they missed what she calls "women's language" (242), which she wishes to emphasize not only because of what it conveys but for the economy of stylistic forms it is informed with (such as ellipsis, litotes, and metonymy). She finds that economy to be in congruity with her own designs, unlike that of some Arab poets whose language she describes as "prodigal."[30] Her focus on oral discourse also entails an attention to sounds themselves, music and noise, along with women's language, a precious "sonorous treasure," as well as silence.[31] In that sense, directing films was not a second-best choice (due to her lack of competence in written Arabic, for example), but showed an aesthetic decision to anchor her work in a language associated with the less prescriptive in terms of linguistic usage, and the less privileged or prestigious within the political spectrum. Likewise, and this is the second reason why not writing in Arabic is not necessarily a sign of alienation, Djebar's increased awareness of hierarchies within Arabic usage and other political discrepancies helped her overcome her misgivings about writing in French, which could thus be made to signal something else beside subordination.[32]

In *Fantasia* and subsequent interviews about that book, Djebar has formulated a number of contradictions inherent in writing in French. By calling a section of *Fantasia* dealing with French "The Tunic of Nessus," in allusion to Heracles, the divine hero who, after having killed the centaur Nessus, was later poisoned or burned by the centaur's blood, still potently efficacious after his death, Djebar seems to concur with the postcolonial writers underscoring the long-standing damage of the imposition of what she calls her "stepmother tongue."[33] The implication of that metaphor is also that French may not be simply discarded, just as the centaur's tunic irremediably stuck to Heracles's skin. As she is prompt to recall in that regard, she did not "choose" to write in French: "Since my childhood, I have been, by my situation of colonized, installed in the French language."[34] This installation is anything but a comfortable and tranquil inhabitation, to the extent that the "enemy's language" has been the instrument of injustice and arbitrariness inflicted on Algerians: "This language was formerly used to entomb my people."[35] The conclusion of *So Vast the Prison,* titled "The Blood of Writing," examines the ways in which "to account for blood . . . that is, for violence."[36] The reference to the tunic of Nessus may then be understood as the political difficulty involved in disentangling the use of French from the memory, and therefore the repetition of that violence, or it may indicate that that violence is perpetuated through means other than colonial occupation, for example through *francophonie,* which many thinkers of the postcolony point out to be the case. Djebar is well aware of the political risks attendant to writing in the language of the former enemy, even though she may boast to have "stolen" it.[37] But the irreducible complication is that the "adverse language" is never simply that; as we have seen earlier, it is also the very element of Djebar's writing: "One way or another, French is not a foreign language to me."[38] The condition of schooled Algerian Arabophones of her generation was one in which French was both distant and familiar, external and internalized. Thus French is not only the enemy's language but also what she terms the "paternal language," in opposition to the mother tongue, to be sure, but also because her father was a teacher of French and supported her education.[39] As such, French is not only stolen but also received as inheritance.

Djebar draws conclusions from that exposure to heterogeneity, which did not merely affect her from without but was also experienced within: it leads her to interrogate separations between the inside and the outside and gives rise to a reflection that could be summarized as a spatial investigation of difference. On the one hand, she often insists on what she calls a "dichotomy of space," a space in which demarcations are visible and evidently felt, in particular because of the colonial partition.[40] From the beginning, her writings (for instance, *Children of the New World, Les Alouettes naïves*) constructed alternation around polarized figures or locations (alternation of narrators, of settings, etc.)—*Fantasia,* which interchanges successively time frames, documents from the colonizer and testimonies from the colonized, locations of men and women, insights from collective and personal histories, constituted no turning point in that respect. Such "territories," as she likes to say, seem at first impenetrable and allergic to one other. But it is only one aspect of the architecture she delineates, because, as we have seen with the example of French as adverse/paternal, Djebar shows that, on the whole, there are always points of passage that defy borderlines, with the consequence that as soon as dichotomy is posited in her work it is immediately problematized or shown to be ineffectual. It is not that Djebar denies difference, but that difference becomes considerably diversified and difficult to account for in oppositional schemas. We have seen that she finds in the cultural history of Arabic in the region a springboard for thinking plurality (linguistic and other) in Algeria; likewise, French, which, unlike the mother tongue, remains arid and cut off from affect,[41] is also endowed with imagining what is not or the impossible: French words learned at school were remote from reality or devoid of referentiality, an uncanny situation that, slightly displaced, can become enabling for thinking along other premises than the immediately given.

Despite appearances, that is, despite the fact that she published in French again with *Women of Algiers in Their Apartment* (1979), Djebar gives no privilege to French, going so far as to claim that her project is to anchor French in vernacular Arabic or orality or remarking on an "affinity of sounds between the French language when it is limpid and my Arabic language when it is spoken," thus definitely interlocking French and Arabic.[42] In that respect, her often quoted statements that French was the "language that gave [her] space," and set the body in motion,[43] must not be misinterpreted as glorifying an intrinsic potential of French. One explanation is that going to school beyond puberty gave her access to the outside. But that could be construed as implying merely that "French" gave her freedom and could therefore obliquely turn Djebar into an apologist of colonization. Instead, receptivity to "space" entails becoming alert to compartmentalization and to thresholds as well as to diverse modes of inhabitation. In *Fantasia,* for instance, written Arabic is tied to a circular exploration in time and space of the secret architecture of the city, while French is linked to detachment and reattachment.[44] If the "apprenticeship" of each language orients the body differently in its outreach, each promotes an exploration of space proceeding from and subverted in writing; in addition, Arabic is consistently tied to history and temporality. Thus it is not that French gave Djebar space whereas Arabic did not, but that bilingualism, and even multilingualism, enabled a spatial interrogation of difference. In that respect, *Fantasia* enacts in French the circular architectural motifs that she ascribes to Arabic writing, through the spiraling reiteration and displacement of scenes, such as the little girl's departure to school with the father repeated at the beginning and at the end.[45] Whereas the first scene takes up the novelistic convention of individual detachment from the community, of a departure from familiar surroundings through the first steps outside and through education ("I cut myself adrift" [5]), the second scene, weighted with all the previous developments of *Fantasia* on the impact of colonization on Algerians, also reattaches the narrator to the group of origin ("isn't it my 'duty' to stay behind with my peers in the gynaceum?" [213]). Thus the circularity assigned to Arabic writing finds a tangential inscription in and overlaps with the back-and-forth structure attributed to French writing. Djebar's position with respect to languages in Algeria has been recalled in this section as a way of approaching her conceptualization of the cohabitation and spatialization of differences.[46] To the extent that Djebar's purpose is to expose what she calls the "permanence of several territories in our Algerian memory,"[47] she is led to confront instances when memory is severed, just as the hand of the anonymous Algerian woman, which she takes to make it hold the *qalam*. In such cases, the very point of writing might seem defeated; in fact, however, gaps in memory, figured by cuts such as the woman's mutilated hand, are not paralyzing but at the core of Djebar's reflection on how to provide a just, though not a seamless narrative about Algeria.

THE TIME OF THE DIFFEREND

With the thought of the *differend*, Jean-François Lyotard addresses the issue of idiomaticity and the possibility of justice in a colonial or postcolonial context. In *The Differend* and elsewhere, Lyotard has recourse to the term with two particular examples in mind: one is the case of a survivor of the Shoah seeking justice and the other is that of a worker seeking redress from his employer in a social conflict. He has also applied the term to the Algerian/French conflict in a way that shows that his thinking of the differend was profoundly informed by his encounter with the injustice of colonialism and of racialized others: "I owed and I owe my awakening, *tout court,* to Constantine [where he taught in high school]. The differend showed itself with such a sharpness that the consolations then common among my peers (vague reformism, pious Stalinism, futile leftism) were denied to me."[48] The differend is a conceptual tool for comprehending the racialization of Europe in the wake of the Shoah and in the grip of decolonization (in Africa and Indochina). In *The Differend* each example involves a scene where a tribunal cannot give justice to what Lyotard calls the victim (as opposed to the plaintiff who may receive justice). The injustice is first and foremost due to the lack of a common idiom between the victim on the one hand and the tribunal and the second party on the other hand.[49] Importantly for Lyotard, injustice is not merely (though it may be that as well) a question of ill will or bad faith on the part of the tribunal: "there is a differend between two parties when the 'settlement' of the conflict that opposes them appears in the idiom of one of them while the tort from which the other suffers cannot signify itself in this idiom" (9). *The Differend* shows that, unlike the damage, the tort cannot be heard because it cannot be said or, more precisely, is not receivable in the idiom of the tribunal, which it shares, on the contrary, with the party against whom the victim is pleading.[50] Lyotard goes on to show that the criteria of receivability rely—silently or not—on the concept of evidence as a demonstrable proof that can be presented. This anchors the understanding of the opposition between true and false or of the connection made between what takes place and what is real. In that respect, Lyotard examines some of Plato's dialogues, which establish rules "proper to . . . a consensus" between the protagonists before the dialogue can be instituted.[51] The terms of the agreement stipulate that an idiom must be shared, but also that there should be a preliminary accord as to the objectives of the dialogue: what is at stake in the dialogue is the search for an agreement (24). This passage complicates any hasty reliance on the possibility of resolving differends through a common idiom, if there is such an idiom. For the preliminary agreement regarding agreement, which seems commonsensical, is also a process of elimination, of exclusion of the other, that is to say, the occasion of a potential or actual differend: "[Materialists] would have to be 'civilized' (*nômimôteron*) before they could be admitted to dialogue. But in fact (*ergô*), . . . one will act as if (*logô*) they were civilized: one speaks in their place, one reinterprets (*aphermèneué*) their theses, one makes them presentable for dialogue" (24). The differend describes two phrases that are heterogeneous and untranslatable. But as Lyotard also says, although or because they are heterogeneous, the two phrases can be "linked" (xii). Rather than being only a sign of homogeneity or continuity, this link also marks rupture and heterogeneity. Likewise, Lyotard says that the differend is "the unstable state and instant of language wherein something which must be put into phrases cannot yet be" (29). It is the space of excess of the "not yet" that constitutes both the injustice and the call for justice in another idiom. Lyotard's point is that the marks of the differend must also be upheld in order to promote its opposite, namely, justice.

Lyotard shows that the search for, and reliance on a common idiom actually rests on the exclusion of some other. Yet, instead of urging the demise of the idiomatic in his delineation of a way out of the differend, Lyotard calls, on the contrary, for new idioms, new phrases to link ("This requires new rules for the formation and linking of phrases"; "bear witness to differends by finding idioms for them" [13]). The answer is not fewer idioms, but more idioms; not more homogeneity, but more heterogeneity. What constitutes the differend or injustice itself is also what, slightly displaced or "new," is the condition of a call for justice and will, if possible, make justice happen. Or in other words, the conflicting phrasing in the differend is what could also put an end to it. With another phrase. Regarding the idiomaticity of the idiom, Lyotard does not decide once and for all between what it makes possible: both the differend and its contrary. The idiom is the problem and its solution. Yet it seems that the question of justice does not only depend on "institut[ing] new addressees" (13), which would assume that once the idiom reaches its destination justice happens or may happen. If *The Differend* cautions time and again against the reductiveness of understanding language as communication, it may also be because it wants to leave untouched something from the time of the differend, the time of the not-yet: this something would be silence, the inexpressible, the unheard-of, what resists formulation or prevents it (as Lyotard shows in the case of the survivor of the Shoah). "To give the differend its due" (13) should also include paying attention to that silence or that resistance, in order for the as yet unheard-of idiom to be just, and not to reiterate the tort in the old terms (which always know what to say), a state of affairs that allowed for the differend in the first place. Giving utterance to this difficult formulation is what is at stake.

When Djebar uses the word *qalam* in her French text, she makes a gesture that may recall what Abdelkebir Khatibi performed in *Love in Two Languages*: "He calmed down [*se calma*] instantly when an Arabic word, Kalma, appeared."[52] Réda Bensmaïa has pointed out that the object of such a writing is not to "'dialect-ize' or 'Maghreb-ize' French,"[53] which, as we mentioned earlier, has been a common strategy adopted by Francophone postcolonial writers to mark in French their difference to French discourse. It could be said that Khatibi's sentence is not opposed to the kind of dislocation of the French idiom in which the foreign word would abruptly interrupt the other language; more precisely, it increases the impact of the dislocation by making it less locatable. What is most defeating for logic, which can accommodate the exotic disruption of an occasional Arabic word, however opaque, within a French text, is that this example ("calma/Kalma") affects the understanding of duality that the very notion of bilingualism (French/Arabic) would seem to imply. On the one hand, the homophony of Arabic and French terms is paradoxically endowed with and entrusted to difference *through* the recognizable harmonious similarity. It remains inassimilable in its very proximity. On the other hand, as Bensmaïa writes about Khatibi, "the task is to found a mode of thinking of the *milieu*" (181), this rather unrepresentable site being in Khatibi's words "a (thought) riddled by its marginality, displaced, and full of silent questions" (181). For Khatibi, bilingualism is not a process of consolidating abundance (in which bilingualism would imply one language + another language). Instead, he posits "an internal bilingualism of every language," which entails that "a foreign tongue is not added to the native tongue as a simple palimpsest, but transforms it."[54] This new space for writing and thought, producing "a dis-identification" (160), inscribes a tangential semantic recognition that implicates, and perhaps risks confusing, one language with another while forbidding stable (re)appropriations.

Djebar's use of the Arabic word *qalam* resembles that process, but it takes it in another direction. To a French speaker hearing *qalam* as *calame* (meaning "calamus" in English), the term designates a writing instrument used by the ancients, a reed pen, a stylus or a quill.[55] The word may also refer to a manuscript that was written with a reed pen. Khatibi relies on homophony to point to difference, or to dissemination rather than bilingualism, where *calma* and *Kalma* unpredictably affect each other's meaning and, by association, evoke terms that almost sound like them, such as the Arabic *kalima* or *klima*. But, in this instance, Djebar seems to promote, on the contrary, the premises of the receivability, to mention Lyotard's term again, of such a term as *qalam*. Unlike *Kalma*, which makes the very bilingual speaker speechless at this undecipherable scene in which two words "observe each other,"[56] *qalam* can be heard and relatively understood by a non-Arabophone Francophone speaker. Yet, at this juncture, receivability, the very milieu or meeting ground for comprehension and understanding, is now turned around, and Francophones find themselves in a position in which that possibility or that site occurs not in French but in Arabic. At the moment of a flash of recognition of convergences, one is already on other grounds. If Djebar's move when using *qalam* is not an attempt to undermine or implode French from within, but to bring the language or the speaker to recognize themselves at the moment when the foreign is heard or read, what are the implications? What is the point of bringing the French to the Algerian site? Again?

Critics have argued that Djebar intersperses the adverse/paternal language with the orality of the "mother" and that she exposes Algerian women's bodies in a French and Algerian masculine space before and after the independence. Yet she has consistently questioned the interests vested in rigid oppositions, which she represents as actually untenable, an untenability that does not prevent them, however, from having real and enduring effects. Redoubling this first movement of deconstitution, Djebar diagnoses a forgetting involved in the occupation of the Algerian site, like Rachid Boudjedra, who talks in *Lettres algériennes* of "amnesia" and of "aphasia" in the relationship of France to Algeria.[57] But in the same way that, in *The Differend*, Lyotard arguably strives to keep in the formulation of a new idiom a mark of reticence or silence, the trace of what could not as yet find a language in the victim's tort, so Djebar does not rush to transcribe the contents of a lost memory, but records its very absence. How is it possible to tell the "memory blank" or the "occulted transmission"?[58] A section of Djebar's *So Vast the Prison* titled "Erased in Stone" can shed light on the dual gesture developed in her work.

ERASURE, OR WRITING FOR THE TRACE

In *So Vast the Prison* Djebar reconstitutes and imagines what happens when Europeans "discover" archeological treasures of Antiquity in the

Maghreb. Edward Said's *Orientalism* examined the complicities of the academic discourse about that region with "European-Atlantic power over the Orient," whether such complicities are actually intended or not, whether they are acknowledged or unconscious.[59] Likewise, Djebar recalls that military invasions of the Maghreb have been accompanied by scholars, from the time of Scipio's Roman army marching on to Carthage to the invasion of the French Army after 1830. Let's recall that the claim that Algeria was profoundly Roman or Latin was expounded at the beginning of the twentieth century by authors like Louis Bertrand or writers associated with the Algerianist literary movement, such as Robert Randau, who argued that Islamic and Arab civilization was but a "décor" under which Latin Africa remained discernible.[60] Roman Africa was, in that view, a way of legitimizing in advance French colonization through the affirmation of a Latin Africa that lived on. Because of such former positions, Djebar's allusions to Roman North Africa are to some readers a sign of nostalgia for the colonial period. Instead, we shall see that while some of the motifs she uses may have once served a colonial ideology, they are invested with an entirely other significance, emphasizing hybridity, multiplicity, as well as a unique link between a location and a multifaceted culture. Not far from the former site of Carthage can be found the archeological ruins of Dougga. Djebar rehearses the repeated finding and forgetting of a monolithic monument, a cenotaph bearing a stone with a bilingual inscription. The happening up against this ancient monument was at first accidental, and for a long time, in spite of several attempts, no information on the site had managed to be successfully passed on. Hardly found, it was already about to be forgotten—first in 1631, then in 1815, 1833, and 1842. The bilingual inscription seemed to call for deciphering, for only one of the languages was found to be unknown. That language was presumably a translation of the first understandable language (Punic); furthermore, its alphabet had, in Djebar's words, "vanished," which made the language a "lost language."[61] Djebar presents a hieroglyphic, opaque language, which turns out after all to be the most familiar, in fact the indigenous language of the region, Berber. For a long time, Berber was considered only an oral language; therefore it was transcribed with Arabic signs. It follows that it was not the language of the inscription that was "lost," since it was still spoken, but the possibility of linking it to a different alphabet. As Djebar also shows, while apparently disused in scholarly circles, the alphabet had in fact become nomadic, kept by Tuaregs who left behind them inscriptions engraved on rocks in the desert, while transporting it with them written on the palms of women's hands (148). The effect of such statements is to refute the immediate association of orality with the feminine. The latter should not be simply aligned with the mother's tongue or with the native supposedly "without writing" as opposed to the colonizer.

In a second move, Djebar contests the hierarchical structure that might be afforded by the bilingualism of the stone: the autochthonous language that goes temporarily unrecognized by scholarly discourses, as opposed to Punic signs, the dominant language that endures. In order to complicate the notion of bilingualism, she frames the time of the erection of the stone as following the destruction of Carthage by the Romans. At that time, though defeated, the military and cultural metropolis Carthage is shown to live on through its language and the scattered books of its libraries among Berbers it had formerly colonized. Inasmuch as Djebar pays heed to the permanence of several territories within Algerian memory, such an instance of linguistic survival against all odds provides a model of cultural coexistence and indexes a political potentiality: dwelling on "linguistic durations after catastrophes is reflecting in my own way on the present of Algeria."[62] For the stone commemorates the death of a Berber king whose people still speak the language and contribute to the culture of Carthage, against Carthage, and indeed after it.[63] But to the bilingualism of the stone ("the language of our ancestors and the others' language"), she adds Latin, the "language of the future" in the region (156). While not scripted, that future language of domination is represented: Djebar stages a scene in which the commemoration in two languages is followed by an improvised oral translation into Latin of the bilingual inscription. It would be possible to interpret that scene as writing in advance the politically charged current linguistic triangle in Algeria (Arabic—itself divided at least in two, dialectal and modern standard Arabic, spoken and written Arabic, etc./Berber/French), if she did not add another twist to her Babelian plot by evoking Polybe, the Greek master of the Roman general Scipio, in exile from his already defeated homeland and witnessing in Greek the destruction of Carthage. These interpolated oral and written passages testify to the need to think the Maghrebian or Algerian site as a multilingual space. At stake in this reconfiguration is the liberation of the speakers in that site from an "illusory duality" and "false bilingualism,"[64] not only because such a duality has codetermined a hierarchy among, indeed a racialization of, language speakers. For if she shows that there is more than one, and even more than two languages in the region, this also happens from a position of dispossession, and the gains (more than one) do not quite add up. In the vein of Derrida's "ex-appropriation," which, as we have seen, is not the same as alienation, Djebar explores the terrain on which to inscribe this condition.

In the episode of the Dougga ruins, Djebar does not break the silence dissimulating the message of the inscription, even though the reader is able to understand its commemorative purpose and some of its effects. She emphasizes the greater relevance of examining the very condition of multilingualism. Even when depicting the scholarly work on the inscription, she focuses on the investigation conducted into the name and functions of the unknown language, and stresses that the end of unreadability happens through the intervention of an other reading the inscription (148). Furthermore, over time, the bilingual stone was dismantled, thus exemplifying multiplicity as well as division. In 1833 it was cut off from the monument and the inscribed part was sent to the British Museum. In 1910, "with the exception of the bilingual inscription, which is still in London, the mausoleum is once again standing, almost intact, but stripped of its double writing."[65] But, fifty years later, further archeological research will demonstrate that "at Dougga there were, in fact, two steles, and that the second—probably the most important—of these had been partially erased" (145). The stone doubles itself, but this time writing (in which languages and which alphabets?) cannot in any simple sense lend itself to the hermeneutic achievements previously accomplished when interpreting the bilingual inscription. On the one hand, Djebar is less interested in the decoding of the message than in the exposure of a linguistic condition that goes beyond bilingualism. On the other hand, the second instance of a lapidary writing that has "almost entirely vanished" (145) serves to emphasize the first point, namely, that the disappearance or lack of content, a content that might itself be felt to be a metonym for cultural plenitude or self-coincidence, is the main focus of analysis. Djebar delves into this spectrality and denounces the poetic and political temptation to fill in the blanks so as to provide keys that would unlock the past and answer for the present (215). Instead, paying attention to vanishing inscriptions epitomizes for her the task of the Algerian writer, which entails "being a writer for the trace" (216). "Trace" means for Djebar the transmission of something that remains elusive and radically defies presentation. "How to testify through writing? The terrain has slipped under your steps" (215). "It is your dispossession that you transmit. Inherit my non-inheritance" (261).[66] Thus Djebar reflects on the transitoriness of the written trace and on the condition of a writing under erasure, which enables her to address differently in her fiction the anguished question posed by the formerly colonized, namely, how to say or to think alterity in the language that has already comprehended the racialized other. Withdrawing or emptying out the content promised to thematization testifies to the inability to recall or present, and that impossibility becomes what is the most urgent to tell.[67]

The very word *trace* used by Djebar may productively be put in conjunction with Jacques Derrida's work on the trace. Djebar's attention to inscriptions in a process of erasure can be related to that thinking. When Derrida writes about the trace, he is first inheriting other scenes of writing (in Freud, Levinas, and Heidegger, for example). In "Freud and the Scene of Writing," Derrida recalls Freud's attempts, before the invention of the Mystic Writing-Pad, to account for the ways in which memory functions, that is, simultaneously for "the permanence of the trace and for the virginity of the receiving substance."[68] Derrida radicalizes Freud's gesture by showing that the very structure of the trace is its own erasure, the erasure of its own presence. "It is constituted by the threat or anguish of its irremediable disappearance. . . . An unerasable trace is not a trace" (230), for if that were not the case, as he writes elsewhere, "it would not be a trace but an indestructible and monumental substance."[69] With the trace, Derrida thinks an other of ontology, what he later called "hauntology."[70] The trace is what arrives through erasure, was never experienced or perceived in its meaning in the present, what therefore does not present itself as such: "Traces thus produce the space of their inscription only by acceding to the period of their erasure. From the beginning, in the 'present' of their first impression, they are constituted by the double force of repetition and erasure, legibility and illegibility."[71] In an economy of traces, what seems to remain or to be retained keeps in itself or is haunted by the mark of an other (the past, but also the future, and the double movement of repetition and erasure); what is called the present or presence is constituted by this relation to the other. This makes the location of the trace untenable if one takes into account the relation of and the relation within the trace to something other than itself, hence the mention of "erasure": "Since the trace is not a presence but the simulacrum of a presence that dislocates itself, displaces itself, refers itself, it properly has no site [*n'a pas lieu*]—erasure belongs to its structure."[72] As Marta Segarra has shown in her examination of Djebar's use of archives and chronicles, the point is not simply to delineate and restore what is occluded, but to puncture "the immutable coherence of writing, and its excluding logic."[73] "Writing for the trace," in Djebar's words, would then be writing in view of that piercing dislocation, *for* it, because it can bring about another relation to (a de-limited) proximity that cannot simply be either opposed or opened to alterity, one that challenges appropriations or inhabits what it contests.

CHAPTER FOUR

Poetic Inc.

Language as Hospitality in Cixous

ALGERIAN JEWS AND LANGUAGE

The presence of Jews in North Africa has long been attested, dating back in some regions to the eleventh century BC. Some Berber tribes converted to Judaism, and, as we shall see in the next chapter, the celebrated Berber queen Kahina who resisted the Arab conquest in the seventh century was said by some chroniclers to be Jewish. Before the French conquest of Algeria beginning in 1830, the Jewish population in Algeria was socially diverse: on one end of the spectrum powerful Livornese-Algerian families established at the beginning of the seventeenth century in Algiers held the monopoly of commerce with Livorno, participating as well in other exchanges between Africa and Europe, along with families of craftsmen, for instance, at the other end.[1] Massive conversions to Islam did not eradicate Judaism in the region, but, under the Turkish Regency of Algiers (1529–1830), Algerian Jews taken collectively were Arabized in their language and culture. "Algerian Jews, *dhimmis*, 'protected subjects' on Islamic land, adopted Arabic whereas some Muslim Berber tribes did not speak it," or they spoke a vernacular Arabic, Judeo-Arabic.[2] It is generally agreed that in spite of their subordinated status as "dhimmis," Jews were on the whole tolerated by the Muslim majority and that Algerian Judaism was infused with Islamic mysticism and practices, so that both communities had culturally much in common.[3] Until 1870, when they became naturalized through the Crémieux decree, Algerian Jews "remained sociologically *indigenous*," the Crémieux decree and the division between Muslims and Jews constituting what Stora has called the Algerian Jews' "first exile."[4] Along with naturalization, Algerian Jews became gradually detached from their Arabic heritage, learned French, and became "assimilated." Analyses vary as to the extent of the impact of assimilation on Algerian Jews' religious practices. In her writings, Cixous, who refers to herself as "a Jewoman" in "Coming to Writing," tends nevertheless to emphasize the widespread acculturation of the Jewish community in Algeria.[5] While doing so, she argues that Jewishness remains a faithful affirmation even though it may be detached from knowledge; being Jewish is equated with saying so, "by Jewsay (*parjuifdire*)," a saying, moreover, that is performed in a given language.[6] For assimilated Algerian Jews, the very word *juif* in French becomes the entrusted repository of Jewishness, the "sole survivor of an extinct verbal population" when all has vanished or been forgotten (115).

The linguistic situation of assimilated Jews in Algeria was unlike that of other North Africans like Khatibi or Djebar in that, as several authors have remarked, the former were cut off from what had been once their mother tongue, Judeo-Arabic. As Jacques Derrida recounted in *The Monolingualism of the Other,* "'ladino' was not spoken in the Algeria I knew, especially not in the big cities like Algiers, where the Jewish population happened to be concentrated."[7] This lack was also unlike that of Jews in other Maghrebian countries, where even though Judeo-Arabic was felt to be "a crippled language," in the words of the Tunisian writer Albert Memmi, in the sense that it was neither spoken nor studied at school, it still subsisted as a mother tongue.[8] It is true that Memmi considered bilingualism to be extremely precarious for Tunisian Jews, and his pages on that subject do not testify to the potential so subtly expounded by Abdelkebir Khatibi, nor do they coincide with Djebar's analysis of writing and language, which we examined in chapter 3. When thrown without a net into the French schooling system and thereby into the French language, Memmi writes that the Jew's "second language, far from complementing his solidly acquired, self-confident mother tongue, dethrones and crushes it" (188). In Memmi's *Pillar of Salt* the narrator "tried to speak this language [= French] which wasn't [his], which perhaps will never be entirely [his], but without which [he] would never be able to achieve self-realization."[9] In exposing what is involved in "achieving *self*-realization" in the language of the *other,* a language always borrowed or appropriated while eluding possession, Memmi's positions regarding language are close to Derrida's and to Cixous's, for instance when stating that the Jew is "deprived of a language, without a legitimate language," or that the Maghrebian Jew is the invited "guest of the French language," though the effects of that deprivation are not analyzed in the same way by the three authors.[10] We have seen in a previous chapter that Derrida's *Monolingualism* responded to the ways in which Khatibi addressed bilingualism, indicating the impossibility of that linguistic position, as far as he and Algerian Jews of his generation were concerned, for lack of an "authorized mother tongue."[11] While noting that the inhabitation of a so-called maternal language is neither natural nor proper, he argues for the singularity of that universal necessity in the case of Algerian Jews (58). I have first recalled the historical constellation in which Algerian Jews were inscribed as far as access to languages was concerned; Derrida's articulation of the mother tongue with motherhood and the mother country will serve as a second point of entry into Cixous's elaboration of a language of writing.

MOTHER TONGUE? WITHOUT

For Derrida, the situation of Algerian Jews in French Algeria was specific to the extent that they were exposed to several "interdictions" as far as access to languages was concerned. In order to have real effects, an interdiction in Derrida's sense does not necessarily entail sanctioning or making some pursuits illegal; instead, dissuasion may take several forms. We have mentioned in a previous chapter the hurdles Algerian students encountered when they wanted to study Arabic at school. Dissuading students from learning some languages so as to marginalize their relevance in Algeria is a form of interdiction that Derrida comes back to more than once in his essay. In particular, it was possible to internalize passively an interdict that did not even need to be pronounced. In addition to cutting students off from Judeo-Arabic and from Hebrew, "not widely taught" (84), which resulted in a handicapped memory (54), the study of Arabic or of Berber was not encouraged. Arabic is called the language "of the other as the nearest neighbor. *Unheimlich*. For me, it was the neighbor's language" (37). Derrida does not mention it at this juncture, but what is uncanny about Arabic also has to do with the fact that this language of the nearest other is also (close to) the language lost through the acculturation of assimilation, in other words, the mother tongue, Judeo-Arabic. The nearest other is the lost mother.

One of Derrida's major emphases in this essay consists in arguing that not only was an originary mother tongue lost, but that no other mother tongue was fully gained in its place. Indeed, for Derrida, another interdict was at work, though differently, in the Jews' access to French: while they had been assigned to French by colonial designs, the legitimacy of its cultivation on their part could be violently put into question (explicitly under the Vichy regime, for example, but implicitly in several ways at other times as well). Furthermore, acquiring French in colonial Algeria (for all concerned, even though Derrida takes then into consideration several channels of appropriation and of legitimacy, "circles of socio-linguistic enclosure at once eccentric and concentric" [41]) induced a discontinuity preventing identification or making it difficult: to begin with, French took its authority from elsewhere and stood for elsewhere, the distant mother country or "the *metropole,* the Capital-City-Mother-Fatherland" (42), with the consequence that even though there was no other language fulfilling that role for Algerian Jews, French was but "a language supposed to be maternal" (41), while, conversely, the mother country was inseparably "the city of the mother tongue" (42). The impossible relation to the French language is marked by the double sense of being hostage, *à demeure* ("enduringly" [17], as the translator rightly proposes, but also, "at home"), and of being "deprived of *all* language" (60), "thrown into absolute translation, a translation without a pole of reference, without an originary language" (61). This is recognized while denouncing, on the other hand, pitfalls in anchoring the irreplaceable foundation of the self in the mother tongue.

In a long footnote, Derrida evokes the relationship of major twentieth-century Jewish thinkers to the mother tongue and the language of the other. Franz Rosenzweig attributes to the Jewish people a depropriation of their own language: "they have no language that is exclusively their own, only the language of the host" (79), but they can appropriate it and love it like their own (82). This separation from a maternal foundation and from autochthony is taken up by Emmanuel Levinas, who, while not being himself cut off from "familiar languages" (91), does not invoke in his work the mother tongue, but asserts instead that "the essence of language is friendship and hospitality" (91). Derrida shows that in Levinas, "language, and above all the 'maternal' idiom, is not the originary and irreplaceable place of meaning" (91). This is not quite the case for Hannah Arendt, attached to the mother tongue with which she said she always kept "absolute familiarity"

(85). Derrida's discussion of Arendt's assessment of the possibility for a mother tongue or a language to become mad, or to be substituted and replaced, starts a reflection on the posited "irreplaceable uniqueness" of the mother as well as of the mother tongue (87). That uniqueness is both affirmed and contested, replacement and supplementarity being shown to operate at the very juncture and location of what is posited as uniquely irreplaceable, the unique being replaced in its place: "the mother as the mother tongue, the very experience of absolute uniqueness . . . can only be replaced *because* it is irreplaceable . . . since she is always unique, she is always only replaceable, re-placeable, suppliable only where there is no unique place except for her" (89).

Such is the sort of madness of language and of the mother tongue that Cixous remarkably addresses in her oeuvre, in ways that confirm Derrida's position, while her specific assessment of French Algeria at times distinctly inflects it. For the historical and geopolitical reasons we have mentioned, Cixous consistently complicates the determination of a mother tongue that would ensure identification and allegiance, especially to the extent that it would be precisely locatable and self-same. As she writes in "The Names of Oran," "I love my mother tongue—but which one . . ."[12] Just as in Derrida's *Monolingualism*, the complex determination of and ascription to a mother tongue are coextensive for Cixous with the issue of the perceived illegitimacy that constrains writing. Being reticent to call any language her mother tongue implies being deprived of a language in which to write legitimately: "Everything in me joined forces to forbid me to write: History, my story, my origin, my sex. Everything that constituted my social and cultural self. To begin with the necessary, which I lacked, the material that writing is formed of and extracted from: language. You want to Write? In what language?"[13] The absence of an authorized tongue in which to write is also linked by Cixous to deracination ("diaspora effect"), which does not provide the aspiring writer with a legitimate anchoring place ("no land, no fatherland" [15]). This internalized interdict is of course not the last word in Cixous's assessment of language and writing, but none of her positions about them would make sense if it were not traversed first. As Derrida acknowledges at the end of his discussion of the mother and the mother tongue, one of the complexities of Cixous's take on language is due to the fact that "this great-French-Sephardic-Jewish-woman-writer-from Algeria, who is reinventing, among others, the language of her father, *her* French language, an unheard-of French language, is also a German-

Ashkenazic-Jewish-woman through her 'mother tongue.'"[14] "Mother tongue" is in quotation marks in that instance in order to reinforce Derrida's point about the problematic uniqueness of the mother tongue and the substitutions it evinces or betrays; for if French is "the language of her father," it could also equally be called her mother tongue that is not one, one she was nevertheless ascribed to in the sense elucidated by Derrida, while German is more precisely Cixous's mother's "mother tongue" than her "own" mother tongue: "In the language I speak, the mother tongue resonates, tongue of my mother."[15] Moreover, thinking through sexual difference is crucially informed in Cixous's work by the very relationship to a language that is not quite a mother tongue, yet, to the extent that it is, inseparably is at the same time the language of the father: "How could sexual difference not be troubled when, in my language, it's my father who is pregnant with my mother?" (23).

Reflecting on how to write in a language that is neither *one's* mother tongue nor one's *mother* tongue, she simultaneously delves into the hospitality and potentialities of a differential space, in contrast to entrenched binary oppositions, which she denounces as having marred the analyses of sexual difference. The conception of stable oppositional difference is shown to coexist with the belief in a "principle of identity, of noncontradiction, of unity" (30), which can have paralyzing effects, including that of maintaining difference at the margin or the periphery. She consistently argues as well that such a distribution of difference along two hierarchical axes is already enabled by language, demonstrating the extent to which grammatical and social rules converge in some of their effects.[16] Instead, Cixous promotes differentiation as nonoppositional difference, a divisibility or multiplicity of parts that do not add up to a totality and, especially, that change positions, which binarism cannot think or represent. Her thinking merges the delineation of a language of writing other than a mother tongue and unlike any other with the determination of sexual difference first apprehended through language. In English, Cixous remarks, "the mother says m'other, my other."[17]

CIXOUS AND LANGUAGE: UPKEEP AND LOSS

Speaking a so-called maternal language becomes an issue that is displaced by that of writing in another language, a different tongue resonating with more than one language. In "The Names of Oran" Cixous celebrates words, the sound of names heard in Oran her native town, which are not words that are not understood, but the ones she cannot write. "Oran was always the book before writing, everything took word, and the word was a name and the names were the precious pieces of a mobile mosaic that I collected."[18] This collection that does not add up to a totality determines a specific relation to Arabic, which has a profound hold on her while remaining ultimately out of her grasp: "I was in this language intangible in its totality, elusive compact, and which I could never hold in my mouth" (186); "And to think that I do not speak Arabic, yet Arabic speaks (to) me" (191). In its obliquity with respect to writing, Arabic, like German, to which it is correlated through some of its sounds (190), signals the lack of coincidence of language to itself, a language marked by an opening to what Derrida called an "unheard-of French" at work in Cixous's oeuvre: "my writing stems from two languages, at least. In my tongue the 'foreign' languages are my sources, my agitations. . . . Prevent 'my language' from taking itself for my own."[19] Exposure to linguistic plurality should not be mistaken for the polyglot's abundant resource in several languages. Instead, two effects of that exposure are emphasized: first, what is called the "hoax" of language and, then, the "disappearance" of words, which is one of several approaches to loss pervading her work: "In loss I am rich!"[20] Language as hoax is apprehended through the father's remarkable ability to handle the various languages within his hearing poetically: "It is a language that makes use of everything it encounters, incomprehensible beyond the apartment, a language of signs and *Witz*, a tongue of apes and cats" (190). In that language, for instance, the playfully inventive "*soulbra*" means "I do not know" through the following displacement, in which the German newcomers to the family find their phrases literally upheld while transferred in a phonetic French, itself requiring a translation into French in order to be understood by outsiders: "Soulbra, from: what is there *sous-le-bras* [under-the-arm]? There is *sueur*, French for 'sweat.' In German: *Schweiß . . . Schweißnicht*: I-do-not-know" (190). Such a treatment of syllables and signifiers, juggling with the sense of words while consistently apprehending it through the senses, is strikingly at work in Cixous's oeuvre.

Conversely, some words have been lost, and if they were ever to return it would be as an unbidden irruption, at the time of their choosing, as it were: "I am waiting for the word milk to return murmuring in Arabic. I'm waiting for it. It shall return. May it return" (194). In *Inside* the father's death is tied to a language left pending, in suspense. The figure of the father is endowed with a rare complicity with words, he is the one "who knew all the words."[21] As a result, "since the time my father fell silent, I have been living on my meager inheritance [of words]" (34). The resistance of words can prove insuperable and their disappearance final, as is narrated in "The Names of Oran," in which the father provides his daughter with two teachers, one of Arabic and the other of Hebrew, shortly before his death. Unable to respond to the injunction of that double legacy, "in the end I took up French as a foreign language."[22] The poetic relationship with the world that the father's words conjured up, remembered but temporarily kept in abeyance because of his disappearance, remains in the end the open-ended inheritance. The revered injunction is not the ability to speak several languages, but to inhabit language as already in translation. Consequently, Cixous's inventive writing should not be interpreted as wordplay for the sake of playfulness. Grammar is both an impassable law and one that induces resistance in the writer, if only because language itself resists. In "Coming to Writing," if "the mother I speak has never been subjected to the gramma-r wolf," circumventing the law in that instance is ascribable to the specific position of the mother's mother tongue within the language of writing.[23] But "to spar; to play" with language (21) is still surrendering to the law, by obeying it otherwise. Thus the imperative is never to correct grammar, but to inscribe in language a difference that is itself incorrigible.

In "Coming to Writing," the reader is invited on several occasions to receive "without metaphor" (20) propositions concerning the relation to the mother and to writing.[24] In such instances, the reluctance to anchor writing in metaphor is tied to the project of being just to things as they are and rehabilitating what is mostly unseen, subordinated, or forgotten. Thinking justly depends on using words that are just to things.[25] Distrusting what ties metaphor with analogy, far from things, she retains from the transfer and the bringing together of differences enacted by that trope what she has called at times a "transfigure." The transfigure denotes and reclaims what is disfigured or denied because it is downtrodden, below and past notice. In *Reveries of the Wild Woman* the dog is an instance of transfigure of "our Algerias."[26] The dog is another ultimate gift by the father, just as that of the two language masters, which also precedes the father's disappearance, in a motif haunting Cixous's oeuvre, consisting in being taken back what has just been given. The dog was received as a substitute sibling, but, in refusing to comply docilely with that position, the dog ends up being treated . . . like a dog. Among the acts of hostility that the brother and sister face in their neighborhood, the dog "suffers our fate and his own to boot" (44). In her very first book, *Le Prénom de Dieu,* Cixous had moved from the simile, sad without being uncommon, of a child "trained like a dog," to another formulation altogether, that of "the child dog": "I believed that the dog was my brother and that my brother was a dog, I loved him dog."[27] Taking up the transfigure, *Inside* warns that the child dog is not a figure of speech but tells an "invisible truth" without metaphor, blurring metaphysical demarcations such as that between the human and the animal.[28] As transfigure of Algeria, the dog is "my brother denied, the most wretched of the gods and most divine among the wretched who shrieked and howled yapped in the Algerian amphitheater swept by violent blue winds."[29]

In the delineation of a language unlike any other, traversed by other tongues, attention is often drawn to the tongue as body part or an organ in the mouth (*Merriam-Webster's Dictionary* specifies, "movable organ"), which can itself be eaten, for example in the case of the veal tongue bought by the grandmother.[30] The bloody tongue exemplifies then in advance the violence of the body politic and points to languages at war with one another, for the fact that the bodily organ can be ripped from the mouth indicates the urge to conquer and silence. In "Coming to Writing," a scene involves a doctor-censor verifying the legitimacy of the would-be writer by inspecting her tongue and being dismayed to find that she has three of them, "and what's more, he doesn't know that I have one or two that aren't attached there, or perhaps just one that changes and multiplies."[31] Thus woman's transgression does not merely consist in speaking but in "opening her mouth," disclosing by that means her (re)movable tongue(s) and displaying a disconcerting/disgusting opening to her inner thoughts, another inside.[32] Furthermore, just as the veal tongue is torn from the mouth so as to be devoured, so is language detachable from a posited foundation or origin. To drive that point home, Cixous insists on the literal passage of words through the mouth. Poetic words are first integrated in their corporeality, just as they are being disseminated from a body. Words are processed by the mouth; they are consumed and swallowed as delicious substitutes of food with an incomparable taste: "I didn't eat, I read. . . . I nourished myself with texts"; "Languages nourished me. I hated to eat what was on a plate. . . . If I tasted anything it was the stuff of speech."[33] Conversely, unethical and politically unpalatable discourse cannot be absorbed and is allergically rejected by the mouth: "Colonized, I decolonized. Bit, ate, vomited up" (19). The reversibility between tongue and language, and between food and words, shows the necessity to incorporate, embody, flesh out the poetic, which, conversely, emanates and uncontrollably erupts from the body. Writing cannot be rooted in the legitimate grounds of the mother tongue or the mother country, but gushes instead from the body that shelters a place greater than it, from "an inconceivable region, deep down inside me but unknown, as if there might exist somewhere in my body . . . another space, limitless" (10).

"THE MOTHER I SPEAK"

Cixous's elaboration of a language of writing is informed by her reflection on loss. Therefore, when Cixous writes phrases like "My German mother in my mouth," or "The mother I speak" (22), she is not collapsing the illegitimate, unauthorized mother tongue with the mother; rather she is promoting a new thinking of the mother that relies on her analysis of the different ways of accounting for loss. Her positions on the mother have been misinterpreted by some, though few, critics as essentialism, in a reading she had already anticipated and written against in "Sorties."[34] Her contestation of social and familial positions ascribed to men as much as to women is undeniable in these texts; one may then understand Cixous's recourse to the motif of the mother as a provisional strategic promotion of the subordinated term and not as a normative prescription or confirmation of biological destiny for all women. More importantly, "the mother" is the angle Cixous uses in her assessment of loss. She argues, on the one hand, that loss is embodied by the mother as a love object whose disappearance is dreaded, and, on the other hand, the mother is defined as a a function of resistance to separation, which also means that in that position cuts and interruption are faced in a specific fashion. In that sense, the phallic economy is structured for Cixous around appropriation and fear of loss, which entails "systems of exchange based on masculine thrift";[35] that logic is opposed to the feminine economy, an inadequate, provisional term since it involves depropriation without calculation and without return. Thus the relation to loss and to upkeep, when reassessed through the feminine, "more and less capable of loss," reconfigures subjectivity, which for the sake of accuracy should rather be called "alterability."[36]

In her readings of Freud, Cixous often calls attention to the posited rupture between the child's early love and later devaluation of the mother, indeed of woman, after the realization that the mother is "castrated." In the 1970s, essays like "The Laugh of the Medusa," "Coming to Writing," or "Sorties," or fictions such as *The Third Body*, revisit the curtailing of "the relationship to the 'mother' *as* intense pleasure and violence."[37] That statement does not deny the ambivalence to the mother that Freud signaled even at the phallic stage of infantile sexuality, but it also refuses two consequences of his position: one is the paralyzing "litany of castration" (891), as the internalization of threats of cuts, and another is the devaluation of the mother, construed by Cixous above all as a relation, a position beyond and outside the role (881), which she sums up as what "resists separation" (882). Resistance to separation is not unlike the function of "the feminine" in general, which affirms preservation and strives to "keep alive the other."[38]

Thus the adoration of the mother's face depicted at the beginning of "Coming to Writing" or in *The Third Body* shows that if love is taught by the mother, or more precisely by the human beauty that it embodies, it also presents itself to the gaze of the child as other, nonappropriable: "I was before it, I sensed that there was a beyond, to which I did not have access, an unlimited place. The look incited me and also forbade me to enter; I was outside, in a state of animal watchfulness . . . the other is there, so close, exists, so far away."[39] Once again, the position of being denied admittance allows for another approach to discontinuity and to separation, which is correlated to the thinking of loss. In other words, when Cixous writes that the "mother" resists separation, the objective is not to reconstruct or recover a homogeneous, continuous relation without cuts, but rather not to repress the time before and beyond the cut or, conversely, to affirm cuts, distance, and discontinuity differently. In that respect her works often touch on the ambivalence to the mother, mentioned by Freud in his essay on femininity, as an example that puts into question the seamlessness of the relation mother/child.[40] In Cixous's accounts, which are opposed to some of the positions of psychoanalysis rather than to psychoanalysis itself, Freud's argument is faithfully rehearsed up to a point, and in the repetition the outcome of the debasement of the mother in Freud is altered or acquires other significance. In *Le Prénom de Dieu* ambivalence thrives on the request by the mother to understand the mother tongue as originating from and returning to the mother without expenditure or dissemination: "My mouth, she claimed, belonged to her. I owed her every word"; in that view the child's tongue "should have been but a spoon, and my mouth, the bowl where she would have poured in advance the gruel of language. . . .

I was only destined to take the spoon and regurgitate already chewed words."[41] Thus Cixous insists that the position of the "mother" must not be mistaken for sterile restitution or payback, because this understanding could also lead to a form of repetitive litany. Put differently, the relation mother-child is not to be founded on reproduction. Furthermore, the aggressiveness to the mother is inseparable in several narratives from the fear of losing one's love, that is to say, the mother, which conversely entails that love is addressed *in absentia* to the departed. The fear of abandonment focuses first and foremost on the mother: "I adored God my mother. Love me! Don't abandon me! He who abandons me is my mother."[42] Even though the father's death might seem to upset that model, its premises remain unchanged; what is radically altered instead is the outlook on sexual difference: "My father dies: thus father you are my mother" (19). Examples of revisions of gender and familial ascription through positions that interchange abound in her texts. In "Coming to Writing," for instance, "my mother wasn't a 'woman' . . . to me she seemed rather like a young man, or like a young girl; besides, she was foreign; she was my daughter" (29). Yet the recommended effort to "de-familialize" or to "de-mater-paternalize" must be achieved by inhabiting the positions of the "mother" as well as the "father" otherwise, rather than severing relations to these positions, which is *a contrario* a gesture she consistently denounces.[43]

The familial must be rethought along with what appears to be the dividing line between life and death. The figure of survival and of resistance to death as the epitome of separation and cut is complicated. Although the mother is the parent that survives, living on is also ascribed to the father, who hauntingly returns, so that far from being opposed, the positions of the mother and the father become respectively conducive to a different form of cohabitation with the self, superimposed to the understanding and experience of loss: "In the end my mother survived my father and my father survived my mother differently. In the end I lost my father and my mother and both were given back to me differently."[44] In death the father is both lost and interiorized, becoming the daughter's "undislodgeable specter" (62), whereas the mother "remains external where I come in" (99–100). This differentiated spatial positioning of survival both inside and outside instigates another reflection on loss. Just as *Inside* had shown that the limit between inside and outside evinced modifications that allowed for a rethinking of belonging and exclusion, so life and death are neither to be thought sequentially nor as strictly distinct from each other. First, death is “a mysterious life,” therefore not the other of life, providing the living with a key to life, and, second, preservation as resistance to death must protect both the living and the dead, “for one may also kill the dead, one may bury them, efface them infinitely. . . . It will be a matter of living and living on.”[45] The returns of the *revenant* punctuate the narrator’s life, and the dead loved one speaks, changes, comes back, and leaves, thus lives on. But such returns are also intimately affecting and altering the daughter, so that death did not merely happen to another outside herself but indistinguishably to herself as well, inside and at the beginning. *Inside* traverses both life and death so as to contest the mode and experience of their disjunction, foregrounding the displacement that occurs within the survivor, sheltering within herself the dead loved one or gathering the shores of life and death in herself all at once: “Death is the temporary disappearance of someone you know well. . . . If nobody knows I am my father, no doubt it’s because people don’t like to mix up the living and the dead, for fear of no longer being sure they’re on the right side.”[46]

In her position of resistance to separation and cuts, the mother is frequently placed on the side of “undivided life” while symmetrically positing that writing is deadly.[47] Thus, for the mother, living is enough and consists in the recognition and acceptance of certain limits (203) and the refusal of self-aggrandizement (102). Her eagerness to feed others is interpreted as a battle in which eating means “killing death and devouring it” (115). The mother also examines what she claims to be the deliberate embrace of death and its consequences for the living in general and living women in particular. *Osnabrück* investigates the impact that “glory,” a noble aspiration, has on the living the glorious dead leave behind, who are “abandoned” (101), as the daughter feared at the beginning of the fiction when her mother’s face temporarily disappeared, and are thus “betrayed” in their own expectations (59). Above all, betrayal lies in the unanimous block of “enemies of life” that are actively opposed to the desire to live with the living: “I consider them as guilty of death” (191). Rather than simply contradicting that life-affirming position, Cixous’s reflection on the language of writing shows, for instance through the distribution she establishes in *First Days of the Year* between “the author” and “I,” the extent to which the author is “my enemy” and on the side of death.[48] Yet, at the same time and in the same text, writing is “my life plus” (92) or “the other life” (97), thus not contrary to life. “Vivre fait livre,” as she untranslatably puts it in *OR*.[49] In such configurations, living and dying, life and death are separated and united at the same time, and the borderline between them becomes unstable and difficult to pinpoint. Recalling the notions of life and death that are endorsed by the mother in priority but not exclusively, since they may be pronounced by all characters without exception, including the "I," serves to problematize the solidity of their polarity and avoid familial and gendered ascription of positions. Life gets reassessed first through ghostly returns, and writing is shown to be both mortal and vital, impelled by a disastrous loss that might also be an unavoidable requirement. Thus the father's death is both a "misfortune" and a "chance"; writing occurs from the condition of "*losing everything*, having once lost everything."[50]

THE LANGUAGE OF THE POETS

The reflection on what and how to write takes its cue from that bifid stance. Cixous indicated in *Rencontre terrestre* that "what orients me is . . . what I may not say. I turn around an absolute interdict."[51] Several of her fictions evince the urge to dissimulate or to silence, a secreting that encompasses the I, at odds and fighting with what is called in *First Days of the Year* a "gesture of avowal," which, however, is not equated with revelation.[52] In her narratives the book "comes" unbidden as an eruption from a region of the body that defies intention and construction. Her fictions consistently elaborate the resistance of the narrative, once named "the Book that I will not write," in which what gets written is not what "I" wants to write.[53] This can be due, as in *L'Ange au secret*, to the fear that the book constitutes a dangerous exposure, since it can bite, maim, or kill: "I am in the jaws of the book."[54] The book is not written, but "writes itself" (67), "unbeknownst to us" (11), which is at best unpredictable and at worst terrifying. Or the figure of a resisting narrative can work against the urge to erase the powerlessness to prevent betrayal, avoiding good conscience but also remaining attentive to what is in the process of being forgotten or disregarded. In that sense the book never ceases (not) to be written, while the resistance of the book brings about another writing: "When I write a book, I am constantly in the process of not writing another book, I move forward by driving backward, on the banks of each chapter that is born lie, helpless, the pages that have expired," so that in the end the book is adopted, rather than authored, and the narrator is "the vanquished survivor of a thousand books."[55] This consequence can be grafted to two considerations: the first is that a release from mastery happens in writing, which must inform the ways in which textuality is performed as well as received and interpreted. As she writes in that respect in *First Days*, "if I ever reached a place . . . it was never the goal I thought I had aimed for, it was always the other" (35–36). Moreover that opening of the unconscious in writing is a "passageway, the entrance, the exit, the dwelling place of the other in me" that must be welcomed.[56] In chapter 6 we will examine Cixous's ethical plea for passivity, understood as dispossession of the self in the face of the other. Let's emphasize at this juncture that passivity in writing is not to be interpreted through preexisting gendered models—Cixous's commentary on the epic queen Dido in "Sorties" makes it abundantly clear (77). While she notes that passivity is "partly bound up with death," she also underscores its underlying affirmation of the other or of the unknown through "a nonclosure that is not submission but confidence and comprehension; that is not an opportunity for destruction but for wonderful expansion" (86).

A correlated question revolves around the form this writing may take, "how does it write itself" (82) and in which language. In "Coming to Writing" the language of the poets is the one "that I speak or that speaks (to) me in all tongues. . . . And this language I know, I don't need to enter it, it surges from me, it flows."[57] Thus the endorsement of that language hospitable to and received in all tongues is Cixous's most consistent response to the lack of an authorized mother tongue. In her texts her multifaceted approaches to a language divorced from autochthony have a political resonance and shed light on her relation to Algeria. On the one hand, Cixous attributes to poetic language the faculty of writing the unthought of phallocentrism and, more generally, of the political.[58] Poets testify to "the other bisexuality" she promotes and investigates in several essays, and bring to the fore the extent to which writing thus construed sides with affirmation: "We have no womanly reason to pledge allegiance to the negative. The feminine (as the poets suspected) affirms" (884). The purpose is then to bring about through fiction what are called "irreducible effects of femininity" (883), or the affirmation that keeps the other alive. On the other hand, poets invest and inhabit the untenable, "poetry involves gaining strength through the unconscious and . . . the unconscious, that other limitless country, is the place where the repressed manage to survive" (879–80). Cixous insists on several occasions on the real sociopolitical effects of the act of writing. For instance, *Prénoms de personne* asserts that "fiction, which is an action, has an effectiveness."[59] Furthermore, "fiction" designates a "non-place," which announces "the elsewhere to come" (5). Thus writing consists, as "The Laugh of the Medusa" puts it, in "dislocating" the "within" of a certain discourse, in deconstituting and desedimenting too well-known topographies or, on the contrary, in showing the ways in which so-called demarcations gather rather than separate.[60] In that respect, Cixous consistently challenges two modes of self-sameness, "whether it be integration-identification with the uncontested myth or theme of the nationalist-nation; or whether it be the same homogenising fusion with a part that resists the whole, a fragment that is constituted as a small whole, a communal core, often self-defensive, for example in Algeria when I was little, the enclaved excluded encircled attacked small-whole constituted as an enclosed space that was the Jewish community."[61]

In this chapter my objective was to examine the ways in which, after exposing the causes of the perceived lack of an authorized mother tongue, Cixous theorizes a language of writing in which that inaugural loss is reappraised in several ways, and in particular through the position of "the mother," defined as the contradictory location of the embodiment of and resistance to loss. In that sense her indication in "How Not to Speak of Algeria" that there is "some subterranean link between my relation to Algeria and my relation to my mother" illuminates Cixous's specific way of upholding discontinuities as the starting point for rethinking being with and for others.[62] Characteristically, contestation, which springs from and responds to the perception of imposed limitations and the experience of linguistic restrictions, shifts emphasis when Cixous addresses poetic language or the language of writing she is theorizing. The position of the mother she exposes in that regard shows that while dividing lines remain arbitrary and inappropriate, not to mention powerless at times to contain what they purport to delimit, it is their very instability that allows a less frontal opposition and at times a form of resistance to them that does not exclude affirmation. In that respect, let us recall that I addressed in part 2 what, for different reasons, forced or motivated Djebar and Cixous to elaborate a language of writing cut off from the mother tongue that took into account, and depended to a great extent, on the various language policies enacted in French Algeria. However, while exposing the multifaceted impact of the colonial project with respect to languages and the mother tongue, Djebar's and Cixous's different corpuses are informed by a comparable strategy, which consists in deriving a promising inhabitation of space based on that exemplary dispossession. Djebar interprets Maghrebian archaeological sites with vanishing inscriptions as a political chance for the postcolonial subject faced with what could be paralyzing gaps in memory, by reconfiguring such textual traces as a model (of writing) challenging appropriation or puncturing dominant discourses; Cixous dwells on scenes of irremediable loss, but also of upkeep and ghostly returns, so as to suggest another approach to interruption and separation that in turn fosters a reflection on the political body, which is not apprehended as homogeneous union but as a set of differences on the verge of conflagrating. As we shall see in part 3, which examines Djebar's and Cixous's assessment of war, and in particular the Algerian war of independence, it is not the issue of enmity that is mostly put into question in their writings, but its presupposed embodiment in one given, recognizable adversary. Foregrounding a multiplicity of fronts on which to struggle is a way of invoking plural differences that will neither be reduced in war nor in the ensuing peace. Against the commonsensical view that differences must be bridged in consensus for peaceful coexistence to prevail, Djebar and Cixous argue for a finer account of differences that require better delineation and accentuation. Djebar examines the ways in which to bear witness to the conflict so as to be just to participants without whom independence might not have been achieved, through fictional resources that break with codes of mimetic representation and allow for unheard-of interpretations of the war that are not voyeuristic or spectacular. Cixous starts with the diagnosis of a belligerent French Algeria and the impossibility and shortcomings of hospitality against that violent background. But instead of repairing the breach in her consideration of the rift between "French" and "Arabs" during the Algerian war of independence, she proposes, on the contrary, in proximity with Levinas, reappraising the separation as infinite ethical distance, a respect that is performed as language. In that sense, what is valorized is shared discourse, and not a shared land, with the other.

PART THREE

Algerian War

CHAPTER FIVE

The Sound of Broken Memory

Djebar's Women Fighters

HEARING HISTORY

The Algerian writer Kateb Yacine pleaded once for an urgent task, that of "making Algerians hear their history."[1] With that phrase, he wanted to promote the rewriting of official history in postindependence Algeria, in particular through the medium he brilliantly illustrated, that of the theater, thus fighting a partial amnesia and producing a counterhistory of Algeria (9). Most historians agree with his diagnosis regarding the writing of Algerian history in Algeria as well as in France. The difficulties they mention are not only empirical (a deliberately hampered access to archives, for instance), though they are that as well. Above all, they are predicated on a "history under surveillance," in the words of Mohammed Harbi.[2] The way of thwarting erasure and oblivion in official and memorial discourses on both sides of the Mediterranean has consisted in promoting pluralism and in assessing the responsibilities of all the participants in the war.[3] In that sense at least, historians as well as other Algerian writers strive to expose what has been left out of representation and interpretation. Charles Bonn has shown that when focusing on Algerian history, Algerian writers writing in French had to come up first with "models of reading the real" in response to a colonial discourse about the Algerian space and to an ethnological interpretation of Algerian society as frozen in time, enacting a "nature" rather than participating in a history.[4] In a 1972 interview in which he recalls some of the issues that led him to write three plays portraying heroic women (the Algerian Kahina and Saout Ennissa and the

French Louise Michel), Kateb makes the point that theater, understood as historical through and through, is a way of fighting amnesia, and that literature directly leads to politics; and he states that writing history in these plays centered on women has meant for him writing about the unknown because of a certain estrangement or a "loss of contact" between men and women.[5] Yet the mother tongue or literally the mother's words—the mother being the first to construct a child's world through "the words of the tribe" according to Kateb Yacine (37)—usher in to a political space that is partly denied to women. Women's contradictory position as strangers to the world they nevertheless give access to is a symptom of their relative, at times desired, exclusion from the elaboration of the political or it signals the denial of their historical role. In spite of their averred contributions, women are somehow always required to prove that they may legitimately inhabit the political.[6] Kateb Yacine claims that Algerians in general are still deprived of their own history. And when he turns to past historiography, such as Ibn Khaldun's *History of the Berbers* (written in the fourteenth century), that testifies to the political prominence of women in the Maghreb, especially the Kahina, a queen who led the Berber military resistance against the Arab conquest of North Africa in the seventh century, he both affirms the cultural legitimacy of women's political leadership *and* shows how contradictorily that heritage is inscribed within collective memory today.[7]

Writing on "the legend of the Kahina," Abdelmajid Hannoum shows the remarkable plasticity of that queen, a historical figure about whom few facts are known, but to whom were attributed over time competing myths upholding different narratives of origin of North Africa. "The Kahina" is then in his analysis an ideological machine that is invested with specific political agendas. In his reading, the "Kabyle, Frenchified, and feminist" Kateb Yacine is drawn to the Kahina in that she stands for a "Berber Algeria," and furthermore a multiethnic, nonreligious Algeria, one in which an "acceptable place [would be] given to women whose role in the war of liberation was equal to that of men."[8] Indeed, Kateb Yacine has said that he concentrated on the Kahina as a "nationalist" commander and has rejected as irrelevant one account of the Kahina according to which she was Jewish.[9] This is a way of claiming that if there was a religious motive for the war that she undertook it must be mainly ascribed to the Arab invaders rather than the Berbers defending their land. In Kateb's play *La Kahina ou Dihya*, first performed in Paris in 1975, the queen insists that religion is "but the veil of conquest" and that she fights for "the free land of Amazigh."[10] Kateb dwells on a controversial element of the Kahina's military strategy, consisting in burning the crops in order to starve the invaders or discourage them, with redoubtable consequences to Berbers themselves. This gesture was recorded in different versions of the Kahina's story by chroniclers who were deeply struck by its desperation or, conversely, its tyranny.[11] According to Ibn Khaldun and other Arab historiographers, this scorched-earth policy contributed to the division that occurred among the Berbers and helped achieve Arab victory. For Arab historians, the act also served to contrast the lawful and prosperous order of an Islamic ruler with the antisocial ruin (*fitna* or disorder, civil war) visited upon a people by a non-Islamic antihero, and especially a female ruler, here the Kahina, while some authors note today that, by extension, women in general are sometimes determined as agents of *fitna*, which puts them on a par with the unbeliever and the foreigner.[12]

In Kateb's play, on the contrary, the Kahina contrasts the invaders' pillage and annexation of her country she equates to its permanent destruction with her provisional and tactical scorched-earth policy, which, though it burns the crops in the present, preserves from a greater future evil "the living earth, / The earth that makes us live, / The free earth of Amazigh"; "Crops are lost / But we can lose everything / The earth remains to us."[13] It is therefore not cruelty to her people or administrative incompetence that causes the Kahina to sacrifice the prosperity of her land but an act of defiance laying bare the irreducible and everlasting aspiration for freedom of North Africa faced with invasion and occupation. Her destruction is reversed preservation, whereas the invaders' apparent care for the population aims at utter dispossession. At the same time, Kateb addresses another recurring component of accounts about the Kahina, attributing to her the gift of prophecy and magical powers (*Kahina* means "soothsayer" or "witch" in Arabic). In that respect, he emphasizes the enduring internalization of negative "racial" traits ascribed by the Arab victors to the vanquished Berbers when he mentions that at the time his play was produced in Algeria a radio series about that heroine represented her "as a bloodthirsty woman who wanted to destroy the country, like a witch" (18), thus reflecting Algerian self-hatred. In his play the free land of Amazigh is associated with the indomitable liberty of Dihya—according to Hannoum, Ibn Khaldun was the first historian to have provided the supposed name and genealogy of the Kahina, "Dihya bint Tabita b. Niqan b. Bawra b. Maskisri

b. Afrad b. Wasila b. Jraw."[14] Dihya refutes associations with magic power, just as she contests the debasing name given to her people by oppressors:

> They call me Kahina, they call us Berbers,
> Just as the Romans called Barbarian
> Our ancestors.
> Barbarians, Berbers, it is the same word, always the same
> As all invaders, they call Barbarian
> The people they oppress, while pretending to civilize them. . . .
> The Barbarians are the aggressors.
> There are no Kahina, no Berbers here.[15]

ASSIA DJEBAR AND THE ALGERIAN WAR OF INDEPENDENCE: WOMEN'S TESTIMONY

With few exceptions, Djebar's fictions arguably always revolve around war, be it the initial 1830 conquest of Algiers, which was the first step of the French colonization of Algeria until 1962 (for example, in *Fantasia*), or the violent conflict of the 1990s (for example, in *Algerian White,* or *La disparition de la langue française*), while she at times extends her temporal span by recalling, for instance in *So Vast the Prison,* wars in the Maghreb that took place in former periods of colonization of the region. This chapter dwells on Djebar's reflection on the Algerian war of independence, which is by far the conflict to which she devoted the most sustained attention, starting with her third book, *Children of the New World,* even though as we have just mentioned, Djebar's approach to war is both attentive to the singularity of a conflict and to its palimpsestic resonance with previous and future wars. While the construction of *Children of the New World,* and of the following book, *Les Alouettes naïves,* allowed her to alternate perspectives between partisans (or other participants in the war) and civilians, she was already particularly intent on conveying the positions of women (resisters and civilians), inasmuch as they correspond to but also differ from those of men, an approach that was confirmed in her later films and fictions.

The period following the war of independence in Algeria shows the extent to which what is consigned to memory is fraught with difficulties. It has been widely recognized that women's participation in combat and resistance has tended to be silenced and left uncommemorated, except in the case of a few celebrated war heroines, which prompts Kateb Yacine to declare that "today these forces are unknown or unconscious."[16] Yet Mohammed Harbi writes that without women "urban terrorism would not have had the same intensity," while in the mountains and the country the Algerian revolution would have been stifled without women's surveillance and logistics.[17] Among the many factors presented by Marnia Lazreg as having contributed to the silencing of women's participation in the war, two are particularly noteworthy. First, women's involvement in military combat or paramilitary activity was limited, whereas women were highly represented in "civilian service" such as the organization of sanctuaries and food supplies.[18] As Lazreg immediately remarks, "The bulk of women's work was less *spectacular*, perhaps even tedious, but equally dangerous" (124, my emphasis). Djebar focuses on this lack of visibility of women's participation, precisely as it coincides with what will become inaudible.[19] The failure to be heard was noticeable after the war, for instance when the government required applications for certification in order to compile a list of war veterans. The difficulty of the procedure that involved a written testimony from supervisors was at times insuperable for some resisters, and for women in particular. Moreover, "in cases where women worked in groups as food and refuge suppliers, only the leader was entitled to certification," which prevented the other participants in the network from receiving benefits.[20] Almost the reverse could happen as far as mudjahidins were concerned: in that respect, Harbi writes that if the list of veterans is not entirely reliable it is partly because the number of enlisted and of casualties was overestimated during the war by some officers at the borders in order to obtain more funding and equipment.[21] Most authors point out that in general women did not index their participation in the war on their own political gains after it, but struggled toward the goal of putting an end to colonization, thereby contributing to the liberation of all Algerians. This disinterestedness was hardly met with reciprocity: during the war, with a few exceptions, such as Zohra Drif during the Battle of Algiers, women were restricted "to sectors where they could neither claim equality, nor accede to the political, nor even acquire power."[22] In addition to the factors explaining why the number of women having participated in the war is certainly only an approximation, several critics have brought to the fore the extent to which many women were dissuaded from engaging in politics after the war and from participating as they wished in the reconstruction of postcolonial Algeria. Writing two years after the end of the war, Fadéla

M'Rabet notes that some fifteen-year old schoolchildren acknowledge women's recent acts of resistance but interpret them as an exception necessitated by the war, which does not justify altering gender roles after it, a view that reflects that of society at large.[23] What has been normalized or occluded in women's history may be reenacted or supplemented by fiction, and fiction acquires thus a political import: far from being a fanciful extrapolation, fiction does not complement so much as shed light on some of the motives or forces at work behind the occlusion or the distortion of historical figures or acts. For Djebar, none of that distortion can be explained without first considering collective patterns impacting both men and women, and without addressing the ways in which individual acts are socially received and interpreted. She has said that fiction allows the writer's preoccupation with a certain time or space to intermingle with its unsaid or its ghosts.[24] This formulation indicates the specific way in which Djebar uncovers what has been historically repressed, giving the elusive and the intangible their due.[25] In her films and fiction Djebar follows in her own way Kateb Yacine's injunction regarding hearing one's history: as we have seen in a previous chapter, she abstains from providing a seamless, totalizing narrative, and her oeuvre displays the evidence of missing links that cannot be fully recovered. Her turn to fiction testifies to a silencing that is itself interrogated rather than entirely lifted. Regarding the idealized narratives of heroic feats circulated after independence, Djebar is prone to denouncing their absence of restraint, their indecent logorrhea and "overvaluation of the verb," and, on the contrary, to valuing "taciturnity," a sense of the secret, or of silence.[26] She attempts, then, to balance what must be affirmed and what may not be said.

Perhaps because Djebar is attentive to the fragile threshold between reserve and revelation, her approach to Algerian women's stories is itself somewhat reticent. Her oft-expressed refusal to be considered the spokesperson of Algerian "Woman" (263) leads her to concentrate in her fiction on singular moments of a woman's life, which she assesses at first as enmeshed in a location and a social network. In the wake of other women authors writing about Algeria, Djebar often illustrates girls and women's complicity and solidarity in a cherishing, protective familial and social circle: "To us, my mother and me, it [our hometown] seemed a haven, a cocoon: and my enchanted child's memory turned it into a place of constant celebrations where gentle, languid women seemed to laze around."[27] Festive celebrations, with their convivial atmosphere and their music and dancing, are particularly emblematic of that affective space. On the one hand, the traditional gestures or language with which these celebrations are enacted particularly compel Djebar's interest. Her attention to the cultural value of reiteration leads to demonstrations of the ways in which, through apparent repetition, women's narratives, songs, or dances acquire unsuspected and unscripted significance. On the other hand, she is also wary of the rehearsed immutability that such traditions or recitals might induce. The family "haven" tolerates few trespasses against collective conducts, and, while still being perceived as "the family cocoon, the warm protection assured me by the affection of a group of women," the narrator adds, as an afterthought, that it is "an affection not without its acrid moments" (292). About the "chain of memories" her fiction deploys, Djebar points out that the transmission providing a counterhistory, though it responds to an ethical inner necessity, can also become a severe constraint: "is it not precisely a 'chain' that fetters as much as it roots down?"[28]

In *So Vast the Prison*, dance is mobilized to figure a dynamics between reiteration and nonconformity. The narrator explains her rejection of the "Western" custom of dancing in couples, and, conversely, her passion for dancing alone, both in deference to a traditional cultural trait and as a challenge to that very code. In the patios or apartments of the mother's friends or family, ritual dancing is performed in a circle of women, where girls and women dance in turn. The formality of such festivities does not exclude spontaneity or inspiration, but within parameters that make abandon legible, such as the grandmother's trance during the musicians' ceremonial chants in *Fantasia*, the performance of the singer of the city intoning a collective mourning chant from which her improvised recitative may unfold in *Women of Algiers in Their Apartment*, or traditional classical Andalusian music, resting, like jazz, on the art of improvisation in *Nulle part dans la maison de mon père*.[29] Djebar is not the first Algerian writer to depict an outpour of emotions when women dance. But it leads her especially to reflect on what constitutes adhesion to a culture. In effect, improvisation is channeled rather than rejected outright; but Djebar often records instances when straying from the accepted mode of improvisation meets with incomprehension. When the young girl of *So Vast the Prison*, for instance, participates in dances, she is led at times to invent "some nervous, hybrid dance" with a "whimsical choreography."[30] Such a creative behavior puzzles its witnesses, some going so far as to interpret it as a collective betrayal, while she understands it as "the challenge my engulfed body made by claiming to improvise movement" (61). This example of self-assertion through improvisation does not amount to a rejection of cultural constraints, however. For one thing, the narrator underscores the internalization of the restriction of visibility on two occasions: when dancing with another in imitation of "Western" custom, she inwardly revolts "others can see!"—and when being watched by her hidden husband while she dances alone in her circle of friends, she feels that he has "unwillingly become a voyeur" (62). Therefore, improvisation is not so much a contestation as a negotiation that must be thrust in the incredulous eyes of others as well as affirmed against one's own misgivings. Improvisation or invention, like a musical variation to which Djebar's texts often lend themselves, is not cut from the terrain that made it both possible and unpredictable.[31] It is true that in Djebar's writings the ground from which improvisation springs can be shown to be uncongenial, reticent, uncomprehending, if not frankly hostile. Her narrators or protagonists are often alone, reduced to yet endorsing "proud solitude," in the margin of the circle of women they nevertheless feel in solidarity with, relishing their role of "witness."[32]

When dealing with the Algerian war of independence, Djebar's approach is also dual, consisting in enabling recitation with a power of disclosure while fighting the effect of "torpor" that reiteration may induce through an emphasis on invention and improvisation, which affirms *and* displaces the first position.[33] This approach does not dissimulate the limitations inherent in the discourse celebrating heroes and especially heroines, having to do mostly with channeling testimony in an exclusive direction or stifling what it is inappropriate to bear witness to. In that respect Djebar writes that the testimony of Algerian women's participation in the war was double-edged: the public applause that they received did not prevent a repression or silencing of their role.[34] She shows that the outcome of their testimonies often was shame or a certain voyeurism of women's tortured bodies, which could also result in women's self-censorship or silence. Djebar looks for alternatives to both consequences. In *Women of Algiers* Djebar favors open and full disclosures shared between women, "about yesterday and today . . . in all the women's quarters" (50), with the implication that a discourse ostracizing woman's involvement in the war has affected the ability of women in general and resisters themselves to pay heed to other women's testimonies. Furthermore, Djebar insists that words recounting that participation should concern unsung heroines, but also be unheard of: "Not the voice of female vocalists whom they imprison in their sugar-sweet melodies . . . [but] the voice that's searching in the opened tombs" (50). As Derrida explains in *Demeure*, testimony testifies to truth and in its name, but its relation to knowledge is heterogeneous to the regime of the proof.[35] There is at least a dual injunction within testimony: on the one hand, "the value of publicity, that is, of broad daylight . . . seems associated in some essential way with that of testimony" (30) and, on the other hand, "the testimony will not simply consist in knowing or making known a secret, in sharing it, but in engaging oneself, in an implicit or explicit manner, to keeping the secret. In other words, the experience of the secret is, however contradictory this may seem, a testimonial experience" (32). Djebar's fiction keeps that double testimonial engagement of shedding light and of respecting a silence and a secret. She is consistently attentive to historical figures or to figures of speech standing for improvisation in Algeria and authorizing it in advance for such discreet practitioners as the narrator of *So Vast the Prison*, just as she investigates the historiographers' inscription of women's active invention that makes "reversal possible," and notes when the record suddenly yields to a deafening silence.[36]

Zoulikha Oudai, the heroic *mudjahida* of her hometown Cherchell, who is noticeably chosen by Djebar in preference to the better-known figure of the Kahina, is such a figure standing for improvisation. One explanation for Djebar's reticence to rewrite or contribute to the Kahina's legend is that the illustrious Berber provides a version of female heroism that remains within "the tradition of the feudal queen-mother (intelligent, a tactician of 'virile' courage)," a tradition she wants to revise so as to counter the erasure of the body.[37] However, as we shall see, Djebar incorporates some elements of accounts of the Kahina that she indirectly quotes and challenges when writing about Zoulikha. Zoulikha disappeared after her arrest by the French Army in the *maquis* or mountains, and Djebar devotes several works to her, including the film *The Nouba of the Women of Mount Chenoua*, dedicated to Zoulikha, the journal of the shooting of the film included in *So Vast the Prison* under the title of the initial synopsis *Arable Woman*, passages from *Fantasia*, and especially *La Femme sans sépulture*, combining, through a frequent device in Djebar, a "documentary approach" with the "imagination and variations that fiction allows," as the foreword to *La Femme sans sépulture* claims.[38] Such variations of medium and approaches on the same theme are themselves part of Djebar's argument regarding the merit of recitation and reiteration, while, in her need to deceive and elude the surveillance of the French police and army, Zoulikha is shown having recourse to resourceful invention and stratagems that also rely on the participation of other women exposing themselves to promote the cause of independence.

THE SOUND OF BROKEN MEMORY

The Nouba was shot some ten years after Gillo Pontecorvo's *The Battle of Algiers* (1967), a film that reconstituted the military battle of 1957 in Algiers and the search for National Liberation Front (FLN) fighters in the Kasbah, the old city in Algiers, on the part of French paratroopers, for the purpose of dismantling their network. *The Battle of Algiers* evokes the political victory of the FLN on the international scene even as the movement seemed to have failed militarily. This victory started when the "Algerian question" was discussed by the United Nations in 1956, and France was condemned by the same organization in 1958.[39] The film stresses the chain of command of the resistance movement and argues that guerrilla warfare is the first step toward a general insurrection, which is made all the more plausible by the temporal elision between 1957 (the Battle of Algiers) and 1960. The end of the film represents the 1960 demonstration in Algiers in support of the FLN, about which several authors have recalled the overwhelming presence of Algerian women. Instead, Djebar's film concentrates on resistance in the mountains, which required a different networking between mudjahidins and the civilian population, mostly women. The script of the film by Pontecorvo drew on the memoirs of Yacef Saadi, a protagonist of the Battle of Algiers.[40] It starts with the claim that not one foot of actual newsreel or documentary of the time was used. The reconstitution of the theater of operations that the Kasbah was dwells on a theatricalization of its *actors*, for instance with Yacef Saadi performing his own role, but also on the transformation of women adopting "European" dress (makeup, clothes) so as to go unnoticed past the French army. Pontecorvo's narrative encompasses the strategies of both sides, but it does not dwell on the inner divisions within the Algerian resistance and unfolds steps toward the liberation from the French and a return of the nation to itself.[41] Quite differently, Djebar analyzes the ruses of memory and its detour through an adjacent narrative in telling the traumas of the war. In her film there can be no return full circle to oneself, one's culture, and one's land. Not only are Djebar's narrators or heroines solitary, they are also "fugitives," and even impossibly "rooted in flight," when they are not haunting a space they seem barely to inhabit.[42] In the film *The Nouba,* for instance, the protagonist Lila has returned home, but uncertainties remain: "But you, after this long absence, are you really back?"[43] This question that is both mundane and troubling indicates that something or someone remains missing, compromising the evidence of the return by the suspicion of an irreducible absence.

Unlike Pontecorvo's *The Battle of Algiers,* Djebar represents few war scenes in *The Nouba,* concentrating instead on its traumatic impact and the ways in which it affects the present. Djebar focuses on the silence in which the main protagonist, Lila, is engulfed, a silence that betrays her inability to communicate her wartime experience, while in the present she suffocates under the expectation of transparence to which she is supposed to conform in her home and social circle. Silence, though it is the consequence of a trauma that is alluded to in voice-over, may also be a strategy to avoid a ready-made interpretation of women's role in the war. While the film was well received in Europe (it was awarded the Venice Biennale Critics Prize in 1979), it was met with some resentment in Algiers, according to Djebar,[44] and interpreted as "feminist revenge" because of its depiction of a paralyzed couple:—literally, since Lila's husband has an accident that puts him temporarily in a wheelchair and, later, on crutches, while, by contrast, Lila enjoys an unimpaired freedom of movement, and figuratively, because of their inability to speak to each other.[45] In his illuminating reading of the film, Réda Bensamaïa notes that it is not only Lila who remains mostly silent, but that his accident left her husband aphasic.[46] Indeed, Djebar does not entirely invalidate her critics' negative judgment when she writes that the film represents "a certain defeat for the man [or *for man*]" or "the frozen present of the couple exposed thus before us."[47] But this understanding is only partial. She first intended to make a film, not about Arab woman, "but of the image of the woman for the Arab man" (304), and this project required a certain distance, hence the immobility of the male protagonist. Here Djebar pursues as well her investigation of *infiçal,* the recommended spatial separation or avoidance between men and women, predicated in principle, though of course not always actually enacted, on a scopic delimitation or a demarcation of space. She puts in question the "devouring gaze" by which woman's existence is often constrained (305). Lila, an architect, says in *The Nouba* that she should build "transparent glass houses" so as to expose and undermine the permanent urge to watch woman.[48] But Djebar felt that her initial project would only have demonstrated woman's "alienation," whereas she wanted to break with woman's condition as a thesis, an object of debate, and especially with objectified woman, which, she argues, is the case "in almost all of masculine cinema, whether Arab or not."[49]

To begin with, of course, the camera is not only "a gaze, that is, 'the' Gaze" (256), but also a "ravenous" (281), "spying eye" (256). In fact, Djebar did not altogether eliminate the initial project of a film about "woman's image"; rather, she superimposed on it Lila's own gaze on others, especially on other women: "In this film a woman walking alone rests her fertile gaze on other women" (310). Djebar may liberate Lila from an all-encompassing male gaze, but she does not liberate woman from the hold or the logic of the devouring gaze. She merely displaces it in order to appropriate it for women. Likewise, while Lila's desire of speaking, but also of being unobserved, may be interpreted as an aspiration to escape the masculine gaze, it also seems to repeat the situation of "invisible" women that is being more generally interrogated in the film. But precisely, as Mildred Mortimer points out, there are many indications in Djebar's works that bypassing the appropriation of the gaze would be detrimental to women, because, as *So Vast the Prison* puts it, they have to "learn to see" (306).[50] Woman's mimicking devouring gaze is only a preliminary response to an attempt to circumscribe her vision, the violence of which is not always latent. Thus *So Vast the Prison* alludes to the narrator's first husband's attempt to blind his wife, and her ensuing separation, travels, and recovery, such a scene occurring in other books as well, for instance in *A Sister to Scheherazade*: "Carefree and relieved to be free; above all happy to have kept my eyes. . . . As a result of seeing new things, multitudinous things, the repetition of landscapes and faces, becoming nothing but gaze!"[51] However, there is a corrective in Djebar, such as her emphasis on solidarity between women, which prevents or limits self-serving appropriation, without the urge to dominate or possess.

Furthermore, even though Djebar puts into question the controlled space and the sense of being permanently watched experienced by women, she aims to do so by "taking into account interdicts regarding the image," which are by the same token interdicts about space.[52] Thus she strives to subvert or inhabit that interdict otherwise instead of attacking it frontally. In that respect Bensmaïa notes that Djebar's film *The Nouba* was "geared to the investigation of a 'world' that was as yet virtually unknown in Algeria:

the world of space and time as perceived by women" and, in addition, a world "in which the male gaze . . . [has] been for the time being suspended."[53] Djebar rejected accusations of artificial exclusion and separation between the sexes in her film. "But how can I respond other than by saying that all I did was show what exists in reality?"[54] In other words, the film gave to see relative gender spatial separation, which, unlike women's space and time, was not "virtually unknown" and should not have been provoking. What may have especially disconcerted some critics was that the film conformed relatively closely to that expectation while defeating it by bracketing man's gaze instead of that of woman and by emphasizing a woman's singular inhabitation of space in a form, moreover, that avoided recourse to psychology and realism. Radicalizing the experience of a sequestered gaze, Djebar explains her understanding of filming as "first closing the eyes to listen better in the dark."[55] The priority of the image in cinema is thus questioned and even devalued in order to rethink the link between image and sound: "First with my eyes shut, to grasp the rhythm, the noises from submerged depths believed lost, then rising back to the surface again and finally, eyes washed clean, seeing everything lit by dawn" (279). In order to see, one needs to be silent and listen; filming entails "turning one's back to images . . . as though blind."[56]

The decision to prioritize hearing over sight in the viewer's experience was perhaps also dictated by the fact that Djebar had initially recorded women's testimonies (twenty-five hours worth of material), some of which were integrated in another text, *Fantasia*, in several sections titled "Voices."[57] One consequence is that her film, consisting in her words in "handling the sound/image through the ear," which echoes Kateb Yacine's injunction of making history *heard,* mentioned at the beginning of this chapter, formally as well as thematically interrogates the interdict and privilege of visibility in the discourse on women.[58] Furthermore, stylistically, the representation of war in Djebar's film did not aim to be "spectacular" (80). Djebar consistently denounces war as spectacle, for example in *Children of the New World* and in *Fantasia,* and values verbal testimony because of the capacity of language to withhold even as it shows. *The Nouba* opens with sounds and actual footage of combat alternating with images of a countryside scene, that of women watching a tree in which a little girl is hidden. Djebar experiments here with a device she will use again in her second film *La Zerda ou les chants de l'oubli* (1982): a disjunction between image and sound, where the sound does not necessarily corroborate the image we watch, although it may open up possibilities of understanding the image differently as an unexpected commentary. The sound follows a logic of its own; it develops in convergence with the image, but is sometimes at odds with it. This is also true of the music, which does not "illustrate" the image.[59] Part of the musical score, for instance, in the first scene of *The Nouba*, was composed by the Hungarian musician Béla Bartók when he visited Algeria in 1913 in order to study its folk music, an interaction Djebar values.[60] In her films, Djebar minimizes as well the importance of the storyline, to which sound and image are not subordinated, and from which they become in effect emancipated. Her film belongs to a form that Bensmaïa calls "a fragmented work."[61] That aesthetic, which eludes totalization, implies that Djebar's project is in itself neither exactly historical nor accurately memorial but precedes both history and memory as one of their possibilities, as a preparation for a work of anamnesis (878).

The first scene, in which a little girl is perched in a tree, is typical of Djebar's treatment of the genre of the documentary and of her construction of the film. For Djebar, a documentary is "a gaze on a space" that becomes inhabited by memory, an inner discourse.[62] In their introduction to *The Image and the Witness*, Frances Guerin and Roger Hallas make the point that a widespread understanding of the image in contemporary visual studies evinces an ambivalence to the image having to do with the recognition of a "mimetic promise" to represent or produce evidence or "truth," on the one hand, while, on the other hand, the image falls under the suspicion of being a "false image" belying its implied veracity.[63] In the case of the documentary, or *documenteur*, in Agnès Varda's formulation, this suspicion explains why the reverence for the referent encapsulated by the image also comes under attack.[64] For example, through the work of editing, in which an image or an interview is followed by archival footage or other interventions, a filmmaker may complicate and even contradict the truth status of the image, pointing to political extrication, rationalization, bad faith, or lying. But ambivalence to the truth of the visual document is particularly strong when images purport to witness traumatic events. "There is a persistent scepticism expressed toward their capacity to remember or redeem the experience of the traumatised victim."[65] Guerin and Hallas trace the legacy of that distrust to the pictures taken by the Allies when they liberated concentration camps, which led to the question of ethical and responsible representation (6). The autobiographical account or testimony was then valued for its authenticity, as "still connected to the body of the sufferer" (7), while it was also endowed with a therapeutic and social value (8). In terms of its relation to truth, the act of bearing witness involved a "relationality between the survivor-witness and the listener-witness" (10). Djebar is interested in this negotiation within the testimonial act between the one who speaks and the one who listens. In *The Nouba* Lila desires to learn to listen to others more than to speak.[66] When testimony is reinforced in the film by a scene enacting it, or followed by a fictional sequence built around Lila, Djebar demonstrates that both testimony and fiction, though they speak of truth and toward it, are more performative than constative, and do not prove so much as embody.

Writing about the work of Alain Resnais and Marguerite Duras in *Hiroshima mon amour*, Cathy Caruth points out that, in declining to make a documentary about Hiroshima, "Resnais paradoxically implies that it is direct archival footage that cannot maintain the very specificity of the event. And it would appear, equally paradoxically, that it is through the fictional story, not *about* Hiroshima but taking place at its site, that Resnais and Duras believe such historical specificity is conveyed."[67] Fiction is thus enabled with the potential to tell the truth of the event. The inscribed return to the geographical location where the trauma took place has also been shown to be particularly significant in addressing its violence, by filmmakers such as Claude Lanzmann for instance.[68] The geography of *The Nouba* is both that of the war and, more significantly for her project, that of the testimonies she recorded about resistance after it, so that the location is both representational and testimonial: "we are in the mountains of Cherchell, the narratives are those that were told me in that province, which was a place of violence."[69] When working on testimonies about the war, Djebar became aware of moments when they yielded to fiction or to a narrative of substitution that became a way of "displacing memory" (90), of managing what was too painful for utterance. Is the result a revelation, even if it is indirect, or does it keep secret what it simply points to as a locus of resistance to utterance? The episode of the little girl in the tree is such an undecidable instance. Mireille Calle-Gruber remarks that the scene "redoubles the narrative while displacing it from sound to image; from documentary to fiction" (89). After that first image at the beginning of the film, one that is enigmatic for the viewer, because what it refers to is cut off from a diegetic chronology, its implicit story unfolds later in the film, once in the form of a narrative told by an old woman, then shown twice, played out in images performing the story. Characteristically, then,

Djebar separates the woman's memory from its visual transcription. Furthermore, the woman narrating the testimony in the film was not an ocular witness of the war violence she recounts. First, before she started the film, Djebar taped interviews of women of her mother's family, and she partly wrote the script on the basis of these recordings. In one of these interviews, which is the basis of the sequence of the little girl in the tree of *The Nouba,* Djebar was struck by the fact that when she narrated her story, which was about her son's execution, the woman insisted instead on her younger daughter's plight. For a whole night, the little girl had been left "alone except for God" (the mother's words in *The Nouba*) hiding in a tree, before being able to jump to the ground and reclaim the body of her dead brother. In *Fantasia,* the resister Cherifa gives a similar (or the same?) testimony. She and her brother were running away from French soldiers when he was hit by a bullet. She hid in a tree, and in the morning she jumped and went to retrieve his body.[70] In that testimony the "new Antigone" (122) is pitied by her elder brother: "My elder brother Abdelkader came up behind me and suddenly said angrily to the other, 'Why did you show her the body? Can't you see she's only a child?'" (121). Djebar focuses on and reiterates a scene that she finds emblematic of women's participation, but especially of their way of commemorating acts of war: the mourning of the son is addressed through the mother's sorrow for the young girl forced to cope alone with her brother's death. That displacement uncovers another way of historicizing the war and its heroes, one that would be oblique and allusive, and bring to light some of its less commemorated actors, like the young girl. In spite of the restraint with which the testimonies that Djebar gathered unfold, one senses her witnesses' deep disappointment having to do with a confiscation of memory for the benefit of a few, which makes Djebar's project all the more timely and necessary. "Alas! We can't read or write. We don't leave any accounts of what we lived through and all we suffered! . . . You'll see other people who spent their time crouching in holes and who, afterwards, told what they've told!" (148). What is important for Djebar to uncover is not primarily memory itself or its contents, but rather "the way of being with [one's] memory,"[71] as well as what is called in *The Nouba* "the sound of broken memory." In Djebar's film, out of modesty, the witnesses would not repeat in front of a camera the story that had been preliminarily recorded (85). This is the second reason why the woman retelling her children's plight in *The Nouba* is not telling her own story. The women who recall their wartime experiences in the film are performing words that Djebar extracted and assembled from her recordings with other women who remain hidden from view (92). By so doing, Djebar stresses that the veracity of the narrative lies in its audition.

Like Djebar herself in preparation for the film, Lila gathers the testimonies of the women of Mount Chenoua who participated in the resistance, just as Zoulikha did at first before joining the *maquisards,* by preparing meals, conveying or hiding medication, money, and weapons. Some resisters like Cherifa also worked as nurses in field hospitals.[72] One of Djebar's relatives is proud of the uniforms she made for the partisans (158). A woman concisely says about the resistance: "The 'revolution' began and ended in my home, as every *douar* in these mountains can bear witness. In the beginning the partisans ate up everything I had. . . . Then Sid Ali arrived and said, 'We're going to let the men hide here, aunt!' " (146). In retaliation, the farm was burned several times by the French army—this act of war is mentioned by several witnesses interviewed by Amrane-Minne as well as in *Fantasia*: "France came and burnt us out," says Cherifa (117).[73] Djebar here obliquely addresses the scorched-earth policy of the Kahina while inverting the queen's gesture. The military strategy that had struck the queen's enemies and people alike with awe is now quite reversed—women support resistance through farming the land and feeding the partisans, while French soldiers burn the land: "But I wouldn't give up. The following days I decided to go and make my fire between some stones and I managed to feed the partisans, just the same!"[74] Another witness says that "we decided that we women would in future cook extra quantities of food, in case it was needed. . . . We agreed we'd bury the food every time" (187). She successfully managed to hide during the war: "I began to go into the hills to help other people; we took food, we washed their uniforms, we kneaded bread" (188). Thus Djebar reframes and contests the cultural commonplace according to which woman's agency is a factor of destruction of the cohesiveness of the group by underscoring her role in nourishing and protecting the partisans. She again addresses the ascription of *fitna,* civil war or disorder, to woman, by inserting in the film a sequence apparently unconnected with the war, but one that well illustrates her approach, consisting in reinterpreting legends and historiography so as to extract from their very misogyny an unexpected feminist potential. Lila asks one woman to tell her the story of Abdel Rahman, the saint of Mount Chenoua.[75] According to the story, he gave protection and abundance to his village until a (foreign) young woman came and caused his blessings to cease because of her unwarranted curiosity. As often in the film, the sequence is narrated before being transcribed visually, and the young woman's curiosity is figured as her forbidden opening of a lidded jar from which birds, or abundance, fly away. This story is then repeated in an intimate scene at night between Lila and her young daughter. In that scene, Lila retells her daughter the story, but thoroughly alters its meaning by turning the young woman's curiosity as disorder and ruin for the village into an improvised disclosure of what was put under cover and repressed. In her account, the birds figure graceful mobility and freedom of action, which she playfully encourages her daughter to emulate. In Djebar's works, birds stand for liberty and improvisation because of their ability to take off. Her female characters are all likely to say: "You see, I flee, I take off, I tear myself off"; but flying away also entails taking risks, for every flight may end in a fall.[76]

ODYSSEUS AND THE SIRENS

A scene of *La Femme sans sépulture* establishes a parallel between Zoulikha, who disappeared after her arrest by the French army during the war, and a mosaic exhibited in a museum in Cherchell, a town located in Zoulikha's zone of combat, and Djebar's hometown as well. The motif of the mosaic is central both to the structure of *La Femme sans sépulture*—the foreword indicates that Zoulikha's story is "at the center of a large feminine fresco, on the model of the very ancient mosaic of Caesarea of Mauretania (Cherchell)"—and to the understanding of Djebar's work in general.[77] This mosaic dating back to Roman colonization represents the scene in Homer's *Odyssey* in which Odysseus has recourse to a cunning trick so as to resist the fatal song of the Sirens. Being bound to his ship's mast while his companions whose ears are stopped with wax row past the peril, Odysseus can hear the song and avoid its mortal consequences, according to the formula of cunning, which "breaks the ordinance by fulfilling it," as Max Horkheimer and Theodor W. Adorno have noted.[78] Several critics have pointed out the recurrence in the *Odyssey* of encounters (including with the Sirens) during which Odysseus and his companions are threatened with oblivion, in particular that of their own country, which becomes in Homer's poetic transcription "forgetting the way home," through drugged meals and amnesiac fruits.[79] The song of the Sirens does not operate like the fruit of forgetfulness of the Lotus-Eaters, for instance. In recalling the recent past (the Trojan war), the Sirens promise, on the one hand, a song that enchants the listener because it enlightens him, making him "well pleased, knowing more than ever / he did; for we know everything that the Argives and Trojans / did and suffered in wide Troy through the gods' despite."[80] But, on the other hand and in return, as Horkheimer and Adorno remark, the Sirens "demand the future as the price of that knowledge."[81] Djebar equally asserts the impossibility or indefinite postponement of the return, but she does not equate it with the dreaded oblivion of the homeland noticeable in the *Odyssey*. In her analysis there can be no return because the stability and permanence of the home supposedly anchoring the self are by no means assured: "actually the only question would be: where to come back truly?"[82] Back in her hometown, as several critics have noted, the narrator of *La Femme sans sépulture* is thus always referred to as a "visitor," "invited guest," "stranger," or, slight concession, "not so strange stranger" (213). There is no equivalent of Ithaca in Djebar. Zoulikha, an exceptional person who was the only woman belonging to the group of young partisans evoked in *La Femme sans sépulture* (192), stands for the nomadic figure who does not come back but traverses the familiar landscape and her time otherwise, renouncing all security and putting her body at risk. She is thereby an anti-Odysseus.

In their study of *metis*, or cunning intelligence, in Greek thought, Marcel Detienne and Jean-Pierre Vernant emphasize its characteristic "pliability and polymorphism, duplicity and equivocality, inversion and reversal."[83] Precisely, Odysseus's subtlety and reversibility have at times been interpreted as shameful evasion. Thus Maurice Blanchot's reading of the *Odyssey* opposes sailors, "men who take risks," to Odysseus's "fortunate and secure cowardliness."[84] Likewise, in "Sorties," Cixous denounces Odysseus as return to the self and to the same, celebrating on the contrary figures like Ariadne, who give themselves without return, in an economy that is neither that of the debt nor that of the obligation. For Cixous, Odysseus is "the Winner: the one who was saved the homecoming man! Always returning to himself—in spite of the most fantastic detours," whereas Ariadne is the one who renounces everything "without calculating," the anti-Odysseus "advancing into emptiness, into the unknown."[85]

Nobody seems to contest Zoulikha's courage and commitment, but this position is still insufficient for Djebar. To the homage, even sincere and respectful, paid by authorities in Algeria to the memory of Zoulikha's acts of resistance, *La Femme sans sépulture* juxtaposes other scenes in order to shed a different light on Zoulikha's decision to expose herself to the unknown and to danger. Throughout her narrative, Djebar emphasizes specific gestures, extending Zoulikha's demonstrations of free spirit and rebelliousness well before the war of independence, but she is especially intent on recognizing a woman's will and power to act. Such are the characteristics of Zoulikha's struggle that she deems crucial to commemorate for the impact they may have today. If Zoulikha should not, of course, be forgotten, her initiative should also be understood accurately, in a way that does it justice, by avoiding participation in a hagiographic discourse that ignores or represses the specificity of Zoulikha's commitment. Some means of paying homage are akin to a second killing. So says Zoulikha's eldest daughter Hania about interviews with journalists regarding the war heroine, while noting in passing the unavowable relief many might feel today about Zoulikha's disappearance.[86] There are several reasons, some of which we have mentioned in this chapter, why official discourse may be reticent about evoking some aspects of women resisters' combat. One reason frequently mentioned by Djebar revolves around the wish, which is not lacking in respect for women, to avoid any voyeurism, even in testimony (of their tortured, raped bodies for instance), and therefore the desire to protect the female body after the fact. But, for Djebar, the preservation of woman's body is a delusion that can serve all sorts of alibis or programs, particularly social conservatism: "Where will we be, if our women, our daughters are mistaken about their role!" (203). On the contrary, Djebar affirms the chance as much as the risk of the opening to what she still names the "exposure" of the body, so as better to reject the anxiety triggered by the reminder of a woman's initiative that is viewed as illegible or inadmissible. In interspersed monologues from beyond the grave, Zoulikha interprets her "time in the *maquis*" as "the perpetual exposure of my body . . . the expenditure without calculation of my physical strength" (175). Zoulikha's body was never returned to her family nor found, hence the title of the book devoted to her, and Djebar proposes several hypotheses to come to terms with her disappearance and unknown burial site: Zoulikha might have been thrown out of a helicopter above the sea (65), and, as we shall see, in some versions of the myth the sea also becomes the tomb of the Sirens after the passage of Odysseus. In another hypothesis, the French army may have exposed her corpse as a warning to the population (202), after which a partisan might have given her a decent, though secret, burial (210). In that scene both Algerians and French are shown to share a similar ambivalence about the female body: it is because they are "afraid" of it that the soldiers torture it (199), while the sight of her corpse makes villagers "afraid," afflicted with the cruelty encountered by female heroism, but also fearful of Zoulikha's body in itself, "of this presence of my arms, of my chest, of my head" (201).[87] In that respect, Djebar often distances herself from the "familial conventions" that the actors of the war of independence relied on—Zoulikha was called "my mother" by the young partisans in the mountains—not because they betray a lack of esteem, but because they risk negating woman's body and instrumentalizing or even neutralizing the singularity of her acts through a collective inscription.[88] In addition, the respect of the partisan who is supposed to have buried Zoulikha is not applauded, as could have been expected, but deplored: "Whereas spontaneously the enemy had found what fitted my fibers, my muscles best: rotting in the open air, with women's youyous piercing me through. No, he buried me! According to tradition . . ."[89] The next chapter will analyze the ways in which Cixous recasts hostility and love as not necessarily opposed; the passage in which Zoulikha protests against her burial confirms a similar approach to enmity in Djebar. That pattern especially determines the construction of *Fantasia*, which analyzes "love of and in war" and imagines future possibilities of contiguity that arose as of the 1830 conquest of Algiers, but will not repeat the violence of the encounter between French and Algerians.[90]

Zoulikha's protest can also be understood in light of Djebar's frequent demonstration that murdered corpses in a state of putrefaction are indicative of the truth of the event, not out of morbidity, but so as to oppose the urge to bury, dissimulate, and thus risk annihilating forever the sinister logic that led to extermination. She recalls, for instance, in *Fantasia* the "fumigations" carried out by the French army in 1845, asphyxiating the population that had taken refuge in caves and refused to give themselves up. That act of war was followed by the "speleology" ordered by General Pélissier to retrieve the bodies, and his archived report of the number of victims: "Bring them out in the sun! Count them!" (73). Here Djebar trusts the sun, not the wish to bury a secret. In 1845 "the corpses exposed in the hot sun have been transmuted into words" (75), including Pélissier's report and Djebar's text. She prefers that exposure of bodies to the decision of another officer, Saint-Arnaud, who ordered the cave to be sealed: "This is death indeed. To be interred in Saint-Arnaud's caves and never exhumed!" (76). Even then, Saint-Arnaud's correspondence with his brother brings the corpses back into the light of inquiry. But Djebar does not merely equate exposition with revelation. The exposure of the body is inseparable from a risk and a future that should not be guarded against. One should check the impulse to bury too fast aspirations that demand to be openly uttered. This vigorous protest against amnesia or selective memory, as well as against a soothingly consensual discourse about women's combat, seems to situate Zoulikha in opposition to Odysseus's calculated prudence.

Yet, if the pertinence of the motif of homecoming in the *Odyssey* is contested in *La Femme sans sépulture*, and if, by the way in which she accepts risk, Zoulikha represents an anti-Odysseus in the sense of Blanchot or Cixous, the figure of Zoulikha is not merely assigned to that position. Instead, she can be located either on the side of Odysseus or on that of the Sirens. This is certainly because Djebar is less severe to Odysseus than the main critics of Homer's *Odyssey* mentioned so far. However, Cixous, for one, avoids good conscience by placing, at times, the I on the side of Odysseus: "But sometimes I was ashamed: I was afraid of being Ulysses, and wasn't I sometimes?"[91] Likewise, the narrator of *La Femme sans sépulture* compares herself to Odysseus,[92] and she does so all the more willingly since she interprets anew the scene of the encounter between Odysseus and the Sirens. It is the scene in its entirety that becomes emblematic of Zoulikha's individual history, which explains why all the protagonists of the mosaic can represent several aspects of her struggle and why it is indicative of a potential narrative of Algerian history told from the perspective of women's resistance.

Zoulikha can be likened to Odysseus because of the multiplicity of her improvisations, which testify to an ability to invent and to adapt that is praised in the case of Zoulikha's epic strategy, once referred to as her "Odyssey" (151). The transformations of her physical appearance abound in the narrative, and the changes in dress that she adopts in order to be taken for a peasant or look like an old woman, for instance, thereby eluding the surveillance of the army and the police, recall Odysseus's numerous disguises in the *Odyssey*, particularly when he appears in Ithaca transformed into an old beggar by Athena. Likewise, Zoulikha's responsibilities change as police searches increase, from the contacts she first establishes between the resistance cells in the city to her permanent removal to the *maquis*. Her activities are always characterized by the urgency of a decision, "of ruses to find, of the face, of the body either hidden or bare . . . I would have to invent" (175).

The analogy of Zoulikha to the Sirens, which is also found in *La Femme sans sépulture*, is less unexpected. Zoulikha was arrested and taken away by helicopter, and the Sirens, winged women of the mosaic in Cherchell, personify that feminine takeoff, that momentum, flight, or freedom, and that tearing off of the prosaic. Zoulikha's disappearance is referred to as a take-off to the sun (122), but from the beginning, her commitment to the resistance is equivalent to "flying away" (109). Likewise, the three Sirens in the mosaic or "women-birds" are described with "long feet of birds ready to fly away above the sea" opposite Odysseus's ship (106). The *Odyssey* evokes only the voice of the Sirens but says nothing of their appearance, while later legends or Greek poems, such as Lycophron's *Alexandra,* insist on the double aspect of the Sirens, whose shape is that of a woman and of a bird. The mosaic in Cherchell is probably inspired by these later versions of the myth. In the *Metamorphoses,* Ovid does not expose the encounter between Odysseus and the Sirens but involves the Sirens in a scene in which he takes up the attributes mentioned by Lycophron and others and wonders what motivated what he takes to be a metamorphosis: "What reason / Was there to give Achelous' daughters feathers / And claws, but let them keep the faces of girls?"[93] Ovid usually records instances of metamorphoses that happen as chastisement, a punishment to a human being or a lesser divinity such as a nymph requested by an offended higher divinity such as Juno. The change of form often entails degradation of the human shape, which becomes animal, vegetal, or mineral. Thus the Sirens are a rare instance in this poem of creatures asking of their own accord for a new form. Out of faithfulness to Proserpina, who has disappeared after her abduction by Pluto (and, unlike Zoulikha, her removal was not up in the sun but underground), they beg the gods to be turned into birds in order to seek her over the waters: "And the gods were kind, and gave them golden plumage" (124). Blanchot deplores the misogynist tradition that only retains from the Sirens of the *Odyssey* "the false voices that must not be listened to" or "the trickery of seduction,"[94] but in Ovid's version the Sirens demonstrate instead an indefectible solidarity with their companion, which, just as in Zoulikha's case, puts their body at risk and to the test. In recognition of their fidelity, they are allowed to "keep the lovely singing voices, / So dear to the ears of men, the human features, / The human voice, the dower of song forever."[95] The figure of the Sirens enables Djebar to take into account both the act of flying away and the voice, but she is also drawn in *La Femme sans sépulture,* as she is throughout her work, to women's friendship, to acts that bind women to one another. Zoulikha is the only woman to have taken off and flown away, a singular heroic history that makes her the "woman bird of the mosaic" par excellence, but the narrator is struck by the resemblance of the Sirens to the appearance that women from Caesarea (the name of Cherchell at the time of Roman colonization) might have had two thousand years ago (106) and wonders whether women would respond in the same way today to the invitation to fly away (109). The question, then, is what such an analogy between Algerian women and the Sirens might imply, a question that Djebar handles by renewing the figure of the Sirens with respect to the poetic traditions in which they appear.

Several critics have been, so to speak, on the side of the Sirens against Odysseus, whose cunning would have forever affected all songs (the poetic in general) and not only that of the Sirens.[96] For Horkheimer and Adorno, the encounter between Odysseus and the Sirens inaugurates, among other things, the passage from art as power to art as contemplation: "The prisoner [= Odysseus] is present at a concert, an inactive eavesdropper like later concertgoers" (34). By curtailing the power of their song with his trick, Odysseus brings about the ruin of the Sirens, as much as that of the mythical figure of art. Moreover, in other evocations of the Sirens, such as the *Alexandra*, the Sirens commit suicide after the passage of Odysseus, that suicide being also a murder: "Of Tethys' son three daughters he shall slay, / Who reproduced their songstress-mother's lays. / From lofty watch-rock they shall leap to death, / And with their wings dive deep in Tuscan waves, / Where Clotho draws them with her cruel thread."[97] Blanchot distances himself both from Homer and Lycophron by positing an imperfection in the Sirens' song, which would not be irresistible because of its faultless beauty, but on the contrary would seduce and be powerful as "a song still to come": "they [the Sirens] did lead the sailor toward that space where singing might truly begin."[98] The song opens up a space that can neither be said nor located; it is a "song of the abyss that, once heard, would open an abyss in each word and would beckon those who heard it to vanish into it" (4). For Blanchot, if the Sirens were vanquished by Odysseus's technical power, and if the *Odyssey* is their tomb, they have also engaged Odysseus there (5). What their song evokes still resonates within the space of art or of literature after their disappearance. But it also still remains to be heard as such.

In *La Femme sans sépulture*, the song of the Sirens certainly has, at first glance, a more expected role, which is to stand for Zoulikha's initiative: "Woman-bird of the mosaic, she seems today, half faded to her countrymen! But her song remains."[99] One may not want to hear that song, which the narrator contributes, however, to saying and transmitting, but it subsists nevertheless. That position already suggests that, unlike in the *Odyssey,* the song of the Sirens in the Cherchell mosaic is uttered, first and foremost, independent of any listener, and its chord is unaltered whether its harmony is heard or not. Djebar proposes reading the scene otherwise than as an altercation with death at stake, even if it is avoided by Odysseus's cunning: for her, the song of the Sirens is not fatal. In the *Odyssey* the confrontation to the Sirens is unavoidable. No other way home to Ithaca is possible. Likewise, in that text, the Sirens, mythical figures of repetition, always watch out for sailors with the same deadly ends.[100] This is not the case with the musical Sirens in the Cherchell mosaic, who are, on the contrary, ready to fly away when Odysseus's ship approaches: "The mosaic does not make the risk of death present. No . . . The scene seems entirely flooded by the magic of music. . . . Musicians ready to . . . fly away, I believe! As for the hero, Odysseus, he listens to them."[101] The song does not strive to trap the other in order to destroy him, but gives itself; one must already want to be in its orbit before having heard it. This implies neither generosity nor sacrifice. The Sirens are ready to fly away and land elsewhere if such expectation and attention are not manifest. Thus the relation between the different protagonists of the mosaic is organized on another premise than in the *Odyssey,* which founds the encounter with the other on domination. Whereas some of Homer's readers emphasize Odysseus's privilege, based on a division of labor that enables him to be the only one to enjoy the song that the sailors do not have the possibility or the authorization of hearing, while Odysseus owes his survival to their physical strength, Djebar, without wholly ignoring this inequality, alters its consequences.[102] In the *Odyssey* sailing past the Sirens is impossible to bypass, but, of course, such is not the case with hearing their song, which is the foundation of the trick. The magician Circe gives Odysseus the choice whether to listen to it or not, thus privileging the safety of homecoming: "melt down sweet wax of honey / and with it stop your companions' ears, so none can listen; / the rest, that is, but if you yourself are wanting to hear them, / then have them tie you hand and foot on the fast ship."[103] For Djebar, as for Circe, Odysseus could have, if not rowed like his companions, at least decided to go like them past the domain of women-birds without listening to them. But the fact that he did not want to do so is interpreted positively by Djebar. Thus Odysseus is "the traveler who did not stop his ears with wax" in the sense that he chose to hear and "never to forget the song of the Sirens."[104]

Listening is no longer a matter of exclusive enjoyment based on privilege, but the recognition that the other has something to say. Conversely, plugging one's ears becomes tantamount to a deliberate torpor and frightened detachment, which seem to the narrator to be a widespread condition today: "in my city, almost everyone lives with wax in their ears . . . having chosen amnesia" (214), an allusion to the history of the region during the war, but also to the violence and murders of the 1990s (218). This voluntary deafness is no longer an act of survival as in the *Odyssey*, but bad faith or injustice, a refusal to hear a certain discourse.

Djebar interprets Odysseus's eager listening to the song of the Sirens as the beginning of the necessary act of reading of the war of independence and its aftermath. Therefore the mosaic is not only the allegory of the history of an exceptional woman, but proposes a model of hearing history (in Kateb Yacine's words) that transcends her. This greater dimension leads Djebar, in a supplementary fold of interpretation, to complicate the notion of passivity, which is not necessarily fruitless in her analysis. It is to be proscribed if it is synonymous with immobility and denial or if, as cunning, it turns weakness into strength and merely reverses power. But passivity can also be something wholly other, an ethics of relationship to the other that is not of the order of annexation, possession, or precomprehension. We will develop that notion of passivity as exposure and deference to the other in Emmanuel Levinas's thought and its inflection in Cixous. For Djebar, the fixed and passive position of Odysseus, tied to his mast, who still wants to listen to what he should never have been in a position to remember, is an invitation to rethink the links between history, memory, amnesia, and anamnesis through the privilege granted to testimony, a silent attention to the words of the other, which she has emphasized throughout her oeuvre. Odysseus bound listening to the song of the Sirens, then, is also in that perspective the man without knowledge desirous of hearing a woman historian (Ovid, in agreement on this point with Homer, refers to the Sirens as "skilled" or knowledgeable) and the other history she is telling him.[105] In this configuration there would perhaps still be room for seduction, but a seduction that would have nothing to do with deception or subjection, but rather with the enchantment of an unheard narrative, infinitely new, addressed to the disinterested attention of someone who wants, more than anything, to hear and let the other come.

CHAPTER SIX

Allergy in the Body Politic

War in Cixous

THE ETHICAL QUESTION OF POLITICS

Cixous's textuality has always been infused with loss, violence, conflict, war, and fights to the death. In her writings, which are anything but appeased or consensual, the reflection accompanying the exposure of violence averts both the absolute rejection and the embrace of violence. Just as Cixous argues that being for life must also be understood as protecting the dead,[1] so she elaborates an account of violence that requires another formalization than the opposition of war to peace, hate to love, activity to passivity. In *Hélène Cixous: A Politics of Writing*, Morag Shiach shows, on the one hand, that Cixous theorizes the *politics* of writing, in the sense that she analyzes the political presuppositions and stakes of philosophical, psychoanalytic, and literary texts.[2] On the other hand, Shiach examines the delineation in Cixous of alternative political economies (21), and she makes the point that Cixous's own writing is strategic and has political import (23). Yet she also notes that the reader should be alerted "to the dangers of claiming any 'definitiveness' for Cixous' readings of any given text" (29) or that Cixous's conclusions can seem "remarkably fleeting, and slippery" (26). Such remarks by Shiach should not be taken as adversarial or critical, but must be related to Cixous's very textuality: one that aims, in Shiach's words, "at opening up theoretical and political difficulties" (29) and at exposing a displacement of or exteriority to conceptual oppositions rather than providing and defining the determinable terms of an alternative economy. This gesture is akin to what Jacques Derrida called "sortie" in *Of Grammatology* and *Dissemination*, one that Cixous forcefully addressed and formalized in her own essay "Sorties."[3] One of the conceptual oppositions that Cixous consistently aims at exceeding in her thinking of the political is that between love and hate. If the political is so persistently associated with the problematic of love in Cixous's fictions, it is because of the recurrence of the motif in the philosophical interpretation of the concept of the political, as Derrida has shown in *Politics of Friendship*, whether one considers, like Aristotle, that "the *properly* political act or operation amounts to creating . . . the most friendship possible" or, on the contrary, like Carl Schmitt, that what constitutes the political is the enemy.[4] Cixous re-marks both discourses; while valorizing or siding with the discourse of love, not hate, she does not uphold love as a figure for the wholeness or unity of the *polis*, but as a force of disruption, of infinite distance and separation. On the one hand, love consists in resisting the overwhelming impulse to fuse with or possess the beloved and, on the other hand, it "is forced to make war on war."[5] In her play *L'Indiade*, for instance, which opposes Gandhi's conception of independence to that of Jinnah, the leader of the Muslim League, Gandhi points out that repulsion names a separation intrinsic to love: "You do not love me? So be it. Let's separate. . . . A separation, yes, but if it is within love."[6]

Furthermore, Cixous's work unfolds as a politics of *writing* in that it accounts for "a politics that must also be a poetics," a position that has at times baffled critics.[7] When Cixous writes, for instance, that she "always thought that History could only be treated poetically," she does not dismiss the political, but remarks that poetry, or fiction, is particularly attuned to, and equipped to convey the nodes of resistance of the political to the univocal.[8] Verena Andermatt Conley notes that when Cixous is asked questions regarding the political in her oeuvre, she prefers using chiasmatic reversals, such as "poetically political, politically poetic," in a formulation that insists on the necessity of apprehending one through the other.[9] The form of such statements is not an evasion, be it poetic, of the political, which, as Cixous often underscores, is already reified and precomprehended. Statements affirming that "my vocation,I must say, is not political" must be understood with respect to what immediately follows: "The ethical question of politics, or of responsibility has always haunted me."[10] Cixous entrusts the poetic with the possible advent of the unthought, of an other of politics, another ethics. In that sense her writing is not simply political any longer, at least to the extent that, as Derrida writes in *Politics of Friendship*, changing the sense of the word *politics* changes politics itself.[11] Furthermore, in her work the political is shown to be what may not be postponed but must be addressed without delay, an untimely interruption pursuing and haunting the "I." Cixous has consistently reflected on that irruptive request of the political, which interrupts the oeuvre or punctuates it, that is to say, is not simply exterior to the work though it may appear to be at cross-purposes with it. One well-known example of that thinking of the political occurs in *To Live the Orange*, which begins with the ethical demand of respecting the thing in itself, here the orange, approached through a reading of Clarice Lispector. In the midst of that "philosophical joy," entranced with and aspiring to the orange, the telephone rings, interrupting that ethical imperative with a demand for another urgent gesture, that of militant political activism: "And Iran?"[12] That interrupting phone call must be immediately attended to—such is the incontestable priority of the political. Yet the opposition between writing and politics is actually denounced in a project that amounts to saying (a saying that is also a doing), "*the love of the orange is political too*" (26). Well aware of the cost and the risk of being misunderstood involved in such a declaration, Cixous emphasizes the necessity of that dual approach. Her particular mode of ethical engagement depends on an external request or a call of the other, while her response is textually enmeshed. Additionally, if there is ample evidence of Cixous's activism,[13] it is also true that the term remains inadequate in its implied voluntarism, a notion that Cixous consistently complicates.

As we have seen in chapter 4, if what she terms poetic language has for Cixous the potential of altering the political, it is because of its distance to representation, or to the reproducibility of the given, and its paradoxical re-presentation of that which "will (never) be presented to us."[14] In her analysis that difference already inscribes heterogeneity within the political. Moreover, one of the powers consistently attributed by Cixous to fiction, which is defined as "an antiland" in "Sorties," precisely consists in thinking contradictory positions at once—which does not mean reconciling them—or in being "on neither one side nor the other."[15] All her texts revolve around the inscription or the interpretation of such alterations or differences. Paying heed to such inscriptions helps, in turn, delineate her political thinking. I agree with the critics who point out that this thinking is resolutely nonsystematic in form, and even more so with those who remark that that very formal (or more precisely, informal) trait signals a political or ethical stance. Pushing the second point further, I argue in this chapter that the constellation of positions kept deliberately discrete is a discursive pattern related to Cixous's ethical stance, which it is therefore possible to interpret. What is guarded against in Cixous's nonsystematic discourse are the presuppositions at work in systematic thinking, such as positing a simple origin or originary principle on which depends a number of determinable derivations. The constellation proposed by Cixous is not homogeneous; it cannot be traced to a single principle, nor evaluated as a set of numbered positions or effects. Without claiming to gather the integral political content of her corpus (which would be difficult, given its disseminating textuality), I examine the process of what some would call her incomplete, and what I will name her interminable, thinking on the political. What has taken some of her readers aback is her way of addressing political issues, one that is not recognized by them as "political." I capitalize, on the contrary, on the conclusions of Cixous's most astute critics, who have shown the shortcomings of the view equating an unrecognizable political position with the lack of any political position; I argue that Cixous formulates a persistent response to alterity, enmity, and war as exposure to allergy, within which is lodged the thinking of war in Algeria in particular.

ALGERIA AS WAR

The Algerian war of independence has generally not been directly thematized in Cixous's works, perhaps with the exception of "Letter to Zohra Drif," although mention of Drif's participation in the Battle of Algiers is only the starting point of a more general reflection on colonized Algeria, with a short coda on postcolonial Algeria. But from the very beginning, for instance in "Sorties," Cixous focused on French imperialism in Algeria and the ways in which it was maintained through violent inequality. All her writings about French Algeria foreground latent hostility or overt violence: "The scene was always war. . . . We always lived in the episodes of a brutal Algeriad, thrown from birth into one of the camps crudely fashioned by the demon of Coloniality."[16] The obligation to be what one is not is loathed and rebelled against when imposed by the French state, while the other condemnation on the part of Algerians, and especially Algerian children, is interpreted as a painful rejection, but a comprehensible outcome, nevertheless, of that forced ascription.[17] In Cixous's texts the diagnosis of

Algeria *as* war determines (the fewer) interpretations of Algeria *at* war. The latter depends on the former, and if Cixous does not address the full circumstances of the Battle of Algiers or abstains from writing about the Algerian war, in which she did not directly participate, she minutely evokes, in contrast, what motivated the conflict. She repeatedly shows that revolution and war were already readable outcomes in the violent text that French Algeria constituted.

The short story "Bare Feet" provides an instance of the awareness on the part of a little Jewish girl of the hatred of an Arab shoeshine boy, when he covers her white sandal, as good as new, with red polish or rather, in the narrator's interpretation of the boy's act of intimidation, with "thick blood."[18] The horror felt at that hostile gesture is all the more poignant since it happened during the Vichy years when Jews were deprived of their nationality, "pariahs," just as Arabs, and thus "had fallen into the just: we were no longer part of the oppressors" (56). Revolving around bare or shod feet and momentous steps, that story associates the father, who had become a podiatrist when he could no longer practice medicine under the anti-Jewish legislation, with the daughter, who used to walk in Oran on the path of the Planters among Muslim tombs, enjoying what she interpreted as familiarity with, and familial approbation from, the dead: "I put my bare feet down on the stones that had known their feet, I stepped where earlier steps had been made, and I went back all the way back to the family of the Creation, the steps hewn into the rock to the size of my earliest ancestors" (53). Thus the little boy's silent verdict resulting in spreading red polish on the girl's white sandal contradicts both the initial natural harmony with the Algerian soil *and* the political identification of the plight of Jews with that of Arabs. The "hospitable company" of the dead, "that sharing of the earth, that acquiescence" (52) of the first part of the story are not presented as a delusion, but they also lose their relevance and become subordinated to the evidence of injustice in the second part, an evidence that is all the more striking since it does not need to be uttered. The boy's interpretation is impossible to controvert: unavoidable and felt to be just. "I confessed. I was guilty. Before his tribunal, the acquittal I had enjoyed since Vichy was of no value whatsoever. . . . We knew everything. . . . I was not innocent. . . . Full of anxiety but not surprised, I stayed, mute, because I couldn't ask him: why do you hate me?" (58–59).[19] This recognition of conflicting Algerias gives rise in Cixous's work to formulations such as "I side with those who are injured, trespassed upon, colonized. I am (not)

Arab," whereby it is impossible to be together or at one with those whose wrongs one nevertheless recognizes or with those whom one sides with.[20] The exposure of such a maddening impossibility is one of the most frequent strands in Cixous's Algerian narratives.

Whenever they delineate hate as a motivated response, the necessity of war is upheld up to a point. Indeed there is no irenic discourse and there are "just war[s]" in Cixous's discourse, above all in the case of the Algerian war of independence, a conflict the commitment to which is said to come "naturally."[21] Even peace, as she writes in one recent fiction, which returns to and develops some of the motifs of "Letter to Zohra Drif" and *Reveries of the Wild Woman*, must not be understood as an avoidance, but an endurance of war, a passage through it: "When there is war, on principle I don't let go, I go all the way toward peace."[22] Furthermore, as the story "Bare Feet" demonstrates, Cixous's narrators consistently ignore good conscience; they refuse to be exculpated and assume responsibility, in an ethical sense making explicit that they accept accountability for a structural fault, regardless of individual guilt.

Emmanuel Levinas addresses the issue of responsibility and of the possibility of justice by rethinking subjectivity, and in particular the autonomy and the priority of the I. Maurice Blanchot, for instance, following Levinas, writes of responsibility as "innocent guilt" toward the other.[23] Levinas rethinks the subject in relation to itself, and in connection with the other, by turning the position of the subject facing the world, "the master of itself as of the universe," into what he calls "*subjectivity as hostage*," a condition in which the other precedes the I in a dissymmetrical relationship.[24] Dissymmetry is for Levinas the requirement for justice and irreplaceable responsibility for the other, which "in its antecedence to my freedom . . . is a passivity more passive than all passivity."[25] Responsibility thus understood radically reconfigures subjectivity; it "separates me from myself (from the 'me' that is mastery and power, from the free, speaking subject) and reveals the other *in place* of me."[26] Likewise, Cixous's Algerian narratives emphasize scenes of separation: first, being "always separated from my true kin as from myself" is the inescapable fatality one is unwittingly ascribed to, on and by all sides;[27] but, in a second step, Cixous upholds separation, including within the self or from a community encompassing the self, as a positive basis for an ethical relation to the other. It goes without saying that the separation in question has nothing to do with segregation but is an experience of passivity and dispossession that affects the self from the beginning: "I did not hate and I let myself be hated by the Arabs. . . . the most passive form of love I have ever known."[28] In Cixous's fictions the awareness of rejection, and the impossibility of being credited for the eager desire of being with or on the side of the colonized, give rise to another consideration of the self, not this time *with*, but *for* the other, irrespective of the self's position and even expropriating the self: "Algeria for the Algerians. Not for me of course."[29] That reflection in Cixous is also articulated to the unstable identification of the I with an "inside" and, beyond, with a problematic localization in general. And yet affirming the coexistence of incalculable alterities or unquantifiable differences always remains politically promising for Cixous. In *So Close*, for instance, the question of "Algeria" gets rephrased as "there are millions of Algerias," and Algeria differs from itself in the seeming unity of its location, since it is possible to think "*in* Algeria *of* Algeria" as potentialities converging but also at variance with it.[30] But the political benefit of such a conception tends to be defeated or to get indefinitely deferred, which leads to the ethical endorsement of the disappropriating deference of the self to the other.

One example in *So Close* illustrating the way in which these two approaches (coexisting differences, the transcendence of the other) are represented and defended in turn revolves around a conversation with Zohra Drif said to occur decades after the independence, in which reminiscing about Lycée Fromentin leads the two former classmates to the shared memory of reading *The Song of Roland*, a Middle Ages epic poem pitting Christian against Muslim warriors. That reading had already been evoked earlier in the book as an instance of the uncomfortable position of the self attempting to straddle competing narratives. *The Song of Roland* induces in the narrator a "mental complication" (65) having to do with which side justice requires one to be on but also with the refusal to conform to the anticipated interpretation of the poem. Reading is not a neutral operation, "conditions on reading *The Song*" are encoded within the poem, but "pirate reading[s]" may also make these conditions less effective, and their outcome less predictable (66). The two kinds of readings (encoded and pirate) have contradictory effects, yet they coexist, being thus somehow both authorized by the book. Another interpretation of *The Song* emphasizes the option of refusing to endorse any side at all and feeling "before each corpse the same pain" instead of having to conform to imposed polarity (66). When upholding singularity in life and in death ("each corpse") *and* commonality ("the same pain"), the narrator avoids ready-made political identification with any self-styled group and remains attached to the potentiality involved in enduring contradiction.

In effect, reading *The Song of Roland* in school is shown to have had immediate political relevance in and out of the classroom: "from Roncevaux I arrived in Algiers" (67). The issue of individual allegiance yields then to another question, revolving around what Zohra's critique of *The Song* would be, "what reading, which I don't know, which I don't see, which I will never know?" (67). This question harks back to the interpretation of the medieval poem, but also depends on the Algerian contemporary backdrop of the class assignment. In that respect, Cixous's evocation of the Battle of Algiers through the lens of Lycée Fromentin can be compared to the beginning of Zohra Drif's testimony about her arrest in 1957. The beginning of *La Mort de mes frères* provides the circumstances that motivated Drif's participation in the resistance and urban terrorism in Algiers and dwells in particular on the lycée as a foundational experience: "We were aware early on of racism, which caused us to be considered different from our European fellow students. . . . In the boarding school where I spent seven years, nothing had ever succeeded in bringing us closer, we the 'Muslims'—this was the name given to us—to the others."[31] Drif insists that the time when she was at school coincided with the anticipation that "Algeria was going to make itself," but without "the majority of Europeans [who] had remained foreigners in our country" (7). In her analysis the racial divisions engineered by French Algeria were predicated upon an association of Europeans with France that deemphasized the actuality and materiality of Algeria, which were, on the contrary, the only elements that Muslims could take for granted: "It was as though [Europeans] had kept on living in France, and better than in France, whereas we lived in Algeria. And when the Revolution started, it was quite natural for Algerians to participate in it" (7–8).[32] Cixous and Drif agree on the very form of racial separation that led to the war, and Drif emphasizes as well that war somehow finalized that constructed separation by taking it to its logical conclusion. Cixous's formulation is close to Drif's evaluation, but it insists on proximity as and through separation: "What brought us close was what separated us the war the same each one on her side."[33]

Cixous develops here another thinking of separation, one that is not based on enmity, but on respect marked by distance from the other. In *Totality and Infinity* Levinas links the aspiration to a radical, also called metaphysical, exteriority that "we must 'let be'" to a reflection on subjectivity "as welcoming the Other, as hospitality."[34] By postulating a desire for the wholly or absolutely other (33), Levinas also examines the conditions in which not to suspend or neutralize alterity by possession through appropriation. In the metaphysical or ethical relation the same respects the alterity of the other through separation and distance (38). *Totality and Infinity* addresses the wholly Other (*Autrui*) as an alterity "prior to every initiative, to all imperialism of the same" (38–39). Instead of exercising power, the I is "the first to give up its place" in ethical subjectivity.[35] Not even the coexistence of the self alongside the other (as well as along a certain limit) or reciprocity are respectful enough of alterity, or the right determination of the ethical relation: "The *relation* between the same and the other . . . is language. For language accomplishes a relation such that the terms are not limitrophe within this relation, such that the other, despite the relationship with the same, remains transcendent to the same."[36] Discourse exemplifies what Levinas names the "face to face" (79), an ethical relation of resistance to contact (197). Moreover, Levinas analyzes both the prerogative of possession as appropriation indicative of the very "*way* of the same" (38) *and* the possibility of welcome or hospitality informing the subjectivity he calls for through a number of spatial examples, such as inhabiting or dwelling. In the following section, I will examine Cixous's theorization of the subject in light of Levinas's positions before turning to the way in which she upholds separation as an ethical relation.

FRONTIERS IN THE VERB TO BE

For Cixous, subjectivity seems to ensure uniqueness and totalization, but she argues in *Prénoms de personne* that the subject is in fact already divided or being returned to its divisibility.[37] Likewise, in "Sorties," in a passage about French Algeria, Cixous opposes two ways of apprehending alterity. The absolute other, in its irreducible otherness, is not localizable and cannot be theorized; it exceeds the place where History has assigned it: "The 'other' escapes me. It is elsewhere, outside; absolutely other."[38] On the contrary, the "empire of the selfsame," or "the way of the same" in Levinas's words, consists in appropriating the other, but also in reducing the "person" to the position of otherness (71). But, while denouncing the philosophical and political reduction of the other to the same as well as a certain conceptual externalization of the other, Cixous also asserts that the exceeding other can break through what is therefore but a purported totality, one that is in fact heterogeneous and fractured by openings to difference, markers of another history (98). Thus "Sorties" demonstrates that while the violence of the selfsame is at work with redoubtable political effects, its project is also at times potentially and on other occasions actually thwarted by the alterity that it cannot abide, but that contests it.

In *So Close* the phrase "my Algeriance" gets rewritten, as if to make the point clearer, as "my exalgeriance," a condition that is due, or rather "owed," to Algeria;[39] there, the unity of a self-same subject is split: "I have frontiers everywhere in the verb to be" (73). As we have seen, the figure of an elusive, unattainable Algeria constantly recurs in Cixous's oeuvre, for instance when the initial pages of a manuscript about Algeria cannot be retrieved, an inability that corresponds to the assessment of an untenable position in Algeria, defying inhabitation.[40] The relation to Algeria is consistently formalized through disassociation and dislocation, and the recurring image pointing to that lack of coincidence is that of an ineffectual search for a door, a gate, or an entrance. *Reveries* emphasizes the convoluted lack of reciprocity in crossing a threshold, entering another house, and gaining admission within, the very sign of racial compartmentalization in French Algeria. For instance, access to the friend Françoise's house is barred, but so is the Algerian nanny Aïcha's house while she comes to look after her employer's children in their own place, this dual impossibility amounting to facing two closed doors, "the Algerian door in the person of Aïcha for one thing, for another . . . the French door visible in the person of Françoise."[41] Although Aïcha is one of the few Algerians truly encountered, "the only Algeria that I was ever able to touch" (51), the connection with her is intermittent and restricted. The narrator notes the difference between being "*on* Aïcha," in daily affectionate contact, and being "*at* Aïcha's" (52), in the intimacy of her home, which never happened.

Such examples of ascribed exteriority help explain why providing evidence of dislocation does not indicate nostalgia for lost plenitude or exilic woe. At the very least, longing for the motherland is the reverse of a wound inflicted by the very country that is missed, but, more radically, there can be no homesickness because there was no home.[42] This does not prevent another form of attachment, as long as it is differentiated from rootedness, such as the "sort of invisible belonging to a land to which I am bound by my atoms without nationality" portrayed in "My Algeriance."[43] In *Reveries algia* (rendered as "searing pain") is a term preferred to *nostalgia*; deracination is divorced from pathos: "The possibility of living without taking root was familiar to me. I never call that exile."[44] On the contrary, even though pain or "algia" is recorded, most of the occurrences recording expulsion or the imposition of an external position upon the self are actually positively assessed in her narratives. This aspect of Cixous's conception of subjectivity may be related to Levinas's proposition regarding rootedness. If Levinas poses existing as inhabiting or dwelling, he adds that home should be construed as "a land of refuge, which answers to a hospitality, an expectancy, a human welcome," and insists that home does not "implant the separated being in a ground."[45] He sides with deracination over implantation or enrootedness, with Abraham over Ulysses.[46] In an essay directed at Heidegger, Levinas writes that technology may be less dangerous than a certain thinking of the Place: "One's implantation in a landscape, one's attachment to *Place* . . . is the very splitting of humanity into natives and foreigners."[47] Elaborating subjectivity as otherwise than being is related by Levinas with thinking a nonplace: "the extraction from essence contests the unconditional privilege of the question 'where?'; it signifies the non-place,"[48] and thinking the ethical distance as language inaugurates an approach to spatiality in which ethics is enacted through exteriority and transcendence.

In *Adieu* Derrida expands on Levinas's remark that home is best understood as a "land of refuge" by noting the implication that "the inhabitant also dwells there as a refugee or an exile, a guest and not a proprietor."[49] For Levinas, the house is already, from the start, "hospitable to its proprietor."[50] When I welcome the Other who presents himself in the house by opening my home to him, in fact it is "the Other who welcomes me in the Home" (170). The Other puts the I into question because, to begin with, the relationship with the Other "puts in question the world possessed" (173). Through Levinas, in *Adieu* Derrida emphasizes the "implacable law of hospitality": "The one who invites is invited by the one whom he invites."[51] The law of hospitality is also implacable in that Levinas contemplates both the possibility of opening oneself and one's home to the wholly other and that of keeping "closed doors and windows."[52] But forgetting the transcendence of the other "evinces the absolute truth, the radicalism of separation" (172–73), and allergy to the other is also commanded by the exceeding law of hospitality.

In her narratives underscoring nonreciprocity, Cixous's analysis of hospitality begins with the diagnosis of a failed togetherness. But in *Reveries* it might seem at first glance that the pattern of double noninvitation (referred to as the Algerian door/the French door) is only contradicted or resisted in places associated with the narrator: they often appear to be the only locations receptive to alterity. In that respect, the figure of Mohamed, mentioned in several Algerian narratives, is exemplary. Mohamed is credited in *Reveries* for initiating (the lost pages of) the manuscript and for being the forgotten Algerian come back "in person."[53] When Mohamed is evoked later in the book, the narrator insists on the social-racial division ("Spanish so-called French German so-called French Jewish so-called French Catholic so-called French") evidenced by the occupation of apartments in the building, and above all by the fact that Mohamed lives in a makeshift refuge at the bottom of the stairs (78). But upstairs the grandmother is the only tenant who bypasses that separation and calls Mohamed in: "She feeds hers. Her who, her what, her host, her guest, her other, he has come, she doesn't know who has come, she fills the tin can. Had there not been the couple Mohamed and Grandma the house would be like an empty tin, no doubt about that, but no one gives it a thought" (79). One recognizes here a proximity to the terms of Levinas's thought on hospitality as well as of Derrida's reading of hospitality in Levinas. At the same time, that specific scene of hospitality (the grandmother's welcome) may not be entirely congruent with the analysis of the self as hostage of the other, or guest of the guest, delineated by Levinas. Although the grandmother is endowed with the unique initiative, one that is not imitated by anyone in the building, of opening her door to the other, this welcome is also sent from high up to the destitute man below her. Thus the couple formed by the grandmother and Mohamed may be rare in a colonial world divided between the so-called French and Arabs, but since the colonial system thrives on binary hierarchies, the hospitality displayed by the grandmother has the potential of ruining the system as much as confirming it.

But other readings are also integral to that scene, which, like many others in Cixous, focuses on the relapse into discursive patterns of colonial paternalism in spite of the very determination to avoid them. At times, one protagonist of her fictions is assigned that overdetermined discourse while another contradicts it. The very name of the Algerian nanny evinces the profound disconnection that French Algeria induces with relation to the other. The brother and the sister believe that they uphold the uniqueness of the name properly designating one person to the exclusion of any other, and that their task is also singular in that it is intended to prevent "the family from ever committing an aggression against proper names the way others always did" (53). But they actually contribute to the general disadequation between name and person by giving another name to the nanny than her actual proper name, Messaouda. It is true that the mistaken name is "Aïcha" and not the pejorative "Fatma" (53) or "Moors" (54) that tended, dismissively, to be given to all Algerian women employees in French Algeria,[54] in a denomination that turns a proper name into a common noun applicable to the generality of Algerian women or, as Cixous writes, playing with the double sense of *propre*—that which is proper and that which is clean—transforming them into "dirty and dirtying proper names."[55] That disjunction illustrates once more the condition of always doing what one does not want to do and being irremediably at fault characteristic of what is summed up as French Algeria: "Now we all know that Aïcha was really called Messaouda. But too late."[56] Thus even though a unique welcome of the other is at times attributed to the protagonist's family, it must also be assessed within a larger demonstration in which the political machine it is part of irrepressibly tends to turn disinterested, open-ended acts into reprehensible, predictable deeds, regardless of one's intentions. In these instances Cixous concurs with Levinas's analysis of hostility as not incompatible with or still deriving from hospitality.[57] She contrasts the ambiguity of voluntary acts with what happens without any prevision: both Mohamed in Philippe Street and the arrival of the three Muslim classmates in Lycée Fromentin are of that order, an event that shattered the present and made the future tangible.

Thus another interpretation of the story of the couple of Philippe Street splits it by concentrating on Mohamed irrespective of the grandmother. In that view, Mohamed's visible but silent destitution is prophetic of an Algeria to come, just as the arrival of Zohra Drif in the class recounted in the same text is coextensive with future Algeria. Mohamed's resilience calls for Algeria, in the sense of "prophecy," expounded by Cixous in *Prénoms de personne,* as "producing events."[58] In the case of the encounter with Zohra and the other two Muslim classmates in Lycée Fromentin, "I saw in bright glimmers how I will never be one theirs. . . . There was a glimmer of history. . . . I began to live for what was going to happen. My prophetic soul. The future, at long last there was one. I made use of it as present, I delocalized past nothingnesses."[59] The reference to Hamlet's exclamation in act 1, scene 5 when told by the Ghost that his uncle murdered his father ("O my prophetic soul") is to be linked with the rending of time signaled by the arrival of the three Algerian classmates. In Blanchot's words in *The Book to Come*, both language and time are shattered in prophetic speech: "it is not the future that is given, it is the present that is taken away, and any possibility of a firm, stable, lasting presence."[60] Thus in Cixous the future is not merely foretold but irrupts in the present, substituting itself to the present and displaying there and then the other "in person," expelling the self from the possibility of colocation: "—You invited me I say. —No way! says She."[61] Or as *So Close* reads: "The door opens, she enters, what I must do is: go out."[62] Cixous proposes to affirm differently the relation to the body politic as nonreciprocity and inner separation, a division externalizing the subject or splitting it. Her evaluation of nonreciprocal asymmetries leads her to promote such a conceptualization for addressing alterity.

SEPARATION AS AN ETHICAL RELATION

In her Algerian narratives, Cixous points out the distinction between being *in* and being *born in* a country so as to indicate the fragility and instability of identification legitimating itself in a posited selfsame origin. The fact of being born in French Algeria enacts disjunction or "testifies to "accidence."[63] *So Close* does not merely dwell on the contested nature of the narrator's tie to Algeria but also on its felt improbability. Even the apparently incontestable fact of being born in Algeria smacks of fiction, triggering "this uncanny and exhilarating strangeness . . . a slight incredulity."[64] But such incredulity and disjunction are not extended to all Algerians. In *So Close* a distinction is posited between the narrator and Zohra: "Zohra as well was born in Algeria I say to myself. There is no doubt. And that is the difference between Z. and me. Between my being born and me there is doubt" (45). In such instances, Cixous does not focus on the consequences of a pattern of exclusion affecting the I. Instead, she concentrates on Algeria irrespective of the self, Algeria oriented and inhabited by the other and for that other regardless of the self.

In statements such as "I have never been able to say anything but 'your home,' or else I say in Al- and that's all I can't land on more than one syllable" (73), Cixous affirms Algeria for Algerians and refuses to adopt the position of speaking for the other.[65] It is when confronting the dissymmetry between self and other, where the other is not another "I" but is unknown and unpredictable, that another thinking of Algeria can be undertaken, not in the mode of a deprivation experienced and undergone in Algeria but based on an Algeria with concerns unmoored from those of the self: "From my side . . . the force of Zohra's impact on my unconscious when Zohra and I met. That I am marked by it does not naturally entail that Z. is equally marked by H."[66] We will return to the question of the name or the first name in Cixous's work; it is already clear that "Zohra Drif," in name and in person, deeply informed Cixous's ethical reflection on Algeria. Likewise, the phrase "*What-is-Zohra-going-to-say*," which recurs in *So Close* (for instance, 43), registers the forbearance not only to speak in the name of the other but also to anticipate what the other will say. Far from constituting and appropriating the other, being occurs for the self from the experience of the face of the other, a Levinassian formulation that Cixous mentions explicitly on several occasions in *So Close* in reference to Zohra Drif: "I thought I saw the face of Zohra Drif. . . . I was waiting for a face" (17). Likewise, in *Reveries*, Zohra's arrival confronts the narrator to "all my algerias face to face."[67]

Derrida writes that, for Levinas, "I cannot speak of the Other, make of the Other a theme, tell the Other as object, in the accusative. I can only, I *must* only speak to the other; that is I must call him, in the vocative."[68] The question of the modalities of the address of and to the other is taken up by Cixous in several texts. In "Letter to Zohra Drif" Cixous conflates in the issue of the address *what* to write, *how to* write ("its form, its tone"), and *where* to send a letter that would be written to Zohra Drif, who had become an underground resistance fighter in the Casbah in Algiers, an uncertainty that *So Close* asserts to be characteristic of "how I had always been in Algeria," not knowing "how, *where*, to reach it."[69] In that sense, the vague mention of "Zohra Drif, Algeria" is the only address available. But the question of destination as specific location is cast aside as a "false question" in "Letter to Zohra Drif," an alibi, so to speak, covering a much deeper impossibility, that of "writing with justice to Zohra, Algeria."[70] The question of justice encompasses both what to write and whom to address in person. In that respect, a distinction is made between the essay published with the title "Letter to Zohra Drif" and the actual letter, a phrase that might not be adequate since it is an impossible, perhaps materially nonexistent letter (88). Likewise, *So Close* upholds the difference between the two: "I had the pointless desire to write to Zohra I say to myself. The enormity of destinerrancy diverted me from it. . . . Years later I did not write a letter to Zohra Drif. I abruptly wrote the 'Letter to Zohra Drif.'"[71] Thus "Letter to Zohra Drif" is said to convey "something of the mysterious

Detour that has always been inflicted on me, the originary malediction weighing on my relation to this native land that has never been my country" (19).

Yet, even in the early "Letter," and perhaps more clearly in *So Close*, other affirmations beyond that "malediction" are recorded as well. The capital point of the letter was perhaps not so much *what* to write and *where* as *how* to *answer* and *to whom*. The answer is said to be impelled by a "message" sent by Zohra, the indirection of which parallels that of the letter to come to Zohra Drif: "Then I read the newspaper: Zohra Drif armed in the Casbah. Alongside Yacef Saadi. It was the message."[72] As we have just noted, if Cixous clearly mentions a diffident response to the call that Zohra Drif encompassed, in person and in action, the delay and confusion that the call provoked must not be merely understood as ideological hesitation. As Derrida mentions in another context, "A call worthy of that name, a call of the name worthy of the name, must give room to no certainty on the side of the addressee"; "The possibility of an originary misunderstanding in destination is not an evil, it is the structure, perhaps the very vocation of any call worthy of that name, of all nomination, of all response and responsibility."[73] Thinking the letter to Zohra Drif as an answer to Zohra is recognizing the other's precedence, paying heed to several modes of response entails reconsidering the fatality of failed encounters, and, finally, thinking of Zohra beyond her metonymical position ("Zohra, Algeria") suggests both taking into account the irreducible uniqueness of Zohra Drif as well as, more radically, suspending in the question of the address the objective of reaching an addressee.

The difficulty of figuring out what to write revolves around words, since what the letter would convey if it could defeats verbalization: "Yes, yes, a letter to Zohra Drif. Something, a hello, a joy. I did not write it. Not with words"; the letter "was a burst of laughter, a jubilation rather than an argued missive."[74] Likewise, even though the two classmates are repeatedly said to have shared no common ground, and not a single word, both have at least felt "the silent weight of fits of anger in the classroom."[75] In other words, what eludes verbalization, though not eloquence, be it silence or laughter, is invested with the force of an affirmation in which the unsaid still asserts and rejoices at the other's freedom: "It was a happiness of relief. The content of this happiness was triumphant. I can thus enjoy a happiness that is not mine, I can be in the freedom of someone else, I can be free because of an other freedom that Z. takes for me" (13). The priority of the other's freedom inflects the narrator's reflection on the ways in which to take up the question of the address. Likewise, keeping language suspended in that instance extends the prophetic dimension of the arrival of Zohra Drif, the significance of which was kept silent, with "no names for it," while the only name that can be justly called is the unique name of the other, in a discourse that does not already know what to say: "In this letter I said: Zohra, then the words went off."[76]

When examining several modalities of response, the narrator turns away from the problem of Zohra's address (*where*) and considers instead the temporality of the answer along with the issue of sender and addressee. On the one hand, "Letter to Zohra Drif" is said to be itself a response, standing for "my Algerian countertemporaneity."[77] On the other hand, the narrator insists as well on the ways in which time affected the letter itself (14), in terms of what it said (or failed to say), but also, which is quite different, in its very project of reaching the addressee: "The fact remains that no one today could say whether I wrote *the letter to Z.D.* in the end or whether I did not write it in the end. I put *time* into it" (14). This passage shows that time inflected the letter at the assumed risk of being late, too late in responding; thus the letter embraced countertemporaneity. And precisely because countertemporaneity is the very temporality reflected upon by the narrator, being too late is not opposed to being on time: "It is too late, finally it is too late, it is my hour" (100). In *So Close* the reader is given to understand that the letter has indeed arrived, in the sense that, in the end, "Letter to Zohra Drif" was actually received by Zohra Drif, who read the essay in English (80). But ultimately that happy outcome through another language is not what impels Cixous's reflection. The crux of her analysis revolves around the remark that the letter becomes detached from an origin, relinquishing the possibility of attesting to an intention of sending the letter, which goes out "unbeknownst to me" (19), as much as it is severed from a destined reception: "I had written a 'letter' to someone who would never read it, I thought" (20). Likewise, the answer that the letter constitutes does not call for a reply in return: "Did I ever expect a response? Which response?" (20). The disseminating gesture of sending out a text without anticipated reception or return is first approached through the notion of the so-called open letter (20) that the published "Letter to Zohra Drif" became. The open letter suspends the possibility of availing oneself of any assurance as to the addressee, or of owning (up to) the letter: "One never knows whose Letter it is" (22). That condition becomes then generalized in the book as irrepressible vacancy in address or an address without address: "—The address? —Never any address I say" (148).

In statements such as "I had thus written this letter addressed to one of the characters of the person Z.D. without the intention of reaching the person" (20), Cixous invites us to think the ethical potentiality in suspending the address. First the proper name encapsulates the other in person, while stopping short of uttering one word beyond that invocation, a silent approach that respects "the speech that was not mine but that should have been theirs" (21). In that case the ethical response consists in keeping the question of the address suspended, as well as the content of the response, and to leave the latter to Algerians that one can then only echo, never precede (21). In that respect, Derrida challenges Levinas's approach to language as ethical relation to the other produced only in the face to face with a reflection on "unconditional hospitality," consisting in "suspending language, a particular determinate language."[78] Unconditional hospitality even suspends calling the other by his or her proper name: "Does hospitality consist in interrogating the new arrival [*l'arrivant*]? Does it begin with the question addressed to the newcomer . . . what is your name? . . . Or else does hospitality begin with the unquestioning welcome, in a double effacement, the effacement of the question *and* the name?" (27–29). Elsewhere Derrida also talks of unconditional hospitality as "a *hospitality of visitation*, which consists in letting the visitor come, the unexpected arrival, without asking for any account, without demanding his passport," opposing that hospitality to "a *hospitality of invitation*."[79] In *Reveries* Cixous mostly examines hospitality or hostility along the lines of a logic of invitation; but in *So Close* the displacement of her focus from invitation to visit or visitation, which, as Derrida explains, "welcomes what arrives as im-possible," constitutes another form of acquiescence to the other.[80] When the narrator adopts the position of "visitor," that posture is approached through a passivity in which the visitor visits as much as is visited, as the translator rightly emphasizes: arriving (not returning) in Algeria is equated to "a kind of visit, I would go and *I would let myself visit, be visited*."[81] There is a shift from the perspective of the uninvited, who remarks the recurrence of being shut out, to an acquiescence in which alterity takes place without the I. Then the call of the other, from which it is impossible to hide or take distance, according to Levinas, promotes welcome as well as a togetherness that was consistently depicted as impossible: "I'm calling you late, says Zohra —Come, I say" (93). Thus the answer to Zohra's "message" consisted in the reception of that call: "I say: Come. It is neither an order, nor an imperative, nor a present, nor a prayer nor an appeal. It is the first word that comes, that may come, that makes come what is going to be the 'we' that ever since the Lycée Fromentin could never be pronounced" (94).

In their respective examination of what constitutes responsibility for the other and the call for his possibility or advent, one that would not already be known and thus recognizable, Cixous and Djebar also interrogate (with different approaches and styles) the position of autonomous subjects with respect to the political body. Starting from the posited distinction between self and other that is consistently denounced for the biased hierarchies that it capitalizes on and conveys, what they end up promoting is a retreat of the self from the scene. It is only after that discreet effacement, that departure, or that bracketing of the self, corresponding to an experience of passivity, that the welcome of the other is felt. As Cixous writes in "How Not to Speak of Algeria," Algerian women "gave me the space to speak from out of my native country,"[82] which does not mean speaking for them. In the following, and last, chapter, the affirmation of an ethical relation based on dissymmetry and extraterritoriality will be tested through Djebar's and Cixous's reflection on the veil. Dissatisfied with the polarized interpretations it often triggers, they insist that some of its associations shed light on social togetherness as spectatorship, and emphasize instead the spectral or the miraculous in their reading of the veil as intermittent interval.

Conclusion

The Logic of the Veil; or, The Epistemology of Nonseeing

ORIENTALIST PARADIGMS

In *Orientalism* Edward Said formalized a European or Western "mode of discourse with supporting institutions" about the Orient, in which he conceded that the Orient in question was not "merely imaginative," but which he investigated above all as a consistent discourse "despite or beyond any correspondence, or lack thereof, with a 'real' Orient."[1] Said also posited that domination over the Orient was partly legitimized by Westerners through orientalizing patterns, imperialist ambitions being mapped onto Orientalist paradigms: "Orientalism is more particularly valuable as a sign of European-Atlantic power over the Orient than it is as a veridic discourse about the Orient" (6). In spite of some critical responses to Said's interpretive model, for instance that of Homi Bhabha, arguing for hybridity and resisting the notion of a hegemonic colonial power in *The Location of Culture*, the currency of Said's view, according to which Orientalism performs the Orient for the West, or is "not about non-Western cultures, but about the Western representation of these cultures," in Ania Loomba's words, remains widely in use today and has been corroborated by several studies.[2]

Numerous scholars have also drawn attention to the extent to which veiled woman has been and still is emblematic of the Orient. In a seminal essay, "Algeria Unveiled," written in 1957 during the war of Algerian independence, Frantz Fanon exposed this function of the veil for the outsider as a representative of both otherness and gender: "For the tourist or the foreigner, the veil delimits both Algerian society and its feminine component."[3] Or one as the other, since the colonized is, as Fanon and others emphasize, feminized by the colonist's gaze in a first symbolic appropriation. Fanon's essay has had a tremendous critical impact, including, as I shall argue, on Djebar. Fanon's political and psychological approach to his ostensible topic (women's participation in resistance and urban terrorism in Algeria) often seems to dictate the very terms of future critical discussions: depicting the "instrumentalization" or multiple strategic uses of the veil on the part of resisters (42), he particularly concentrates on women's unveiling. We will return to his analysis in that respect; let's note at present that Fanon does not merely report instances of tactical unveiling, but takes unveiling to be revealing a nascent Algeria: *l'Algérie*, which is feminine in French, unveils herself, in Fanon's words, in order to reveal a certain truth, or *aletheia*. Precisely "Western" concepts of the veil emphasize as well that the veil veils something, the thing itself, or its absence, and sometimes, too, that the movement of unveiling is inseparable from an understanding of the veil in that unveiling constitutes the veil as such.[4] In that sense, one always finds oneself inscribed within some culture of the veil. In their respective reflection on the veil, Djebar and Cixous converge in their articulation of the motif of unveiling to the asserted continuity between seeing (*voir*) and knowing (*savoir*), interrogating the equation mentioned by Martin Heidegger of the "visible and hence knowable."[5] Both address the issue of cognition and revelation by seemingly adopting a strategy of unveiling; yet the epistemological objective of disclosure of a hidden truth or cognitive content is both attained and derailed in their texts, since what is gained from their thought on the veil does not only consist in exposing what is secreted behind it but also in shedding light on some disregarded effects of veiling as well as on some implications unveiling remains blind to.

DISCOURSES ON THE VEIL IN ALGERIA

The veil is consistently touched upon throughout Djebar's works. Yet the concluding essay of *Women of Algiers in Their Apartment*, "Forbidden Gaze, Severed Sound," written in February 1979, arguably synthesizes her views on the issue, and a later fiction, *A Sister to Scheherazade*, published in 1987, also explicitly addresses the veil as a cultural sign encompassing and affecting all social participants. The first text was written at a time when the phenomenon of reveiling, analyzed, for example, by Marnia

Lazreg and Leila Ahmed, was felt to have become a visible trend in Algeria and other Muslim countries.[6] In order to understand Djebar's position accurately, it is useful to situate her argument with respect to that trend and to the legacy of critical essays such as Fanon's "Algeria Unveiled."

In a study published in 1966, Germaine Tillion argued that veiling was not to be understood simply as "a Muslim phenomenon."[7] On the one hand, she mentioned "the zigzag path of an invisible frontier" in "the Mediterranean fringe of Christianity" (167) in order to point to a large geographical compass in which gendered division in the occupation of public places could be observed, while her study aimed to "unearth customs far older than the Muslim faith, and to determine their limits" (174). Likewise, she underscored various veiling practices within a given country, and in particular differences between cities and the countryside, for instance in Morocco and in Algeria (172).[8] Djebar often mentions as well diverse practices, representative of different social circumstances and locations, occurring within one and the same period. But her work concurs with Ahmed's point that, if covering was once "normal dress" for all women in Muslim societies, there was a period starting at the beginning of the twentieth century, doubtless as an outcome of the colonial encounter yet encapsulating widespread aspirations within Muslim societies for modernity as well, when unveiling became a metonym for a new social and political order.[9] When the promises of that era, recast by Islamists as a deluded Westernized, secular, feminist age, failed or fell short of those hopes, the veil started reappearing to indicate the desire for other sociopolitical implementations, Ahmed notes (46–47). Thus, what has irked critics about what I initially referred to as a widespread Western association between Muslim women and the veil is not the inaccuracy of the perception, provided it is properly historicized. In that respect, Lazreg remarks that the veil is a marker of gender division in the eyes of secular Westerners and of its advocates today.[10] But a frequent critique of the Western perception of the veil is that it does not correctly assess its significance or that it ignores the dynamic and contradictory meanings it can be made to uphold: the West is either accused of interpreting the veil through Orientalist models in which woman's body is erotically dissimulated so as to be displayed and appropriated by a master or a viewer, or charged with harboring ulterior motives of domination in tendentious moral outrage at veiled women's conditions when the veil is denounced as an instrument of women's oppression. In the second case, as Ahmed argues, not only is veiling a visible sign of difference, but it is also taken to denote the cultural inferiority and backwardness of Islamic societies.[11]

In his polemical essay written in order to publicize and valorize the resistance of Algerians against France, Fanon gathers both claims (veiling as erotic enticement, as oppression). The Algerian history he unfolds starts with French colonialism and is separated in two by the watershed moment of the Algerian revolution; or more precisely, while colonialism is said to conceive of itself as eternal, the Algerian war of independence interrupts that static time and inaugurates a new temporality.[12] Fanon emphasizes a point that has gained much critical currency: colonizers claim that the practices of the colonized are oppressive to women and archaic—and even a throwback to the colonizers' own successfully overcome past, with the implication that the colonized are trapped in immutable thought and behavior, whereas Europeans are said to evolve and progress. In that respect, Said has shown that the foreign and the distant are interpreted as "versions of a previously known thing" in Orientalist paradigms.[13] The colonizers' campaign against veiling was seemingly caused by such conceptions; yet, in another highly influential argument, Fanon underscores the shallowness of the colonizers' feminist and modernist claim on behalf of the colonized, with the result, as several authors have since argued, that feminism has at times been tainted by association as neocolonial. For Fanon, before the Algerian Revolution, unveiling women was a strategy used by the colonial administration in order to demoralize Algerian society and profoundly upset its culture, under the pretense of emancipating women. Fanon repeatedly uses a sexualized lexis to describe this aggressive strategy: "we must first conquer women . . . behind the veil under which they are hidden"; "Algerian woman [is] conceived of as the support of the Western penetration of native society."[14] Thus he diagnoses in Europeans aims of political, sexual domination *and* the philosophical, metaphysical induction that the veil hides something, the truth or kernel of Algerian society. In his study of colonial postcards from the beginning of the twentieth century, Malek Alloula agrees with Fanon that Europeans' reaction to the veil takes the fantasized form of lifting it. Faced with a thwarted "scopic desire," the colonial photographer aggressively responds by unveiling women and giving "figural representation to the forbidden," claiming to take snapshots of a society to which he has no access.[15]

The crux of Fanon's argument consists in asserting that this strategy of dominance triggers in turn a reaction of resistance on the part of

Algerians; in other words, Algerians are said to react to Europeans' reaction. Whether deliberately (to serve his point) or by mistake, Fanon misconstrues the relevance and function of the veil, asserting that before the colonists' investment in unveiling women, the veil was "an element among others" or an "inert element" of Algerian culture; conversely, colonizers insist that Algerian woman is "turned by Algerian man into an inert object."[16] While recognizing that the veil is part of the traditional dress in the Maghreb (14), Fanon proposes that there was no prior Algerian social or religious affect before colonizers meddled both with Algeria and with veiling. Instead, veiling is viewed above all as a response, and Fanon also mentions a position attributed to the leaders of the FLN according to which "what was essential was that the occupier should constantly come up against a united front" (48). While Fanon attributes "a historical dynamism" to the veil throughout colonization (45), it is especially during the war that its use is said to have escaped uniformity and passivity; not merely reactive any longer, "the veil is given up in the process of revolutionary action" (46). Noticeably, Fanon does not mention the multiple positions regarding the adoption and/or removal of the veil by Muslims earlier than the war of independence, which other authors have on the contrary brought to the fore from another point of view. Indeed there is for Fanon a rule as far as the psychology of colonization is concerned: first action devolves to the occupying forces and determines at best passive resistance (26); in a second step resistance gives rise to action and unpredictable initiatives (46). That pattern makes it difficult to account for the long time it took the French to achieve the total conquest of Algeria in the nineteenth century because of strong pockets of resistance. Throughout his description of the second temporality, starting with the Algerian Revolution, Fanon shows that the colonized mimic the colonizers' desire in order to deceive them. The colonized take on the very weapons of colonial discourse, which is precisely predicated, in Homi Bhabha's analysis, on mimicry.[17] On the one hand, the veil can be, in Fanon's words, "instrumentalized, turned into a technique of camouflage, into a means of struggle," the question being whether the veil is not an instrument in every case, as several authors have pointed out in their discussion of the veil as mediation and adaptation.[18] For example, women would carry a bomb under their *haïk* or wear European clothes on other occasions, as one scene of Gillo Pontecorvo's *Battle of Algiers* represented, conforming thus apparently to the colonizers' desire to unveil them. The painter Eugène Fromentin, who visited Algeria shortly after the conquest of Algiers, had been struck by the "national" conformity between the architecture of the Arab city and the dress of its inhabitants.[19] Extending the metonymy, Fanon analyzes the Casbah in terms that evoke the protection afforded by the veil on a woman's body: "The protective mantle of the Casbah, the almost organic curtain of security that the Arab city weaves around the native is withdrawn, and the uncovered Algerian woman is launched in the city of the conqueror."[20]

For Fanon, the diversity of Algerians' uses of the veil meant first that the colonizer had been profoundly deprived of the power of initiative, and secondly, that Algerians had no strong investment in the veil itself (46). In their tactical use of the veil during the revolution, they had proved they could go beyond a tradition in which they were, in Fanon's analysis, paradoxically confined by an aggressive modernization that they could only reject because it was proposed by the colonizer. In effect, Fanon oddly suggests that the revolution has succeeded in westernizing Algerians where the French colonists had failed, because "new attitudes, new behaviors, new modalities of being" have been actively embraced as a means of struggle (46). In that respect, one significant pattern of new Algeria involved for Fanon a reappraisal of gender, to be founded not on separation but on togetherness: "The male militant discovers the female militant and together they create new dimensions of Algerian society" (41). Yet, a few years after the Algerian independence, Tillion, for one, noted that while the veil had played various strategic roles during the war, it could not be said that its use had been relinquished after it.[21]

In her concluding chapter of *Women of Algiers in Their Apartment*, Djebar agrees that the colonizers' denigrating gaze on Algerian culture has induced a variety of responses from Algerians. But she does not subscribe to Fanon's view that the investment in veiling was ever merely reactive; she addresses it as an indigenous cultural element, but not as an immutable heritage that would never have undergone any material or ideological modification. And while she agrees with Fanon that the history of the veil is dynamic, the catalyst for change is not ascribable in her view to the single factor of the Algerian war of independence. In her demonstration Djebar often encompasses Algerian practices within a transnational Muslim culture of long historical duration, also in contact with other, non-Islamic nations, with the implication that Algerian culture is neither simply autochthonous nor identical to itself. In that respect, her discernible difference to Alloula's positions in *The Colonial Harem* sheds light on her own project.

Alloula does not only blame the colonial photographer's mise-en-scène for producing an "ersatz reality," which would be a commonplace, but for failing to render gendered spatial division by juxtaposing "two perfectly heterogeneous spaces without any regard for a social equilibrium that it can neither understand nor accept"; as a result, Alloula claims that women, who were invisible or hidden, become "violated."[22] Djebar consistently illustrates the fragility of the oppositions that Alloula relies on with so much certainty. She contests, for instance, the supposed inevitability of Alloula's alternative "invisible/violated," which constructs woman's hiding from view as a premise to "social equilibrium." Furthermore, Djebar does not consider cultural artifacts such as photographs as a reflection of actual social practices, but as indicative of a political potentiality. Delacroix's paintings *Women of Algiers in Their Apartment,* which she discusses in her own *Women of Algiers,* are in that sense exemplary of an impossible social practice (a male outsider visiting a harem) that nevertheless took place, an occurrence allowing for a reading of the actual and symbolic gendering of space that is quite different from Alloula's. As we have seen throughout this book, instead of presupposing a unique model of native cultural authenticity devoid of hybridity and so homogeneous that it would entertain no inner divisions, Djebar is on the contrary intent on challenging the notion as well as the reality of a "dual hegemonic discourse" from within and from without.[23]

As far as the veil in Islam is concerned, numerous studies have analyzed its sacred and secular origins and historicized its adoption and its usage.[24] When its multifaceted spiritual, social, political, psychological significances are unfolded in such studies, it appears that they have generated from within the Muslim world multiple discourses, including feminist discourses, which, therefore, are not simply a belated importation extraneous to the culture.[25] Djebar is not intimidated by the label of feminism, but prefers nevertheless to carve a different position, acknowledging that there is not a single hegemonic Muslim discourse about women or about veiling, but from the beginning a mixture of heterogeneous, at times contradictory positions: the studies or fictions that expose the complexity of such variegated discourses reflect on inherent potentialities as well as actual past or present practices within "native culture."

In some books such as *La Beauté de Joseph* or *Far from Madina,* Djebar's approach seems indebted to the reappropriation of religious space undertaken by authors like Fatima Mernissi. Asserting the emancipating message of the Quran enables feminist critics to demonstrate that misogyny is due to subsequent political alterations of the initial egalitarian Quranic message. Their initiative also stems from the widespread evaluation, in Malek Chebel's words, that "political identity in Arab countries must first take into account the unavoidable preeminence of Islam."[26] Djebar's approach does not minimize the forceful link between the political and Islam, but she also mobilizes other resources than foundational sacred texts to reflect on women's socialization. This is why she turns to Muslim culture, imbued with religious tradition but exceeding it as well.[27] At all events, Djebar's discussion of veiling in her oeuvre is rarely if ever involved with the veil as religious sign, even in the few books explicitly dealing with sacred texts or traditions. Instead, Djebar focuses on the culture of the veil inasmuch as it informs sociability, in a way that is not simply gendered in the feminine, but involves society as a whole. In order to nuance frequent Western associations of the veil with coercion and the oppression of women, Djebar first demonstrates that wearing the veil allows women to go out and to socialize outside the domestic sphere. In that sense, the veil is a contradictory spatial marker, denoting at the same time privacy and publicity, seeing and nonseeing, dissimulation and exposure.

TESTIMONY: SIGHT AS VOICE

In the last chapter of *Women of Algiers*, she examines the symbolic significances attributed to the veil, as Fanon had done before her, by focusing on Europeans' as well as Algerians' investment in the veil as the very site or sight of femininity. But her reading of Algerians' views in particular illuminates some aspects that were left dormant in Fanon's interpretation or that were excluded from his focus altogether. Fanon recorded two categories of dreams about the veil by his patients while he was working as a psychiatrist in Algeria. One dream material was uncovered during his therapy sessions with Algerian women. "Impression of a body torn apart, put adrift; the limbs seem to lengthen indefinitely. When the Algerian woman has to cross a street, for a long time, there is an error of judgment as to the exact distance to traverse. The unveiled body seems to escape from itself, to fall to pieces. Impression of being poorly dressed, and even of being naked."[28]

Djebar does not refer to Fanon, but one passage of her essay seems to address some of these points while rectifying his conclusions. In particular, what Fanon interpreted as the symbolic language of the dreams is actually shown to reflect the various ways his patients refer to the veil in their language: "Dialectal Arabic transcribes the experience in a significant way: 'I no longer go out *protected* (that is to say, veiled, covered up),' the woman who frees herself from the cloth will say; 'I go out *undressed*, or even *denuded*.'"[29] These last words echo Fanon's terms, "poorly dressed, and even naked." The removal of the veil as (a figure of) nakedness is therefore one of the reasons invoked for its necessity, or its comfort and protection. But Djebar, who seems to agree here with Fanon that unfamiliarity with being unveiled entails a difficult occupation of space—"the gait becomes stiff" (139)—is far from consistently upholding that position in the rest of her oeuvre. In *A Sister to Scheherazade*, for instance, which develops a dual, contradictory assessment of veiling, much more typical of Djebar, Hajila does not experience any difficulty when she tries for the first time since childhood to step outside without a veil.[30] That book, which could be misconstrued as a plea for unveiling, emphasizes instead the need for women to protect one another and promote another woman's desires. The recommended tender watch of one woman over another makes the question of the veil irrelevant; thus, Hajila removes her veil, while the unveiled Isma strives for a discreet return to herself metaphorized as veiling: "The second wife stands on the threshold, devouring the space: and now the first one can put on the veil, or dissimulate herself" (159).

Djebar insists that women's recommended invisibility was not a post-1830 novelty in Algeria, while agreeing that colonization gave added legitimacy to the veil. "When the foreign intrusion starts in 1830—an intrusion maintained at all costs at the thresholds of impoverished seraglios—, to the gradual appropriation of space outside symmetrically corresponds the increasingly muted freezing up of interior communication: between the generations, and even more, between the sexes."[31] She often argues that during colonization the veil or the harem functioned as what is called in *Fantasia* a "bulwark," a location or institution construed as the ultimate bastion of resistance to occupation.[32] What is denounced is not the necessity of repulsing the colonizer, including through tactics of retrenchment, but the fact that women have to bear the brunt of that strategy, a point also made by Lazreg in her incisive reading of Fanon's "Algeria Unveiled."[33] Not opting for a religious explanation, and in contrast with studies like Alloula's, which rightly criticized the representation of the harem in colonial postcards but avoided discussing its actual institution, Djebar looks at the veil and at the harem as gestures of protection warding off a danger embodied by women.[34] Her psychological and political analysis focuses on some other factors involved in hiding women from view (at least in fantasy if not always in reality), ascribed to circumventing their possibility of seeing, itself interpreted as bearing witness. Djebar's argument traces the motif of the gaze as voice in her reading of the veil, and exposes the perceived consequences of woman's unconstrained sight in the Algerian space.

Fanon opposed Europeans to Algerians when examining the ways women are watched, the former "wanting to see" and the latter "not seeing" them.[35] For Djebar, for whom that distinction is debatable, the issue is to understand instead why seeing woman's body can be both fascinating and apprehended. She argues that if the veil shields woman by constituting a "garment in itself," it also by the same token prevents her from revealing "the other eyes of the body (breasts, sex, navel)."[36] Woman's body presents to the onlooker a specific experience of exposure, that of a multiplicity of feminine gazes, which Djebar interprets as particularly disquieting, even threatening to man. Therefore, the wish to preserve woman's modesty, to prevent her from going out "naked," is at the same time inseparably linked to man's anxiety about being seen by woman. Certainly, glimpsing woman's forbidden eyes, her breasts, her sex, her navel, is dishonorable, but at the same time, the construct of woman's body as the location of a multiplicity of eyes figures the profound repugnance felt by man at being watched by woman. In that respect, Zimra rightly notes that "one does not have to go very far to see in this threatening eye a variation of the Medusa figure, of which Cixous has made so much."[37] Furthermore, not only does the feminine eye become in itself a sign of immodesty, it also challenges men's "scopic exclusivity."[38] Fanon also emphasized that veiled women see without being seen and that frustration stemmed from the lack of reciprocity of the gazes; a remark that may be linked to Derrida's elaboration of the "visor effect," where the lack of reciprocity in the act of being looked at by someone who cannot be seen induces a power differential, making the one who is seen "blind by situation."[39] Thus woman's gaze is posited as blinding and appropriating the predominantly masculine space.

Conversely, the threat of a male outsider/voyeur looking at the "naked" woman is a risk that is easier to understand and better remedied than the unexpected results of woman's gaze. Djebar shows this by recounting the emblematic visit negotiated by Delacroix to an Algerian dignitary's harem in 1830, shortly after the French occupation of Algiers, which demonstrates that the theme of the "stolen gaze" is less difficult to cope with when man, not woman, is the culprit. In that respect, Fanon mentioned a second category of dreams by European men in which "the rape of the Algerian woman is always preceded by the tearing of the veil," and her flight "inevitably leads the male to 'women's apartments.'"[40] The allure of an exotic community of women standing for feminized Algeria is confirmed in Delacroix's diary recounting his visit to the harem: "It is beautiful! It is as it was in Homer's time! Woman in the gynaeceum looking after children, spinning wool or embroidering splendid fabrics. This is woman as I understand her!"[41] The trespass constituted by Delacroix's forbidden gaze may also be minimized by a consideration exposed several times in *Fantasia*, whereby not all men's gazes are equivalent; in that sense, women's modesty is not deemed compulsory with non-Muslims because "they are blind" or do not "really have a gaze."[42] This shows that Algerians could at least respond to the candid misogyny of a Delacroix standing for foreign intrusion with their own principles of inclusion and marginalization. In independent Algeria the point is for Djebar to reclaim a cultural call for invisibility that would not be equated with gendered subordination or colonial oppression.

For Djebar, woman's threat consists in linking the visible with the knowable. When recalling heroic acts of war during the French conquest, she shows that women's part involved an ocular and oral reporting and witnessing of the battle: traditionally, "woman was watching, woman was shouting: the gaze-that-was-witness throughout the battle."[43] But history has also preserved specific acts in the history of Algerian resistances of the nineteenth century, which represent "women warriors, out of the traditional role of spectator" (143–44). "The Song of Messaouda," which is still heard in the Algerian South, commemorates the story of a young woman, Messaouda, who is said to have changed the course of a battle fought in 1839 by exposing herself to the enemies out of the walls of the fortress, addressing thus the almost defeated soldiers: "Where are the men of my tribe? Where are my brothers? Where are those who used to sing songs of love to me?" (143). They came to her rescue and won the day: "Be happy [*messaouda*], here are your brothers, here are your lovers!" (143). Djebar finds compelling cultural potentialities in this oral tradition, which she interrogates inasmuch as it imagines a community. First this story of unveiling, or exposure of woman's body to strange men, is not followed by the representation of a threat to her male relatives and lovers or to the community at large. On the contrary, it is a story of fulfillment for both men and women: woman's happiness is celebrated "in a mobility that is both improvised and dangerous, in sum creative" (144). In her reading of the song, Djebar also argues that the shared happiness that exalts woman's body and her participation in the war may be due to the happy outcome of a victorious battle, enhancing the perception of common objectives. Moreover, if it is true that during the war of independence Algerian women exposed their bodies like Messaouda, what happened to many of them (rape, torture, or execution) caused an unforeseen boomerang effect on women. The war heroines experienced a double repression, first by the French, then again by their countrymen, who after having denounced the tortures of their fellow female warriors, seem to be saying now, according to Djebar, "We have paid enough for that unveiling of words!" (151). The exposure of women's tortures is apprehended as an unbearable infringement, not on women's bodies any longer, but on the social body, perceived to be endangered because their location within the culture was disturbed and did not allow them to be preserved. Djebar and others have actively promoted woman's gaze and/as voice against that position. Yet, her reading does not suggest in the final analysis that women will be given their unrecognized due when disclosing what the veil covers. Instead, she investigates the urge to veil what has always been in plain view or symbolically acknowledged (for example, in "The Song of Messaouda") but remains somehow unseen and unheard.

In that respect, her stance precisely consists in denouncing both a lack *and* an excess of visibility. If, as we have seen throughout this book, anonymous mobility is particularly felicitous in Djebar's writings, it is also because anonymity is a metonym for invisibility (both words denoting the veil in the language), or posits the onlooker's indifference or "blindness." The determination to control or "preserve their image" is shared by veiled and unveiled protagonists of Djebar's fictions—a concern, as she recalls in *Fantasia*, that is customarily associated with the modesty involved in wearing a veil.[44] Her unveiled heroines often imagine themselves to be alone in their ability to see, but they also claim to be unseen and are disappointed when others fail to take note of the invisibility they aspire to (126). Characteristically, Djebar names such a yearning "symbolic reveiling" (127). The endorsement of symbolic reveiling is the recurring reverse of Djebar's denunciation of "the sharpness of twinkling, lingering gazes" as far as woman is concerned.[45] The benefits of invisibility are therefore taken for granted by Djebar; what she requests is that at least women be unwatched or inaccessible on their own terms and at best that the effects of being with others, and consequently of watching and of being watched, cease being so traumatically experienced.

Furthermore, *A Sister to Scheherazade* examines the impact of the urge to keep woman's body from view on the community in terms that suggest the risk of a general paralysis affecting all social participants: on the one hand, men are "never free of fetter . . . bound fast by fears of the tribe, swathed in all the anxieties handed down to [them] by frustrated mothers, shackled by all [their] obsessions with some ill-defined elsewhere!"; and women are equally "swaddled in their mothers' anguish."[46] Apparently not concerned by the requirement of invisibility, men's own gaze is constrained or blinded. *A Sister* also implies that while woman's veiling/unveiling has been overscrutinized, man's own relation, and perhaps aspiration, to invisibility has not been examined with equal attention. At all events, Djebar's statement indicates the extension of a paralyzing surveillance and generalized imprisonment beyond the harem walls. Her entire oeuvre is skeptical of the figure of the married couple and at times of other couples such as the mother/daughter, which she identifies with the "harem restored" (145). The preferred ethical configuration she promotes is the twin or bifid position of sisters expounded in *A Sister to Scheherazade*. The possibilities out of the social bind, which harnesses men as well as women, are already written in the cultural text, and Djebar promotes a close reading of these inscriptions. Other potentialities cannot be written about or seen, since they will be impro*vised*.

COMING TO SEEING: VISION, TRUTH, KNOWLEDGE

We have mentioned in a previous chapter that in her Algerian writings Cixous denounces the "imperialist blindness" to the inequities of the colonial system, a "first spectacle" that requires blindness to be interpreted politically.[47] Her essay "Savoir" approaches blindness, lucidity, and vision through another analytical angle, which provides, however, a confirmation of her political reflection. "Savoir" apparently tells the story of an unveiling, recalling an eye surgery that cured the narrator of extreme nearsightedness. The essay repeats and transforms passages of an earlier text of Cixous's, *Messie*, or is, in Derrida's words, its poetic double, "almost contemporary, through the operation, the 'miracle' and the mourning it names."[48]

Derrida's essay "A Silkworm of One's Own" constitutes in turn a philosophical double of Cixous's "Savoir." And this double session is named *Veils*. Effects of intertextuality and cross-references do no stop here, for *Veils* retains palimpsestic inscriptions of previous explorations of blindness by the two authors. Derrida's *Memoirs of the Blind*, which, among other things, recalls his own healing of facial paralysis, an illness causing the loss of the "blink" of the eye, or "this moment of blindness that ensures sight its breath,"[49] is mentioned in his reading of "Savoir," and Cixous has often investigated the condition of "writing blind" (for example, in the essay bearing that title). Likewise, in "Savoir," Cixous examines what she calls "coming to seeing," recalling the terms of her former "Coming to Writing."[50] "Writing Blind" emphasizes the writer's "distracted" gaze from the phenomenal world, the necessity of not seeing the world so as to attempt "to see what is secret."[51] Thus blindness is also a "kind of seeing," and even "the precondition for clairvoyance" (140), whereas those who see are blind to another vision, darkly expounded through writing: "what we call the day prevents me from seeing. Solar daylight blinds me to the visionary day" (139). These positions are indebted to a long tradition, which Cixous reiterates, while operating decisive displacements. Our first objective in the following section is to examine the ways in which the effects of eye surgery invoke the veil but address differently some of the philosophical scenes of its interpretation. By focusing on what, if anything, ties knowledge to vision (a vision that would know what it does, what it means to see, or knowledge as true vision, vision as the truth of knowledge), Cixous takes up, but does not leave intact, a thought that has privileged visibility, light, unveiling in or as the manifestation of truth. Dwelling in the interval between blindness and sight, her reflection turns, on several occasions, to issues that are tied to the philosophical discussion of the senses, such as the sensible quality proper to each sense, or the combination/substitution, as opposed to the autonomy of senses, which we will also mention in passing as a response to tradition.

Is the kind of knowledge (*savoir*) involved in Cixous's investigation of extreme myopia or near-blindness, and its cure by a "miraculous" laser surgery, of the same order as Denis Diderot's inquiry in *Letter on the Blind for the Use of Those Who Can See* (1749)? Diderot's *Letter* starts thus: "I was sure, Madam, that the woman-born-blind, whose cataracts M. de Réaumur has just had removed, would not teach you what you wanted to know. . . . He only wanted to perform the unveiling in front of eyes of no consequence."[52] At stake for Diderot is the possibility for the blind to assess vision speculatively, which is also, at the same time, poetically, rather than empirically. Thus the judgment of those who have just recovered their sight is distrusted in these terms: "I should have less confidence in the responses of a man seeing for the first time than in the discoveries of a philosopher who had meditated long and hard on the matter in the dark or, to speak the language of poets, had gouged out his eyes in order to know more easily the workings of vision" (204). Diderot does not look for the truth of vision in the "unveiling" of the eyes. He does not trust the passage from blindness to vision, or "the first time" of seeing, to disclose the mechanism of vision. In that respect he (who used to be nicknamed Plato by his friends) remains within the Platonic interpretation whereby acceding to a (greater) source of light requires becoming accustomed to it, for initially the eyes are blinded by it. Thus the blind is paradoxically blinded as he recovers sight, but Diderot argues that blindedness is only temporary. Just as Plato according to Heidegger's reading of the allegory of the cave, Diderot stresses that a sense can be educated or "teach itself" (211). But he also proposes that speculation competes with and may even surpass sensory experience in theorizing knowledge. Several examples of his essay show that, whether derived from the senses or from speculation, judgment may be in error (because senses may be deceiving us or because we infer wrong conclusions from right premises), which shows that knowledge is a process of revision rather than an outcome (219).

For Cixous, the passage from blindness to vision tells as much about nonseeing as seeing: remaining speculatively at the interval between both, she addresses anew the "first time of seeing," which, unlike in the tradition, does not involve an initial and temporary blindness, but registers the pang of deprivation concomitant, as we shall develop later, with seeing that one does not nonsee.[53] For, if the recovery of sight is celebrated in "Savoir," first as seeing what was so far unseen "*with-the-naked eye*," myopia is not addressed univocally.[54] When it is referred to as bondage, when the myopic narrator "lived in the cave of the species. . . . She was a prisoner, lunar, from birth," for instance, Cixous is revisiting Plato's allegory of the cave in *The Republic*.[55] Its citation in Cixous's "Savoir" could be said to follow an inner necessity, since it constitutes one of the philosophical first scenes of the relation of knowing to seeing. The allegory tells the story of prisoners, detained since childhood in a cave, who are unable to see things as they are and take the visible shadows of things to be things themselves.

Likewise, myopia hides or veils bodies in "Savoir": "Myopia was her fault, her lead, her imperceptible native veil" (3). Just as prisoners in the cave have "necks in bonds," so the "lead" binds the narrator.[56] Derrida, who discusses the allegory more directly in *Memoirs of the Blind*, writes that it provides the semantics of the European *idea* in its relation of seeing to knowing.[57] Conversely, when describing the prisoners chained in the cave, "The Platonic speleology itself develops . . . an 'image' of all possible blindnesses" (13) as well as a link between bondage and sightlessness (40). Plato's allegory considers what would happen to a man first released from his chains, and then from the cave, who could progressively see not only men and things in themselves but at last "the sun itself by itself in its own region—and see what it's like."[58] It finally depicts the return of the man to the cave, where he is exposed to ridicule and even to the danger of being killed when he attempts to free the prisoners (195–96). The visible things outside the cave figure "ideas," or what is as such, "being showing up in its 'e-vidence' (*Aussehen*)," while the sun stands for the Idea of ideas, their cause, the Good or "that which makes all ideas visible."[59]

For Heidegger, the allegory tells the essence of *paideia*—which he translates as *Bildung*, or "formation" (166)—as unveiling. In that sense, the myth tells us Plato's doctrine of truth. Both share "a unity of essence" (167), in that *paideia* never leaves behind once and for all the absence of formation, but constitutes a "constant overcoming of lack of formation" (171). Likewise, truth as *aletheia* is the constant conflict over the latent, or is the unveiling, unconcealment, nonoccultation, nonlatency of being, in Heidegger's reading of the Greek thinking of the essence of being as being-hidden: "the unhidden must be torn away from its occultation. . . . Truth is thus a wresting away in each case, in the form of a revealing" (171). The story examines a series of passages from the cave to the outside and back, and in that respect does not only figure *paideia* as a passage but as a "turn" toward another region. Heidegger emphasizes that in each passage the eyes have to accustom themselves to brightness or to darkness, which means a change of direction and orientation (166). The adaptation to a new orientation disturbs man's way of thinking. *Paideia*, then, does not consist in the absorption of knowledge by an empty recipient, but in the process of being transferred from one region to another where being itself appears (167), as can be gathered from one of the paraphrases Heidegger proposes for *paideia*: "leading man toward the turning around of his essence" (166) or "toward that which appears in its proper form" (170).

In Heidegger's reading, Plato's doctrine of truth expounded in the allegory is itself a turning around. It constitutes a turning point in Western thinking after Plato in that it is said to leave behind the understanding of truth as *aletheia*. The turning point may be sensed in Plato's recourse to the allegory in order, in Heidegger's words, to make the essence of *paideia* "visible and knowable" in the sensible forms of a recounted story (167). From Plato on, *aletheia*, or the arrival of being to presence, becomes, in Heidegger's analysis, subordinated to the *idea*, that which appears and is visible in its luminosity or shining forth (173). In other words, there is a shift of emphasis in the essence of truth from the *unveiling* of being to the exact apprehension or *perception* of the unveiled (176). "Insofar as the access [to the unhidden or to the unveiled] is necessarily carried out through 'seeing' [or achieved as 'vision'] unhiddenness [or unveiling] is yoked into a 'relation' with seeing, it becomes 'relative' to seeing [or 'sight']" (173). What becomes required is "correct vision" (176) or "the correctness of assertion" (179), the conformity or *adaequatio* with what must be seen or the "agreement of the act of knowing with the thing itself" (177). The transformation of the essence of truth, for Heidegger, also implies a change in the locus of truth, which is now at a second remove from being. It is not, as it was with unveiling, the "fundamental trait of being itself. Instead . . . henceforth it will be a characteristic of the knowing of beings" (179).[60]

Cixous examines the relationship of vision to truth and knowledge by recalling that, from the standpoint of knowledge, the one who sees is as blind to what constitutes vision as the visually impaired: "But what does it mean, to see? Who sees? Who believes they know how to see?"—"Do the seers know that they see? Do the non-seers know that they see otherwise? What do we see? Do eyes see that they see?"[61] In the knowable, Plato writes, the Idea of ideas, or the Good, may be seen at last—"with considerable effort"; "it is hardly (only with great pains) really seen at all"—but, as Derrida reminds us, not so visibility itself or the condition of sight, which remain invisible.[62] No knowledge of vision can be gained through the trope or the experience of visibility. Thus knowledge as to seeing (usually put into question and significantly uttered negatively in "Savoir"—"she had not known the day before") is conveyed as continuity without intermediary of the eye's touch with the world.[63] The enjoyment of vision is not primarily conveyed as ophthalmic potency, but through the synesthesia of ocular apprehension: "the world is given to her in the hand of eyes" (9). Cixous's oeuvre offers a great many examples of such figures, which put into question the proper sensible quality attributed to each sense. One of her instruments for probing sensory capacity and the knowledge derived from the senses is the telephone, a recurring motif in her texts. She concentrates on the sense of touch to elaborate on the sort of contact involved in this means of communication. Thus, in *Messie*, the cat "phones" the narrator by hitting its paw on her leg, a phatic contact that encrypts a silent message; whereas one associates that apparatus with the sense of hearing sounds and voices, the phone is instead posited as the line of contact between two lives, a sensory receptor ascertaining that the other is alive and well.[64]

In "A Silkworm of One's Own," Derrida comments twice on Cixous's motif of "touch" in connection with the eyes, which is attuned, as we shall develop later, to his own thinking of the event to come "without the glory of a luminous vision" or without reference not only to the veil but to sight or visibility in the apprehension of the event.[65] In other works, however, Derrida emphasizes that "optical or scopic primacy always . . . rests on a figure of touch, on a haptic basis" and, as he does in *On Touching*, that there is a great philosophical tradition, which he calls "tactilist" or "haptocentric," "that accords an absolute privilege to touch and does not let itself be encroached upon by the possibility . . . of any vicariousness of the senses."[66] But Cixous does not valorize the sense of touch over vision. Instead, when equating seeing with a hand touching, she keeps the seer within the condition of blindness, she avoids the plenitude or the enjoyment/possession/having (*avoir*) of the seer seeing, since she confers to sight determining attributes of blindness. In "Savoir," vision deliberately and tactfully circumvents tropes of visibility, and seeing retains the memory of blindness, a position that inquires into the kind of knowledge evoked by the title of the essay and, moreover, wonders whether knowledge is a relevant term for such an investigation. Her essay is rather of the order of testimony, which, as Derrida writes in *Memoirs of the Blind*, "substitutes narrative for perception" or of the order of an avowal (*aveu*), which "always says that it knows it is blind [*aveu-gle*]."[67]

MOURNING THE UNSEEN

Thus it does not follow that in "Savoir" blindness is "known" in all its effects and its possibilities better than, before, and instead of vision. Cixous remarks that nonseeing can be mourned after vision is gained: "Seeing, there was a world which she did not nonsee any more. And as if a veil had been torn, she then felt around her heart the contraction of mourning: I have lost my myopia!"[68] Therefore, seeing is not, or not simply, the plenitude one might expect it to be, so that its enjoyment is addressed through negative periphrases: "Is *seeing* the supreme enjoyment? Or is it: no-longer-not-seeing?"[69] In that sense, seeing depends on the recognition of a loss or a deprivation, or, in Derrida's words in *Veils*, "We have to *learn from her* . . . that the vision of seeing . . . was from the origin in mourning of the unseen" (50). Cixous's unusual word *invu,* translated as "unseen," is equated with the unheard-of, underscoring thus her point that "*invu* was an invention" (10), or what precedes knowledge. As we have already noted, blindness is both the sign of election of visionaries *and* a sensory prison, a misfortune and good fortune at the same time, which explains why the eye surgery is said both to be a gift and to ruin the "gift in reverse" that myopia constituted.[70] But the reason why the recovery of vision challenges the thinking of the passage is that myopia in itself was already an "interval," a "daily frontier-crossing" between the I and the world, a go-between objectified in "spectacles" and "non-contact lenses."[71] "The non-arrival of the visible at dawn, the passage through not-seeing, always there has been a threshold" (12). At the same time, myopia collapsed the separation of the I from the eye: "Her myopia was her own foreigner, her essential foreignness, her own accidental necessary weakness" (10). The foreign within was also her own belonging, what was most proper to her, and myopia was both accidental and necessary, another impossible colocation that we have often underscored in Cixous's textuality, in which the other is experienced both as the most remote and "as undetachable from her as her blood from her vein, it was she, she was it" (11). In that sense, myopia is mourned as the mourning of the other within, of the no other than herself, yet not her self. Is this movement, then, of the order of *aletheia,* in Heidegger's sense of a struggle between latency and nonoccultation? Or is the structure of *paideia* described here, in Heidegger's interpretation of an ongoing victory over its absence?

Cixous retains from that thinking the chances afforded by the *passage,* as that which is not simply a passage *into* and does not merely leave anything behind—"The link between the thing that passes and the thing that remains needs to be ceaselessly thought through"—insisting that speculation must occupy the space of the interval: "Between the visible and the invisible there is something else."[72] To what extent does such a passage constitute an unveiling? If it is true that myopia is at times called a veil, Derrida has also noted the ways in which, in Cixous, the veil does not work as a cover that can be lifted or dropped, but as a stitch, a point of suture that inextricably weaves the inside and the outside of the eye: "It holds, touches, pulls, like a lead, it affects and sometimes tears the skin, it wounds, it penetrates under the epidermic surface, which a veil never does when it suffices to veil one's gaze."[73] Thus, for Derrida, Cixous's corpus "has parted with the veil, that corpus knew, from the operation of the other, how to part with veiling as much as unveiling" (83). It could be argued that when Cixous refers—once—to unveiling in "Savoir," myopia is not taken to be hiding the gaze, or preventing the eye from seeing, but that the surgery still functions as *aletheia*, since myopia is revealed in and of itself: "Suddenly myopia, 'the other,' the unwelcome, unveiled itself: the other was none other than her sweetheart, her modest companion born. Her dear secret" (11). But as the last sentence of the passage proposes, in a formulation also found in "Writing Blind," to the extent that myopia is a secret, it is immune to revelation even as it is disclosed, constituting an alternative to appearance, visibility, representation or presentation, of another order than the order of knowledge: "Even when it is avowed, the secret is not aired."[74] For the secret is what is kept silent and not necessarily what is unknown. The movement of unveiling of the eye surgery exposes what was concealed—the very workings and location of myopia as that which defies the difference between what is one's own and what is extrinsic—yet the secret remains.

THE VERDICT; OR, THE UNFORESEEABLE

Cixous's notion of the passage is associated with Derrida's thought of "the event without truth unveiled or revealed."[75] To the question of or about *truth* (for example, the truth of vision), Derrida substitutes a reflection on the *verdict*, which he weaves in and out of Cixous's texts. If "verdict" links "the same word, the true of truth, or the veridicity of *veridictum* . . . to the semantic motifs of the veil (revelation, unveiling)" (55), it can also be articulated in "Savoir," and through the event of the eye surgery, to Derrida's own thinking of the messianic: "*Savoir* indebts itself, recognizing its debt, to an event that remains unique, forever unique, forever heterogeneous to every language, that is [*à savoir*], the operation that gave her her sight back" (79). The verdict, "always of the other" (46), is tied to the irruption of a unique, unanticipated event, or what Derrida calls in other essays the messianic, hence Cixous's title, *Messie*, "singular like an absolutely unforeseeable verdict, absolutely, that is with no relation to fore-sight, nor therefore to sight. Life or death question, but one that is decided otherwise than by tearing . . . anything like 'veil.' This coming would have to come from elsewhere, at its date, like an operation of the other, entrusted to the other" (41).[76] For Derrida, the operation from/of the other parts with the movement of revelation, veiling or unveiling, with prevision or sight, and any story/history of the eye. In that sense, in *Memoirs of the Blind*, Derrida ends his reflection on blindness by dwelling on tears, which make the gaze "indifferent to its blurred vision"; if the truth of the eye is not vision but tears, "savoir" should be distinguished from any "voir ça" (*knowledge, seeing that*).[77]

In *Messie* the "abrupt possibility of seeing had been invisibly liberated by the arrival [in a woman's life] of the cat," for whom living is "going and seeing, seeing, seeing."[78] Likewise, the castle, poetically figuring (Kafka's) Prague, which in Czech names the "threshold" (43), the crossing, or the passage, is said to have called for and necessitated eye surgery. Thus both the cat/castle (*chat/château*) embody an injunction to see: "In order to see the castle better, she decided to be done with her myopia and without hesitating she made an appointment with the Surgeon" (117). The operation comes from the other's intervention and returns to the other. The revision of the limit, which is rather a threshold, an opening as well as a closure, between animality and humanity, is a persistent strand of Cixous's *Messie*, but for my purposes here it may be pointed out that the relation of the *chateau* to the verdict and to the messianic in Derrida's sense rests on their remaining short of or in excess of vision. "The cat had come as pure event" (68) in that its arrival was unforeseeable. As for the attempted visit of Kafka's grave, it is exemplary of the understanding of the event as that which escapes prevision: "Knowing perfectly . . . that one cannot see what one wants to see, I went to the cemetery to see what I could not see" (126), or, in Derrida's formulation in *Veils*, "What knowledge does not know is what happens."[79]

"Savoir" strives to occupy what Cixous calls the "*pas encore*" (18) of the event (at the same time *another step* and *not yet*), a space that is also a time and another name for the "*pas*sage."[80] The *pas encore* is not visible, nor can it be said to have taken place. In that respect, as we have argued, the event of surgery does not posit a strict separation between before (blindness) and after (seeing); neither is the passage in Cixous a link between two radically heterogeneous orders. Therefore the event is not an event of "firstness." It is both taken back, in effects of iterability, and, since it has not finally and once for all happened, it is going on or still to come. The day after surgery is a threshold in the sense that it holds seeing in reserve, not yet, while remembering blindness, not any longer: "Because it was that day she was seeing, from her myopia that, going away, was still there a little" (8). The interval, the threshold is the untenable location in which what is promised must also be kept untouched and deferred.

We have seen that the motif of the veil, whether it is inherited from Algerian cultural and social practices or from Orientalist discourse, is also shown to be part of a philosophical tradition: on the one hand, truth is conceived as an unveiling, as the thing in itself appearing out of hiding or being seen without error (in Heidegger's reading of Plato); on the other hand, the *hijab* in the Quran relates to a "visual/spatial/ethical concept," which Mernissi explains as "an act that divides space in two parts and hides one part from view."[81] Both Djebar and Cixous approach what is being disregarded in such elaborations. Djebar puts into question the endurance of that spatial model by focusing on a less discussed desire for invisibility, which she extends to the entire polity, and calling for the irruption of the unforeseen, or the impro-*vised*, in the light of day. In her narratives the public space can (or might) accommodate privacy, the being together of different bodies that would not be compulsively watched, which does not mean that they would be unseen. But this requires another interpretation of publicity, dissociated from the spectacular. Conversely, the social use of the veil leads to a reflection induced by the spectral lack of reciprocity between the one who sees while she cannot be seen and the one who is looked at. That disconnection may be endowed with positive effects if it is reassessed as unthreatening colocation, which does not exclude disinterested contact with others, yet deters from or invents preferred modes of interaction. In Cixous's philosophy the turn to the visible is enthusiastically embraced, but what the surgery brings about is not quite of the order of a luminous revelation. On the one hand, the successful surgery risked obscuring what was left behind, which is nothing less than the apprehension of the self (myopia was I, thus I am now lost, but, at the same time, myopia was foreign to me, thus I was/am not selfsame). What sort of political animal do such disjunctions establish? On the other hand, the swift decision leading to the surgery, dissociated from the will since it came from the other ("the cat"), makes the narrator see, but above all reflect, on the unforeseeable. We have often noted that Cixous consistently problematizes boundaries, substituting to the determination of impassable limits the figure of thresholds and doors, portals or gates (such as the ones separating, but also linking, inside and outside in *Inside*), or the thinking of the interval in *Messie* and "Savoir." What the example of the surgery's aftermath demonstrates are the different temporalities of the event, on the one hand, which exceeds time, and of the interval on the other, a time lag or indefinite spatiotemporal extension in which acts are suspended and that corresponds to the time of thinking. There is an ethical motive as well in being attentive to what remains to arrive within what comes to pass or in proposing to "keep forever the world, suspended, desirable, refused."[82]

In a recent essay, Jean-Luc Nancy shows the extent to which the terrain of the political has shifted, or the place of "politics" is no longer identifiable, which makes it "necessary to rework the entire topography."[83] We have seen that this is what Cixous and Djebar consistently do. The discernible ethical position that emerges from their writings should not be opposed to politics. In her own reflection on the ethics of dissensus (the title of her book), Ewa Ziarek shows that ethics is itself a site of contestation, holding an irreducible dimension of antagonism in politics.[84] She also argues that the point must not merely be to recover ethics "as a new 'ground' for politics," but instead to redefine both (215). The recognition of a contested space marked by plural histories is a way of opposing discourses of hegemony, presuppositions of unity, or oversimplistic dualities. Stylistically, we have seen that both Cixous and Djebar endow negative traits (such as disarticulation, dislocation, discord, and exclusion) with an affirmative ability to transform the political. In their works the ties to the political body are not marked by rupture but rather by discontinuities and disconnections that do not preclude certain returns. The inhabitation of the world by the I, as Mireille Calle-Gruber has pointed out for Cixous, is marked by intermittence, of which she gives several sensory examples, such as the blinks of the eye, the flickers of light, or syncopation.[85] In their texts Djebar and Cixous show the limits of some versions of political discourse endorsing the model of the community or the city: their writings evidence their distrust of such models, while proposing other conditions for being together. Nancy underscores that the notion of "politics" has subsumed all forms of living together and that what should be asserted is the distinction "between the political sphere and other spheres of existing 'in common.'"[86] He proposes that the "with" should be upheld, since politics is posited as "the possibilising of a we" (13). But instead of thinking the community as a multiplicity of individuals, he puts forward the notion of a multiplicity of modalities exceeding politics (11). While ushering in the urgency of action, Djebar's and Cixous's works prefigure the field of its inscription. The purpose of *Algerian Imprints* is to show that Cixous and Djebar respond to various forms of oppression and foreground the ways in which power impacts bodies and sites. But, at the same time, they derive from their experience and their analyses the positive valence of "a community of social de-liaison," as Nancy, quoting Derrida, recalls (13). Through their transformative writings, Djebar and Cixous construct social/textual connections that recast the political on the basis of de-liaison, where politics takes place: elsewhere.

Notes

INTRODUCTION

1. Bensmaïa, *Experimental Nations,* 6.

2. See for instance about Cixous and Djebar: "While there is a certain degree of continuity from one text to another (and even from one motif to the next within the same text), there is also *development*" (Rice, *Time Signatures,* 2); about Djebar: "My reading of Djebar's relationship with French philosophy will portray her evolution . . . as a gradual shift away from a positioned Algerian identity or genealogy, through a discovery of Algeria's singular-plurality, and ultimately to an ongoing preoccupation with its loss" (Hiddleston, *Assia Djebar,* 4–5); about Cixous, Martine Motard-Noar discerns "evolutions, at times contradictory, of Cixous's texts" (*Les Fictions d'Hélène Cixous,* 12).

3. Derrida is quoted in Cixous and Jeannet, *Rencontre terrestre,* 16. Mireille Calle-Gruber talks of two "'epochs' of writing" in Djebar, though she does detect similarities between the two (*Assia Djebar ou la résistance de l'écriture,* 8, 9).

4. Rice, *Time Signatures* and *Polygraphies*; Babayan, "La représentation de l'exil dans les oeuvres de Djebar et de Cixous."

5. One of the short stories in Djebar's *Oran, langue morte* has a quotation from Cixous's "Sorties" as an epigraph, no doubt in deference to the fact that Cixous was born in Oran (Djebar, *The Tongue's Blood Does Not Run Dry,* 11). Other more indirect quotations may be found in *Nulle part dans la maison,* where "ma langue de lait" (309) recalls Cixous's "languelait" ("*Coming to Writing,*" 22). She also refers to that essay in Djebar, *Ces Voix qui m'assiègent,* 26.

6. See, for instance, Shiach, *Hélène Cixous;* and Conley, *Hélène Cixous: Writing the Feminine,* in the case of Cixous; Donadey, *Recasting Postcolonialism;* and Clerc, *Assia Djebar,* among others, in the case of Djebar.

7. Cixous, "My Algeriance," 155.

8. Cixous, *Reveries of the Wild Woman*, 22, "My Algeriance," 167, 170.

9. See Barclay's *Writing Postcolonial France*, the subtitle of which is *Haunting, Literature, and the Maghreb*; O'Riley's reading of Djebar's novels, titled *Postcolonial Haunting and Victimization*; or Hiddleston's chapter, "Haunted Algeria," in *Out of Algeria*.

1. THE GRAVITY OF THE BODY

1. Cixous and Jeannet, *Rencontre terrestre*, 26.

2. Cixous, "The Laugh of the Medusa," 875, 886.

3. Cixous, "Sorties," 68.

4. Cixous, "The Laugh of the Medusa," 882.

5. Zimra, "Writing Woman," 79, 81.

6. Stevens, *L'Ecriture solaire d'Hélène Cixous*, 255–74; Djebar, *Fantasia*, 156.

7. "Flying is woman's gesture–flying in language and making it fly. . . . It's no accident that *voler* has a double meaning . . . women take after birds and robbers just as robbers take after women and birds." Cixous, "The Laugh of the Medusa," 887.

8. Djebar, *Nulle part dans la maison*, 405.

9. Djebar, *Fantasia*, 22.

10. See Déjeux's study of "circulating woman" in Djebar: *Assia Djebar*, 21.

11. Kateb, *Le Poète comme un boxeur*, 41.

12. Cixous, "My Algeriance," 159; Cixous and Jeannet, *Rencontre terrestre*, 129.

13. Cixous, *Inside*, 7; Conley, *Hélène Cixous*, 12–16; and Shiach, *Hélène Cixous*, 72–76 have provided insightful readings of *Inside*, especially the ways in which the positions of "inside" and "outside" cease to be opposed and serve to interrogate the limitations of the thinking of spatiality.

14. Cixous, *Inside*, 29.

15. Cixous, *Le Prénom de Dieu*, 9.

16. Cixous, *Inside*, 13.

17. Cixous, "My Algeriance," 159.

18. See Babayan, "La représentation de l'exil," chapter 2.

19. Djebar, *Nulle part dans la maison*, 48; Cixous, *Reveries of the Wild Woman*, 9.

20. Le Clézio, "Assia Djebar," 233.

21. Djebar, *Les Alouettes naïves*, 9.

22. Jacques Derrida writes that what is at stake in "the scene of orientation" is finding "the most appropriate and direct path for the best question, the path that advances, that proceeds in order to accede and does not return to its starting point by going round in circles in its own footsteps" (*The Beast and the Sovereign II*, 67). This concern with orientation also "engages the body proper of a questioner who is walking, of a question on the march that *goes*, that comes and goes, always risks com-

ing back, going around in circles, being sent back over its own steps" (ibid.). See also Derrida's "law of the wheel" and remarks on circularity (ibid., 119, 120).

23. Djebar, *Nulle part dans la maison*, 50.

24. Sanson, "Mon père, cet autre," 319.

25. Djebar, *Fantasia*, 180.

26. Djebar, *Alouettes naïves*, 187, 189.

27. Djebar, *Women of Algiers in Their Apartment*, 139.

28. Cixous, *Reveries of the Wild Woman*, 30.

29. Djebar, *Nulle part dans la maison*, 358.

30. De Man, *The Rhetoric of Romanticism*, 68.

31. Rousseau, *The Confessions and Correspondence*, 5. Here are the criteria: "If I have happened to use some inconsequential ornament, this has never happened except to fill out a gap occasioned by my lack of memory; I may have assumed to be true what I knew might have been so, never what I knew to be false" (ibid., 5).

32. Lejeune, *On Autobiography*, 25, 26.

33. De Man, *The Rhetoric of Romanticism*, 70.

34. Lejeune, *On Autobiography*, 26, 15.

35. De Man, *The Rhetoric of Romanticism*, 68.

36. Gabara, *From Split to Screened Selves*, xi.

37. Cixous and Jeannet, *Rencontre terrestre*, 31; Cixous, *Portrait du soleil*, 127.

38. Cixous and Calle-Gruber, *Rootprints*, 178.

39. Cixous, *"Coming to Writing,"* 47; Cixous and Jeannet, *Rencontre terrestre*, 92, 150.

40. Cixous, *Three Steps on the Ladder of Writing*, 61.

41. Cixous and Jeannet, *Rencontre terrestre*, 123, 21.

42. Derrida, *H.C. for Life*, 119.

43. In his reading of Cixous's *Manhattan*, Derrida also stresses the undecidable line between the body (*corps*) and the corpus that installs "an unarchivable which itself hesitates between fiction and memory." Derrida, *Geneses, Genealogies, Genres, and Genius*, 10.

44. Djebar, *Women of Algiers in Their Apartment*, 168.

45. Khatibi, "Diglossia," 158.

46. Djebar, *Women of Algiers in Their Apartment*, 172.

47. Djebar, *Fantasia*, 156.

48. Montaigne writes that he speaks of himself "because I find [the subject] so sterile and meager that no suspicion of ostentation can fall upon me." Montaigne, *The Essays*, 754; Rousseau replies to the anticipated objection that, being a man of the people, he has nothing interesting to say by arguing, "in whatever obscurity I might have lived, if I have thought more and better than Kings, the history of my soul is more interesting than that of theirs." Rousseau, *The Confessions and Correspondence*, 586.

49. Cixous, "Coming to Writing," 16, 12–13.

50. Chikhi, *Figures tutélaires*, 134. Dominique Fisher argues that "many of Djebar's writing practices . . . are in fact commonly found in the classical and popular Arabic literary repertoire." Strand, "Assia Djebar's *La Femme sans sépulture*," 343.

51. Chikhi, *Figures tutélaires*, 130.

52. Djebar, *Fantasia*, 215. See also her remarks on the brutal impact of autobiography in Djebar, "Violence de l'autobiographie."

53.

> Autobiography, the writing of the self as living, the trace of the living for itself, being for itself, the auto-affection or auto-infection as memory or archive of the living, would be an immunizing movement . . . but an immunizing movement that is always threatened with becoming auto-immunizing, like every *autos*, every ipseity, every automatic, automobile, autonomous, auto-referential movement. Nothing risks becoming more poisonous than an autobiography, poisonous for oneself in the first place, auto-infectious for the presumed signatory who is so auto-affected.
>
> Derrida, *The Animal That Therefore I Am*, 47.

54. Djebar, *Women of Algiers in Their Apartment*, 169. See also her "Violence de l'autobiographie," 92, and *Fantasia*, 62, as well as Gabara's reading of the gesture of keeping hidden what is narrated in Djebar (*From Split to Screened Selves*, 113).

55. Djebar, *Fantasia*, 156.

56. Gauvin, *L'écrivain francophone à la croisée des langues*, 33.

57. Gabara, *From Split to Screened Selves*, 96. In spite of his stimulating reading of *Fantasia*, I would differ from H. Adlai Murdoch when he mentions the "alternation between the presentation of the events of the 1830 invasion and the presentation of writing as autobiography" ("Rewriting Writing," 76), for it could be argued instead that history is not the other of intimate subjectivity but one of its aspects. Conversely, Gabara shows the pitfalls of interpreting Djebar's project as "polyphonic autobiography" (*From Split to Screened Selves*, 120).

58. Guillot, "Assia Djebar," 181.

59. Djebar, "Violence de l'autobiographie," 92.

60. Le Clézio, "Assia Djebar," 238. *Forty* or the autobiographical number. See "You know that I wrote *Fantasia* when I was over forty."

61. Gabara, *From Split to Screened Selves*, 105.

62. Cixous, "The Laugh of the Medusa," 877.

2. GOING TO SCHOOL IN FRENCH ALGERIA

1. Nora, "*L'Histoire de France* de Lavisse," 2:317, part 1.

2. Gosnell, *The Politics of Frenchness in Colonial Algeria*, 55.

3. Stora, *Histoire de l'Algérie depuis l'indépendance*, 56.

4. Derrida, *Monolingualism of the Other*, 44.

5. Cixous, "Letter to Zohra Drif," 85.

6. Djebar, *Fantasia*, 185.

7. Azéma et al., "Liberté pour l'Histoire."

8. The generation of positivists founded "history-science on the basis of the document, by erecting the archival piece as a warrant of truth and criterion of scientificity, by conferring to it the definitive dignity of the proof" (Nora, "*L'Histoire de France* de Lavisse," 343). But this could only be achieved by symmetrically "suspecting sources and deliberately installing oneself in reconstruction" (341).

9. Stora, *La gangrène et l'oubli*, 247.

10. Nora, "The Era of Commemoration," in 3:637; Weber, *Questioning Judaism*, 27.

11. Coquery-Vidrovitch, Manceron, and Noiriel, "Les historiens n'ont pas le monopole de la mémoire."

12. Derrida, *Archive Fever*, 76.

13. Djebar, *Fantasia*, 177. In that respect, see Gabara's reading of Djebar, *From Split to Screened Selves*, 105.

14. Droz and Lever, *Histoire de la guerre d'Algérie*, 21; Bourdieu, *The Algerians*, 121.

15. Droz and Lever, *Histoire de la guerre d'Algérie*, 21.

16. Camus, "Misère de la Kabylie," 921.

17. Gosnell, *The Politics of Frenchness*, 46, 49.

18. Stora, *Histoire de l'Algérie coloniale*, 105. In 1954 Mouloud Feraoun fondly evoked "the teacher of the *bled*" in *Jours de Kabylie*, 127–36.

19. Gosnell, *The Politics of Frenchness*, 49.

20. Kateb, *Européens, "Indigènes" et Juifs*, 255, 256.

21. Stora, *Histoire de l'Algérie coloniale*, 105.

22. Gauvin, *L'écrivain francophone*, 28.

23. Le Clézio, "Assia Djebar," 233.

24. Le Sueur, *Uncivil War*, 72, 55. Hafid Gafaïti and Djamila Saadi-Mokrane point out that since the schooling of Algerian children had been minimal during French colonization despite the colonizers' claims about "assimilation," the use of French became paradoxically generalized in the first decade after independence, because of the programs of education that were implemented in earnest. Thus children taught by Algerian teachers trained in French or by French *coopérants* (volunteers) learned French before the policy of Arabization was launched in schools in 1964. Gafaïti, "The Monotheism of the Other," 24; Saadi-Mokrane, "The Algerian Linguicide," 53.

25. Kateb, *Européens, "Indigènes" et Juifs*, 194.

26. Stora, *Gangrène*, 23.

27. Kateb, *Européens, "Indigènes" et Juifs*, 190.

28. Cixous, "My Algeriance," 162. Stora mentions the opposition to the 1870 decree on the part of some Army leaders, Europeans and Muslim elites, *and* that of

Jewish religious authorities who denounced the decree as a project of acculturation. Stora, *Les Trois exils,* 53, 54. In his study of Algerian Jews at the beginning of French colonization, Joshua Schreier also notes that many Algerian Jews resisted what they perceived as "a new and intrusive governmental effort to rescind previously enjoyed prerogatives" (Schreier, *Arabs of the Jewish Faith,* 20), including colonial attempts to control religious schools (21).

29. Derrida, *Monolingualism of the Other,* 84.

30. Kateb, *Europeans, "Indigènes" et Juifs,* 191.

31. Derrida, *Monolingualism of the Other,* 15.

32. Stora, *Les Trois exils,* 88.

33. Cixous, "My Algeriance," 168.

34. Zytnicki, "Un épisode de la vie politique," 63, 65.

35. Stora, *Les Trois exils,* 87; Zytnicki, "Un épisode de la vie politique," 68.

36. Cixous, "Letter to Zohra Drif," 85.

37. Dick and Kofman, *Derrida,* 87.

38. Stora, *Les Trois exils,* 88.

39. In contrast, Michel Abitbol opposes such reactions of the Muslim elites to others recorded in the country, which were more favorable to the abolition of the Crémieux decree, with the caveat that these positions were reported by the French Administration. Abitbol, *Les Juifs d'Afrique du Nord,* 64.

40. Djebar, *Nulle part dans la maison,* 33, 31.

41. Cixous, "My Algeriance," 164. See also Cixous and Calle-Gruber, *Rootprints,* with a picture of the store (181).

42. Cixous, *Reveries of the Wild Woman,* 72.

43. Cixous, "My Algeriance," 159.

44. Dib, "Encounters," 105.

45. Djebar, *So Vast the Prison,* 263.

46. Cixous, "My Algeriance," 161. One notable exception to such hostility is found in a passage in *Reveries* in which the father, "an arabizarre," picks up two hitchhiking Algerians in his Citroën. They bless him and call him "brother" in French, and he reciprocates by calling them "brothers" in Arabic (Cixous, *Reveries of the Wild Woman,* 25).

47. Derrida, *Monolingualism of the Other,* 14.

48. Cixous, "My Algeriance," 156.

49. Cixous, *Reveries of the Wild Woman,* 24, 80, 81–82.

50. Cixous, "My Algeriance," 171.

51. Derrida, *Monolingualism of the Other,* 37.

52. Cixous, "Letter to Zohra Drif," 85.

53. Cixous, *Reveries of the Wild Woman,* 70, 71.

54. Even though Cixous seemingly addresses a general condition, she does take into account differences between colonial schools: "My brother, a student at Lycée

Bugeaud, in town, had the good fortune of being in a theater where everything was said. Insults flew. There were Jews and Muslims amongst the colonialist majority. So they could fight it out, a great relief in the thirst for justice." Cixous, "Letter to Zohra Drif," 86.

55. Cixous, *Inside*, 18. See also: "We knew everything" (Cixous, "Bare Feet," 58).

56. Cixous, "Letter to Zohra Drif," 85–86.

57. Cixous, *Reveries of the Wild Woman*, 70–71. "That invisibility to which I refer occurs because of a peculiar disposition of the eyes of those with whom I come in contact. . . . You often doubt if you really exist. You wonder whether you aren't simply a phantom in other people's minds." Ellison, *Invisible Man*, 3–4.

58. Simone de Beauvoir, who wrote about the collective complicity that tainted her in spite of herself during the Algerian war (*Force of Circumstance*, 652), denounces the operation of rendering harsh realities more palatable through paraphrases or softening euphemisms as part of the falsification required by most in France: the Algerian war, to begin with, was called "pacification" by the authorities (337); torture was justified as "exorbitant legality" (379); or the famous phrase "peace for the brave," a so-called generous offer proposed by the French government to Algerians, "to Algerians meant capitulation" (455).

59. Cixous, "Letter to Zohra Drif," 85.

60. Cixous, "My Algeriance," 160.

61. Cixous, *Reveries of the Wild Woman*, 71; Cixous, "My Algeriance," 168; Cixous and Jeannet, *Rencontre terrestre*, 103.

62. Cixous, "My Algeriance," 171.

63. Cixous, *"Coming to Writing,"* 22.

64. Cixous, "My Algeriance," 172.

65. Cixous, *"Coming to Writing,"* 24, 23; Cixous, *OR les lettres de mon père*, 16.

66. Cixous, "Letter to Zohra Drif," 87; Cixous, *Reveries of the Wild Woman*, 85.

67. Cixous, "Letter to Zohra Drif," 88.

68. Cixous, "My Algeriance," 153.

69. Cixous, "Letter to Zohra Drif," 87.

70. Cixous and Calle-Gruber, *Rootprints*, 204.

71. Djebar, *Nulle part dans la maison*, 35.

72. Harbi, *Une vie debout*, 14.

73. Djebar, *So Vast the Prison*, 272.

74. Djebar, *Nulle part dans la maison*, 41.

75. Gauvin, *L'écrivain francophone*, 26.

76. Djebar, *Fantasia*, 3; Djebar, *Nulle part dans la maison*, 43. See Gabara, *From Split to Screened Selves*, 100.

77. See for example in Djebar, *Nulle part dans la maison:* "I was immediately felt to be an exception, I, a girl with a European appearance but without being so" (116); "I felt privileged" (143); "I felt apart, compared to French girls of my age" (175).

78. Gauvin, *L'écrivain francophone*, 28.

79. Djebar, *Nulle part dans la maison*, 180.

80. Cixous, *Reveries of the Wild Woman*, 57.

81. Le Clézio, "Assia Djebar," 236.

82. Djebar, *Fantasia*, 215.

83. Gauvin, *L'écrivain francophone*, 29. Gafaïti points out that, "in 1938, the French government went so far as to classify Arabic as a foreign language" (Gafaïti, "The Monotheism of the Other," 23).

84. Djebar, *Nulle part dans la maison*, 104.

85. Djebar, *So Vast the Prison*, 302.

86. Djebar, *Nulle part dans la maison*, 105–6.

87. Le Clézio, "Assia Djebar," 240, 241.

88. Zimra, "Writing Woman," 68. See also Danielle Marx-Scouras's analysis of Djebar's critics of her first novels, which were accused of an "exclusive preoccupation with sexual problems indecent at a time when Algeria was subject to a merciless war" ("Muffled Screams/Stifled Voices," 172), and Djebar's reply to the accusation (quoted by Zimra, "Writing Woman," 70).

89. Le Clézio, "Assia Djebar," 236.

90. Derrida, *Monolingualism of the Other*, 58.

91. For instance, "I am on the side of Moses, the one who does not enter. Luckily" (Cixous, "My Algeriance," 170); "Luckily, once this holy outsiderization was stopped by the American landing, it did not stop in our minds or bodies" (Cixous, *Reveries of the Wild Woman*, 72).

3. VANISHING INSCRIPTIONS

1. Roos, "Colonial Culture as Francophone?" 17; Senghor, *Le Dialogue des cultures*, in particular the chapter "Du métissage biologique au métissage culturel."

2. Gosnell, *The Politics of Frenchness in Colonial Algeria*, 48.

3. Fanon, *Black Skin, White Masks*, 18.

4. Hale, *Ecrits d'Aimé Césaire*, 407.

5. Fanon, *Black Skin, White Masks*, 27.

6. Césaire, *Discourse on Colonialism*, 67.

7. Sartre, "Black Orpheus," 121.

8. Glissant, *Introduction à une poétique du divers*, 55.

9. Hale, *Ecrits d'Aimé Césaire*, 406. Abdelkebir Khatibi makes a related point when arguing that Stéphane Mallarmé's writings are an exemplary instance of literature already in translation from French into French (*Jacques Derrida, en effet*, 44). He urges Maghrebian writers writing in French to take up the process of translation at work in literature, not through derivation or imitation, but by situating themselves in its midst: "Maghrebian literature is a translation from French into French, and not,

as one tends to think, a transcription from the native language into French" ("Diglossia," 158).

10. Césaire, *Discourse on Colonialism,* 77; Senghor, "What Is 'Negritude'?" 137.

11. Ibid., 76–77; ibid.

12. Glissant, *Introduction à une poétique du divers,* 125, 17.

13. For instance: "What the thought of the trace has already taught us is that it could not be simply submitted to the onto-phenomenological question of essence. The trace *is nothing,* it is not an entity [*étant*], it exceeds the question *What is?* and contingently makes it possible." Derrida, *Of Grammatology,* 75.

14. Djebar, *Fantasia,* 215 (my translation). Blair's translation reads, "the enemy's language"; and in "Collective Autobiography" Geesey proposes "adversary language" (155).

15. Djebar, *Ces Voix qui m'assiègent,* 216.

16. Djebar, *Fantasia,* 226.

17. Derrida, *Writing and Difference,* 230.

18. Gracki, "Writing Violence," 836.

19. For a discussion of this specific passage in *Fantasia,* see Turk, "*L'Amour la fantasia*; Donadey, "Assia Djebar's Poetics of Subversion" (in which Donadey refers to an unpublished paper of hers, "Writing the Trace: Assia Djebar's *L'Amour, la fantasia* as a Bilingual Palimpsest"); Gracki, "Assia Djebar"; Marx-Scouras, "Muffled Screams/Stifled Voices"; Zimra, "Disorienting the Subject"; Geesey, "Collective Autobiography."

20. Djebar, *Ces Voix qui m'assiègent,* 216. Hafid Gafaïti, who also aims to complicate the issue of the opposition between Arabophones and Francophones, writes that the policy of Arabization adopted in the years following the independence "was in large part originally conceived and often carried out by *Francophone* leaders, administrators, and civil servants" ("The Monotheism of the Other," 25).

21. Khatibi, *Love in Two Languages,* 66. Jacques Derrida quotes that passage from Khatibi in *Monolingualism of the Other,* 36; ibid., 2.

22. Mortimer, "Entretien avec Assia Djebar," 199.

23. In *Algeria in Others' Languages,* Hafid Gafaïti and Djamila Saadi-Mokrane point out social and political complexities in the wake of the teaching of Modern Standard Arabic as opposed to the vernacular Arabic or Berber spoken in Algeria, amidst the persistence to this day of the use of French in some sectors of public life and in publishing. However, they strongly differ in their appreciation of the reception of modern standard Arabic by Algerians. According to Saadi-Mokrane, it is not understood by most ("The Algerian Linguicide," 46, 51), whereas Gafaïti is more nuanced and emphasizes generational differences: "it is certainly not the case for the majority of the postindependence generation, for whom Arabic has been the language of instruction" ("The Monotheism of the Other," 42).

24. Valensi, "The Scheherazade Syndrome," 142–43.

25. Bensmaïa, *Experimental Nations*, 3, 2.

26. Gauvin, *L'écrivain francophone*, 19.

27. Le Clézio, "Assia Djebar," 232.

28. Bensmaïa, *Experimental Nations*, 15.

29. Le Clézio, "Assia Djebar," 234.

30. Djebar, *Fantasia*, 214.

31. Djebar, *Nulle part dans la maison*, 174. See also Djebar, *Ces Voix qui m'assiègent*, 179, 180.

32. Le Clézio, "Assia Djebar," 243.

33. Djebar, *Fantasia*, 214.

34. Le Clézio, "Assia Djebar," 233.

35. Djebar, *Fantasia*, 216, 215.

36. Gauvin, *L'écrivain francophone*, 33.

37. Djebar, *Fantasia*, 216. Djebar makes a parallel between an early scene of the conquest, in which a messenger transmitting words from the enemy is killed (33), and the situation of the Maghrebian writer writing in French today (215): "Any writing of the Other, when transported, becomes fatal, since it is a sign of compromise" (33).

38. Le Clézio, "Assia Djebar," 234.

39. Mortimer, ""Entretien avec Assia Djebar," 201; and Gauvin, *L'écrivain francophone*, 26. In *Fantasia*, the language of Others or tunic of Nessus is also referred to as a "gift of love from my father" (217).

40. Djebar, *Fantasia*, 184.

41. Gauvin, *L'écrivain francophone*, 33.

42. Mortimer, "Entretien," 201; Le Clézio, "Assia Djebar," 236–37. See also Anne Donadey's analysis of Djebar's "subterranean languages" ("The Multilingual Strategies of Postcolonial Literature," 29).

43. Gauvin, *L'écrivain francophone*, 25; Djebar, *Fantasia*, 181.

44. Djebar, *Fantasia*, 184.

45. "A little Arab girl going to school for the first time, one autumn morning, walking hand in hand with her father. A tall erect figure in a fez and a European suit, carrying a bag of school books" (ibid., 3); "My father, a tall erect figure in a fez, walks down the village street; he pulls me by the hand" (213).

46. See Khatibi's similar formalization of "Arab space" as "a collection of territories and civilizations" ("A Colonial Labyrinth," 11), an example of which is found in the coexistence of the medina (Muslim old city) and the mellah (Jewish old city), mirroring each other while cultivating difference (9). The labyrinthine structure of each also shapes thinking and memory through what Khatibi calls a "psychology of detour" (9).

47. Gauvin, *L'écrivain francophone*, 21.

48. Lyotard, *Political Writings*, 170.

49. Lyotard, *The Differend*, 49.

50. In "Force of Law," Jacques Derrida posits a heteronomy of right or law to justice. An act of justice does justice first of all to "singularity, individuals, groups, irreplaceable existences, the other or myself *as* other, in a unique situation" (in *Acts of Religion*, 254). Justice occurs, if it does, in the language of the other (245).

51. Lyotard, *The Differend*, 43.

52. Khatibi, *Love in Two Languages*, 4.

53. Bensmaïa, "Multilingualism and National 'Character,'" 167.

54. Khatibi, "Diglossia," 157, 158.

55. See Djebar's *Ces Voix qui m'assiègent*, in which *qalam* is written "calame" (184) or, in *Le Blanc de l'Algérie*, *kalam*, 261.

56. Khatibi, *Love in Two Languages*, 4.

57. Boudjedra, *Lettres algériennes*, 57.

58. Djebar, *Ces Voix qui m'assiègent*, 140.

59. Said, *Orientalism*, 6.

60. Bertrand, *Les Villes d'Or*, 6.

61. Djebar, *So Vast the Prison*, 146–47.

62. Gauvin, *L'écrivain francophone*, 20. Likewise, in contemporary Algeria, "After more than a century of French occupation—which ended not long ago in such butchery— a territory of language subsists between two peoples, between two memories" (Djebar, *Fantasia*, 215).

63. Djebar, *So Vast the Prison*, 159.

64. Djebar, *Ces Voix qui m'assiègent*, 56.

65. Djebar, *So Vast the Prison*, 145.

66. For another approach to Djebar's elusive representation, see Jane Hiddleston's chapter "Haunted Algeria" in *Assia Djebar: Out of Algeria;* and Michael O'Riley's *Postcolonial Haunting and Victimization.*

67. Djebar recalls that, at the Quranic school, each time students had memorized a *sura* (excerpt of the Quran), they washed off the slate on which it was written, erasing the *sura* in order to make space for another (Gauvin, *L'écrivain francophone*, 27). Elke Richter examines Djebar's take on writing under erasure and asserts that, unlike Derrida or Levinas, Djebar does not "subscribe to the idea of the totality of absence" in her conception of the trace ("Sur les traces de la trace," 251). Such a reading overlooks the structural mark of absence in presence in Derrida's analysis of the trace. Derrida does not say that absence is "total," but that presence is open to something more and other than itself.

68. Derrida, *Writing and Difference*, 200.

69. Derrida, *Margins of Philosophy*, 24.

70. Derrida, *Specters of Marx*, 10.

71. Derrida, *Writing and Difference*, 214, 226.

72. Derrida, *Margins of Philosophy*, 24.

73. Segarra, *Leur Pesant de poudre*, 220.

4. POETIC INC.

1. Taïeb, *Etre juif au Maghreb,* 23; Schreier, *Arabs of the Jewish Faith,* 197.

2. Stora, *Les Trois exils,* 12. "What some call 'Judeo-Arabic' is . . . not an Arabic-Hebraic synthesis, but for the most part, a quite particular form of spoken Maghrebian Arabic, some features of which are found in other sedentary vernacular languages in the Maghreb" (Taïeb, *Etre juif au Maghreb,* 69–70).

3. Deldyck, *Le Processus d'acculturation,* 11–12, 17.

4. Taïeb, *Etre juif au Maghreb,* 9; Stora, *Les Trois exils,* 13.

5. Cixous, "Coming to Writing," 7.

6. Cixous. *Portrait of Jacques Derrida as a Young Jewish Saint,* 75.

7. Derrida, *Monolingualism of the Other,* 55.

8. Memmi, *The Liberation of the Jew,* 182.

9. Memmi, *The Pillar of Salt,* 105.

10. Memmi, *The Liberation of the Jew,* 185, 191.

11. Derrida, *Monolingualism of the Other,* 31.

12. Cixous, "The Names of Oran," 187.

13. Cixous, "Coming to Writing," 12.

14. Derrida, *Monolingualism of the Other,* 93.

15. Cixous, "Coming to Writing," 21.

16. On language and sexual difference in Cixous, see Motard-Noar, *Les Fictions d'Hélène Cixous;* Sellers, *Language and Sexual Difference*; Conley, *Hélène Cixous: Writing the Feminine*; Negrón, *Lectures de la différence sexuelle*; Stevens, *L'Ecriture solaire d'Hélène Cixous;* Bray, *Hélène Cixous;* Marder, *The Mother in the Age of Mechanical Reproduction.*

17. Cixous, "De la scène de l'Inconscient," 19.

18. Cixous, "The Names of Oran," 185.

19. Cixous, "Coming to Writing," 21.

20. Cixous, "The Names of Oran," 190, 193.

21. Cixous, *Inside,* 18.

22. Cixous, "The Names of Oran," 191. See Marder's discussion of a "prior, primordial 'translation'" in Cixous's texts (*The Mother in the Age of Mechanical Reproduction,* 214, and in the rest of her chapter).

23. Cixous, "Coming to Writing," 22.

24. "This face [= the mother's face] is not a metaphor" (ibid., 2); "I nourished myself with texts . . . without metaphor" (20); "If you give me the breast, I am your child . . . and you are my mother. Metaphor? Yes. No. If everything is metaphor, then nothing is metaphor" (50).

25. Cixous and Calle-Gruber, *Rootprints,* 11.

26. Cixous, *Reveries of the Wild Woman,* 42.

27. Cixous, *Le Prénom de Dieu,* 26, 126.

28. Cixous, *Inside*, 23.

29. Cixous, *Reveries of the Wild Woman*, 42.

30. Cixous, "The Names of Oran," 186.

31. Cixous, "Coming to Writing," 33.

32. Cixous, "The Laugh of the Medusa," 880.

33. Cixous, "Coming to Writing," 20.

34. See Cixous, "Sorties," 81. Morag Shiach recalls the arguments of Cixous's critics in *Hélène Cixous*, 17–24.

35. Cixous, "The Laugh of the Medusa," 882.

36. Cixous, "Coming to Writing," 39; Cixous, "The Laugh of the Medusa," 889. See Abigail Bray's remark that, for Cixous, "the feminine does lack, but what 'she' lacks is the fear of lack" (*Hélène Cixous*, 8).

37. Cixous, "The Laugh of the Medusa," 882.

38. Cixous, "Sorties," 86. On the question of affirmation in Cixous and her reading of Freud and Marx, see Conley, *Hélène Cixous*, 11.

39. Cixous, "Coming to Writing," 1.

40. "A powerful tendency to aggressiveness is always present beside a powerful love, and the more passionately a child loves its object the more sensitive does it become to disappointments and frustrations from that object" (Freud, "Femininity," 124). See for instance in Cixous, "BECAUSE I HATE HER, MY MOTHER IS NO MORE" (*Inside*, 42); or "antimaternal sickness" (*Reveries of the Wild Woman*, 13).

41. Cixous, *Le Prénom de Dieu*, 22, 23. See also: "I had to be indebted. . . . I had to say thank you [*merci*] instead of saying mother [*mère*]" (26).

42. Cixous, "Coming to Writing," 19.

43. Cixous, "Sorties," 89, 90. In an interview, Cixous indicates that "I thought that any woman who wrote was supported by a paternal instantiation . . . in the 1970s . . . when feminist women imagined that there was no father, that one could be without father" (Cremonese, *Dialectique du masculin et du féminin*, 136). See also Djebar's observation: "Western, European feminism claims at first to be a struggle against the father, against the image of the father. Yet I could tell that in the situation of the colonized, in the Maghreb, fathers had played the part of intercessors" (Gauvin, *L'écrivain francophone*, 26).

44. Cixous, *Osnabrück*, 181.

45. Cixous, *Inside*, 12; Cixous, "De la scène de l'Inconscient," 20.

46. Cixous, *Inside*, 42.

47. Cixous, *Osnabrück*, 104.

48. Cixous, *First Days of the Year*, 101, 103.

49. Cixous, *OR les lettres de mon père*, 72. See Derrida's remarkable reading of the absence of contradiction between living and dying in Cixous (Derrida, *H.C. for Life*, in particular 16–17, 24).

50. Cixous, *First Days of the Year*, 49; Cixous, "Coming to Writing," 38.

51. Cixous and Jeannet, *Rencontre terrestre,* 138.

52. Cixous, *First Days of the Year,* 28.

53. Cixous, *Manhattan,* 41.

54. Cixous, *L'Ange au secret,* 47.

55. Cixous, *First Days of the Year,* 102, 36.

56. Cixous, "Sorties," 85–86.

57. Cixous, "Coming to Writing," 21.

58. Cixous, "The Laugh of the Medusa," 879.

59. Cixous, *Prénoms de personne,* 5.

60. Cixous, "The Laugh of the Medusa," 887.

61. Cixous, "How Not to Speak of Algeria," 161–62.

62. Ibid., 165.

5. THE SOUND OF BROKEN MEMORY

1. Kateb, *Parce que c'est une femme,* 9.

2. Harbi, *L'Algérie et son destin,* 41. See the role of the Algerian Centre National d'Etudes Historiques in the production of official history since 1974 (Stora, *Histoire de l'Algérie depuis l'indépendance,* 56–57) and, on the French side, see Maschino, "La colonisation telle qu'on l'enseigne," 8–9.

3. Harbi and Stora, *La Guerre d'Algérie,* 12. See also the analysis of amnesia in Dine, *Images of the Algerian War,* 215.

4. Bonn, *Le Roman algérien de langue française,* 21, 25.

5. Kateb, *Parce que c'est une femme,* 39, 38.

6. Among the essays devoted to Algerian women's contribution to the war and their political and social action in postcolonial Algeria, see in particular M'Rabet, *La femme algérienne;* Louis, "Les Algériennes"; Daoud, *Féminisme et politique au Maghreb;* Lazreg, *The Eloquence of Silence;* Amrane-Minne, *Des Femmes dans la guerre d'Algérie;* Gadant, *Le nationalisme algérien et les femmes.* Other authors such as Rezzoug ("Ecritures féminines algériennes") or Mosteghanemi (*Algérie*) analyze the ways in which Algerian women writers address the war or the political, in French and in Arabic. One of the most frequently discussed political struggles involving women in postcolonial Algeria is their organized opposition to the 1984 Family Code.

7. For a similar approach regarding Islamic queens, see Mernissi, *The Forgotten Queens of Islam,* which revisits women's leadership in Muslim memory and historiography, and Djebar, *Far from Madina,* in which fiction complements historians' accounts of the first centuries of Islam dealing with "daughters of Ishmael," so as to "fill in the gaps in the collective memory" (xv).

8. Hannoum, "The Legend of the Kahina," 200–1. See also Jean Déjeux's discussion of the multifaceted literary heritage of the Kahina (*Femmes d'Algérie,* 75–118).

9. Kateb, *Le Poète comme un boxeur,* 106.

10. Kateb, *Parce que c'est une femme,* 57.

11. Ibn Khaldoun, *Histoire des Berbères,* 1:341.

12. See Hannoum, "The Legend of the Kahina," 10; and Mernissi, *The Forgotten Queens of Islam,* 44; Daoud, *Féminisme et politique au Maghreb,* 16.

13. Kateb, *Parce que c'est une femme,* 57, 55.

14. Hannoum, "The Legend of the Kahina," 29.

15. Kateb, *Parce que c'est une femme,* 58–59. Ibn Khaldoun provides etymological explanations for the term *Berber,* such as: "Their language is a foreign idiom, different from any other; a circumstance that gave them the name Berbers. . . . In Arabic, the word *berbera* means a mixture of unintelligible sounds" (Ibn Khaldoun, *Histoire des Berbères,* 1:168).

16. Kateb, *Parce que c'est une femme,* 39.

17. Harbi, *Le F.L.N.,* 198; Daoud, *Féminisme et politique au Maghreb,* 142.

18. Lazreg, *The Eloquence of Silence,* 124.

19. In her study of women in the French Resistance, Margaret Collins Weitz evokes a similar "invisibility of women": "Despite the risks women undertook, continuities between their resistance assignments and their lives both before and after the war obscured the *exceptional* nature of their actions" ("As I Was Then," 1).

20. Lazreg, *The Eloquence of Silence,* 120.

21. Harbi, *L'Algérie et son destin,* 109.

22. Ibid., 97. About Zohra Drif's responsibilities, see Amrane-Minne, *Des Femmes dans la guerre d'Algérie,* 137.

23. M'Rabet, *La femme algérienne,* 21, 22. Several women fighters' testimonies collected by Amrane-Minne underscore a profound discrepancy between wartime and its aftermath; for example, Fatma Baïchi says, "Even my brothers, even the youngest with whom I was a partisan during the war, encouraged my husband not to let me go out: 'It is over now, you must not let her go out anymore, it is not as it was before'" (Amrane-Mine, *Des Femmes dans la guerre d'Algérie,* 123); and Mimi Ben Mohamed reports discussions among mudjahidins: "The fact I was in the *maquis,* that they agreed on. One had to help, one had to do everything, but tomorrow after independence . . ." (46).

24. Djebar, *Ces Voix qui m'assiègent,* 233–34.

25. See the study of amnesia and the construction of national identity in Donadey, *Recasting Postcolonialism,* 1–11. Dana Strand writes that, for Djebar, "historical accuracy can only be achieved through a creative reconstitution of that part of the past that has been previously repressed," including "the distorting effects of the silencing of women" ("Assia Djebar's *La Femme sans sépulture,*" 343). Michael O'Riley analyzes "the recovery of occulted colonial history and its dilemmas of place and positioning from the perspective of postcolonial haunting" in Djebar's work ("Place, Position and Postcolonial Haunting," 67).

26. Djebar, *Ces Voix qui m'assiègent*, 66, 156, 155. In a special issue of *World Literature Today* devoted to Assia Djebar in 1996, several authors rightly emphasize silence (Marjolijn de Jager, Valérie Budig-Markin) or the ocular/spectacular in Djebar's works (Mildred Mortimer, Laurence Huughe).

27. Djebar, *So Vast the Prison*, 248.

28. Djebar, *Fantasia*, 178.

29. Ibid., 144; Djebar, *Women of Algiers in Their Apartment*, 86; Djebar, *Nulle part dans la maison*, 125. Nada Elia draws attention to what Djebar calls "the fourth language" or the dancing body in trances in *Fantasia* (*Trances, Dances, and Vociferations*, 22).

30. Djebar, *So Vast the Prison*, 61.

31. See the five "movements" of the third part of *Fantasia*, "fantasia" being a Western musical term (ibid., 111), as well as referring to a North African parade (52). A nouba is a classical Andalusian symphony, but also "a story that each person tells, taking turns" (Gabara, *From Split to Screened Selves*, 98). *The Nouba of the Women of Mount Chenoua* emphasizes the lyrical form and follows the required divisions of that classical composition. Djebar wrote the final nouba in the film (Calle-Gruber, *Assia Djebar ou la résistance de l'écriture*, 206). "Invention" is also an instance of musical composition (such as Bach's inventions).

32. Djebar, *So Vast the Prison*, 310; Djebar, *Fantasia*, 143. On solidarity as different from "unified identity," see Hiddleston, "Feminism and the Question of 'Woman,'" 96.

33. In *Children of the New World*, published in 1962, torpor is "apparent" and intended to deceive the colonizer (Djebar, *Children of the New World*, 106). But in *La Femme sans sépulture*, *torpeur* rhymes with *peur* ("*fear*") forty years after the independence (Djebar, *La Femme sans sépulture*, 152).

34. Djebar, *Women of Algiers in Their Apartment*, 44–45.

35. Derrida, *Demeure*, 27–28.

36. Djebar, *Far from Madina*, 17.

37. Djebar, *Women of Algiers in Their Apartment*, 144.

38. Djebar, *La Femme sans sépulture*, 9.

39. Pontecorvo, *The Battle of Algiers*; Stora, *Histoire de la guerre d'Algérie*, 22; Harbi, *Le F.L.N.*, 266.

40. Yacef Saadi describes his reliance on women as bomb carriers and particularly mentions Samia Lakhdari, Zohra Drif, and Djamila Bouhired (*La Bataille d'Alger*, 1:282–86). The first two young women were Hélène Cixous's high school classmates in Algiers.

41. Harbi's work has contributed to revising the myth of the unity of the FLN by foregrounding its internecine divisions. He has also been critical of the strategy of the FLN underlying the Battle of Algiers (Harbi, *Le F.L.N.*, 198–99, and *L'Algérie et son destin*, 152).

42. Djebar, *So Vast the Prison,* 176.

43. Djebar, *The Nouba of the Women of Mount Chenoua.*

44. Djebar, *Ces Voix qui m'assiègent,* 103.

45. Cixous, Calle-Gruber, and Djebar, *Au théâtre au cinéma au féminin,* 87.

46. Bensmaïa, "*La Nouba des femmes du Mont Chenoua,*" 878.

47. Djebar, *So Vast the Prison,* 178, 280.

48. Djebar, *The Nouba of the Women of Mount Chenoua.*

49. Djebar, *So Vast the Prison,* 305.

50. Mortimer, "Reappropriating the Gaze." See also Anne Rocca's detailed study on visibility and the body in Djebar's work (*Assia Djebar*).

51. Djebar, *So Vast the Prison,* 317.

52. Cixous, Calle-Gruber, and Djebar, *Au théâtre au cinéma au féminin,* 95, 82.

53. Bensmaïa, "*La Nouba des femmes du Mont Chenoua,*" 877.

54. Quoted ibid., 884.

55. Djebar, *So Vast the Prison,* 205.

56. Cixous, Calle-Gruber, and Djebar, *Au théâtre au cinéma au féminin,* 83.

57. See Donadey's comparative analysis of *Fantasia* and *The Nouba* (*Recasting Postcolonialism,* 51–62).

58. Cixous, Calle-Gruber, and Djebar, *Au théâtre au cinéma au féminin,* 84.

59. Bensmaïa, "*La Nouba des femmes du Mont Chenoua,*" 882.

60. Cixous, Calle-Gruber, and Djebar, *Au théâtre au cinéma au féminin,* 93.

61. Bensmaïa, "*La Nouba des femmes du Mont Chenoua,*" 880.

62. Cixous, Calle-Gruber, and Djebar, *Au théâtre au cinéma au féminin,* 80.

63. Guerin and Hallas, *The Image and the Witness,* 2, 9.

64. Varda, *Documenteur.*

65. Guerin and Hallas, *The Image and the Witness,* 2.

66. Bensmaïa, "*La Nouba des femmes du Mont Chenoua,*" 878.

67. Caruth, *Unclaimed Experience,* 29.

68. Guerin and Hallas, *The Image and the Witness,* 16.

69. Cixous, Calle-Gruber, and Djebar, *Au théâtre au cinéma au féminin,* 93.

70. Djebar, *Fantasia,* 121.

71. Cixous, Calle-Gruber, and Djebar, *Au théâtre au cinéma au féminin,* 84.

72. Djebar, *Fantasia,* 130.

73. About the initial period of French colonization, Raphaëlle Branche writes that "scorched-earth tactics and razzia were systematically enacted" by the French army (*La torture et l'armée,* 26). Harbi points out that "practices that will occur during the war of Independence were broken in on a large scale [during the colonization of the country]" (Harbi and Stora, *La Guerre d'Algérie,* 35).

74. Djebar, *Fantasia,* 147.

75. Djebar, *The Nouba of the Women of Mount Chenoua.*

76. Djebar, *Nulle part dans la maison,* 364, 239. See also Cixous: "Flying is woman's gesture—flying in language and making it fly. . . . It's no accident that *voler* has a double meaning. . . . Women take after birds and robbers just as robbers take after women and birds" ("The Laugh of the Medusa," 887).

77. Djebar, *La Femme sans sépulture,* 9. Mildred Mortimer has equated Djebar's work with a mosaic ("Entretien avec Assia Djebar," 205). The mosaic in *La Femme sans sépulture* has also been interpreted as a mise en abyme of Djebar's relation to colonial and postcolonial history (O'Riley, "Place, Position, and Postcolonial Haunting," 78–80).

78. Horkheimer and Adorno, *Dialectic of Enlightenment,* 67.

79. Lattimore, *The Odyssey of Homer,* 139; Horkheimer and Adorno, *Dialectic of Enlightenment,* 32–33.

80. Lattimore, *The Odyssey of Homer,* 190.

81. Horkheimer and Adorno, *Dialectic of Enlightenment,* 33.

82. Djebar, *La Femme sans sépulture,* 150.

83. Detienne and Vernant, *Cunning Intelligence,* 46.

84. Blanchot, *The Book to Come,* 4.

85. Cixous, "Sorties," 74, 75.

86. Djebar, *La Femme sans sépulture,* 48, 84.

87. Clarisse Zimra also notes that Djebar "reinscribes the female body as transgressive in both the Orient and the Occident: posed, painted and celebrated, because it can be tortured, butchered, and dismembered" ("Disorienting the Subject," 167).

88. Djebar, *La Femme sans sépulture,* 209. Conversely, women resisters' testimonies show that "familial conventions" can also be strategically upheld to assert autonomy and the power of decision. About her participation in the Battle of Algiers, Zohra Drif said that "Algerian woman is so present in family life, so indispensable, that when there is a war, her relatives appeal to her. Indeed, woman's place is the one that she wanted to take and that her abilities gave her. In my opinion, the important fact is that we have proved that if we decide to undertake an action, there are no truly absolute hindrances in our society" (Amrane-Minne, *Des Femmes dans la guerre d'Algérie,* 138–39).

89. Djebar, *La Femme sans sépulture,* 210.

90. Djebar, *Fantasia,* 55.

91. Cixous, "Sorties," 74.

92. Djebar, *La Femme sans sépulture,* 214.

93. Humphries, *Ovid's Metamorphoses,* 124.

94. Blanchot, *The Book to Come,* 4.

95. Humphries, *Ovid's Metamorphoses,* 124.

96. Horkheimer and Adorno, *Dialectic of Enlightenment,* 59.

97. Mooney, *The Alexandra of Lycophron,* 75.

98. Blanchot, *The Book to Come,* 3.

99. Djebar, *La Femme sans sépulture,* 214.

100. Horkheimer and Adorno, *Dialectic of Enlightenment,* 58.

101. Djebar, *La Femme sans sépulture,* 107–8.

102. See Blanchot, *The Book to Come,* 4–5; Horkheimer and Adorno, *Dialectic of Enlightenment,* 34. Furthermore, Horkheimer and Adorno note that Odysseus owes his survival to Circe's prophecies about the Sirens, Scylla and Charybdis, which "are ultimately of advantage only to male survival" (73).

103. Lattimore, *The Odyssey of Homer,* 186.

104. Djebar, *La Femme sans sépulture,* 214.

105. Humphries, *Ovid's Metamorphoses,* 124.

6. ALLERGY IN THE BODY POLITIC

1. Cixous, "De la scène de l'Inconscient," 20.

2. Shiach, *Hélène Cixous,* 6 (my emphasis).

3. The brief title of Cixous's essay, "Sorties," is translated as "Sorties: Out and Out: Attacks/Ways Out/Forays." The translator of Derrida's *De la grammatologie* proposes "departure" for *sortie* (*Of Grammatology,* trans. Gayatri Chakravorty Spivak, 162), and that of *La Dissémination,* "exit" (*Dissemination,* trans. Barbara Johnson, 336).

4. Derrida, *Politics of Friendship,* 8, 114.

5. Cixous and Calle-Gruber, *Rootprints,* 111; Cixous, "*Coming to Writing,*" 24.

6. Cixous, *L'Indiade,* 82. See Derrida's analysis of love as "drive of appropriation" (*Politics of Friendship,* 65), to which is opposed "disappropriation" (64).

7. Kamuf, "To Give Place," 75. Kamuf analyzes a resistance to Cixous's writings that takes the form of a denunciation of Cixous's politics as socially irrelevant, mythological, utopian.

8. Cixous, "De la scène de l'Inconscient," 28.

9. Conley, *Hélène Cixous: Writing the Feminine,* 139.

10. Cixous and Calle-Gruber, *Rootprints,* 6.

11. Derrida, *Politics of Friendship,* 67.

12. Cixous, *Vivre l'orange,* 20, 22.

13. See the biographical information compiled by Mireille Calle-Gruber in *Rootprints,* 209–13.

14. Cixous, "Fiction and Its Phantoms," 38.

15. Cixous, "Sorties," 72, 73.

16. Cixous, "My Algeriance," 156.

17. "Two hates shared the hearts differently between themselves. One of them, which I will never forgive, the colonialists' hate, was made of the scorn from which thieves and usurpers, like all despots, forge deceitful arms. In response there was

the other one, which I forgive, even until today, the hate with eyes burning with tears of the humiliated and deprived, the hate of the 'Arabs' for all that was collected in the 'F' group. I was the first person to side with that uprising hate, I cried Friend! Friend! and they tore me to pieces" (ibid., 162).

18. Cixous, "Bare Feet," 59.

19. See Mouloud Feraoun's *Journal* written during the Algerian War, which provides remarkable reflections on the relations between Europeans and Algerians in terms that can be linked to Cixous's; for instance: "We have been co-existing for a century without the slightest curiosity. The only thing left to do is to harvest this deliberate indifference that is the opposite of love" (Feraoun, *Journal 1955–1962*, 42).

20. Cixous, "Sorties," 71.

21. Cixous, "Letter to Zohra Drif," 87.

22. Cixous, *So Close*, 75.

23. Blanchot, *The Writing of the Disaster*, 22.

24. Levinas, *God, Death, and Time*, 181. See Sarah Hammerschlag's reading of uprootedness in Levinas in *The Figural Jew*, 117–65.

25. Levinas, *Otherwise Than Being*, 15. The subordination of freedom in Levinas is thus articulated to a reappraisal of the will and of action. For instance, "Political theory derives justice from the undiscussed value of spontaneity" (Levinas, *Totality and Infinity*, 83), or the radical passivity of the I "is not even opposed to activity, for it is beyond the passivity that would merely be the reverse side of the act" (Levinas, *God, Death, and Time*, 162).

26. Blanchot, *Writing of the Disaster*, 25.

27. Cixous, "Letter to Zohra Drif," 83.

28. Cixous, "My Algeriance," 171.

29. Cixous, "Letter to Zohra Drif," 87.

30. Cixous, *So Close* 45, 7.

31. Drif, *La Mort de mes frères*, 7.

32. Feraoun concurs with Drif: "The French have remained foreigners. They have always believed that they were Algeria. Now that we feel that we are rather strong or that we see them as a bit weak, we are telling them: No, gentlemen. We are Algeria. You are foreigners on our land" (Feraoun, *Journal 1955–1962*, 42).

33. Cixous, *So Close*, 120.

34. Levinas, *Totality and Infinity*, 29, 27.

35. Levinas, *God, Death, and Time*, 162.

36. Levinas, *Totality and Infinity*, 39.

37. Cixous, *Prénoms de personne*, 6.

38. Cixous, "Sorties," 71.

39. Cixous, *So Close*, 49.

40. For examples, see Cixous, *So Close*, 24, and *Reveries of the Wild Woman*, 4, 5.

41. Cixous, *Reveries of the Wild Woman*, 70.

42. Recalling that in French, Heimweh is translated as mal du pays, Cixous notes, "Or ce mal, c'est aussi le mal que vous (a) fait le pays" (Cixous, *Prénoms de personne,* 33), translated as "But this *mal* is also the evil that the country did to you" (Cixous, "Fiction and Its Phantoms," 34).

43. Cixous, "My Algeriance," 154.

44. Cixous, *Reveries of the Wild Woman,* 7; Cixous, "My Algeriance," 167. In spite of her title, Lynn Penrod agrees that "the very concept of exile 'from' is one, which, in Cixous's case, would be difficult to argue" (Penrod, "Algeriance, Exile, and Hélène Cixous," 136).

45. Levinas, *Totality and Infinity,* 156.

46. Derrida, *Adieu to Emmanuel Levinas,* 129.

47. Levinas, "Heidegger, Gagarin and Us," in *Difficult Freedom,* 232.

48. Levinas, *Otherwise Than Being,* 8.

49. Derrida, *Adieu to Emmanuel Levinas,* 37.

50. Levinas, *Totality and Infinity,* 157.

51. Derrida, *Adieu to Emmanuel Levinas,* 41–42.

52. Levinas, *Totality and Infinity,* 173.

53. Cixous, *Reveries of the Wild Woman,* 4.

54. See the old woman's quip in Djebar's *Women of Algiers:* "in our country all *fatmas* are called Fatma!" (Djebar, *Women of Algiers in Their Apartment,* 36).

55. Cixous, *Reveries of the Wild Woman,* 54. See Derrida, who ties the proper name to his reflection on hospitality (Derrida, with Dufourmantelle, *Of Hospitality,* 137–39).

56. Cixous, *Reveries of the Wild Woman,* 53.

57. See Derrida, *Adieu to Emmanuel Levinas,* 95. Derrida recalls Benveniste's analysis of "the foreigner (*hostis*) welcomed as guest or as enemy," a contiguity about which he coins the term *hostipitality* (Derrida, with Dufourmantelle, *Of Hospitality,* 45).

58. Cixous, *Prénoms de personne,* 258. For Mohamed as "prophet," see Cixous, *Reveries of the Wild Woman,* 79.

59. Ibid., 85.

60. Blanchot, *The Book to Come,* 79.

61. Cixous, *Reveries of the Wild Woman,* 86.

62. Cixous, *So Close,* 89.

63. Cixous, "My Algeriance," 153.

64. Cixous, *So Close,* 45. The issue of strangeness in connection with being born in Algeria could be related to Albert Camus's well-known treatment of the question in *L'Etranger,* translated as *The Stranger* or *The Outsider,* but meaning as well "the foreigner."

65. In "How Not to Speak of Algeria," Cixous explains why she has not written on postcolonial Algeria: "I thought: at long last Algeria is free and independent;

I am not going to appropriate it now in writing. . . . I voluntarily abstained from writing on Algeria for ethical and political reasons" (Cixous, *Volleys of Humanity,* 164).

66. Cixous, *So Close,* 44.

67. Cixous, *Reveries of the Wild Woman,* 85.

68. Derrida, *Writing and Difference,* 103.

69. Cixous, "Letter to Zohra Drif," 87–88; Cixous, *So Close,* 15.

70. Cixous, "Letter to Zohra Drif," 88.

71. Cixous, *So Close,* 69.

72. Cixous, "Letter to Zohra Drif," 87.

73. Derrida, "Abraham, the Other," 7, 34.

74. Cixous, "Letter to Zohra Drif," 87; Cixous, *So Close,* 15.

75. Cixous, *So Close,* 13.

76. Cixous, "Letter to Zohra Drif," 86, 88.

77. Cixous, *So Close,* 20, 19.

78. Derrida, with Dufourmantelle, *Of Hospitality,* 135.

79. Derrida and Roudinesco, *For What Tomorrow . . .,* 59.

80. Derrida, *Paper Machine,* 194.

81. Cixous, *So Close,* 106, 26.

82. Cixous, *Volleys of Humanity,* 165.

CONCLUSION

1. Said, *Orientalism,* 2, 5.

2. Loomba is quoted by Cass, "Interrogating Orientalism," 27.

3. Fanon, "L'Algérie se dévoile," 14. Haakon Chevalier translates Fanon's title as "Algeria Unveiled" instead of Algeria unveils itself (or herself), thereby weakening the emphasis on resisters' agency reflected in Fanon's essay.

4. Derrida, "A Silkworm of One's Own," in Cixous and Derrida, *Veils,* 31–32.

5. Heidegger, "Plato's Doctrine of Truth," 174.

6. Lazreg, *Questioning the Veil.* The question of visibility, which echoes the Western perception of "the generic image of the veiled Muslim woman" (Kemp, *Voices and Veils,* 1), is conversely explained by Leila Ahmed as a strategy of Islamism, the emergence of which she examines in Egypt: "Most notable and visible was their signature commitment to gender segregation and thus also to the presence of the hijab as mandatory for women" (Ahmed, *A Quiet Revolution,* 100).

7. Tillion, *The Republic of Cousins,* 174.

8. On the veil as a sign of "urbanity," see Mernissi, *Dreams of Trespass,* 120. Regarding changing veiling fashions, see Ahmed, *A Quiet Revolution,* 83, 101; and Soueif, "The Language of the Veil."

9. Ahmed, *A Quiet Revolution,* 125, 40, 89.

10. Lazreg, *Questioning the Veil,* 48, 49.

11. Ahmed, "The Discourse of the Veil," 43.

12. Fanon, "L'Algérie se dévoile," 33.

13. Said, *Orientalism,* 58. For the need to historicize what is assessed as regressive archaism, see Mernissi, *Beyond the Veil,* ix.

14. Fanon, "L'Algérie se dévoile," 16, 21.

15. Alloula, *The Colonial Harem,* 14.

16. Fanon, "L'Algérie se dévoile," 15, 26, 16.

17. "Mimicry emerges as one of the most elusive and effective strategies of colonial power and knowledge" (Bhabha, *The Location of Culture,* 85). Bhabha recognizes the ambivalence of the discourse of mimicry in that "colonial mimicry is the desire for a reformed, recognizable Other, *as a subject of a difference that is almost the same, but not quite*" (86).

18. Fanon, "L'Algérie se dévoile," 42. See Homa Hoodfar's discussion of strategic uses of the veil in Iran against imposed gender roles on the part of the state (Hoodfar, "The Veil in Their Minds and on Our Heads").

19. Fromentin, *Une Année au Sahel,* 31. See also Lyotard's *La Guerre des Algériens,* in which the social unity of the population in the medina is said to be "made concrete in the very topography of the traditional cities: they appear as closed and impenetrable, but only to the adversary, to the foreigner" (212).

20. Fanon, "L'Algérie se dévoile," 32.

21. Tillion, *The Republic of Cousins,* 172, 173.

22. Alloula, *Colonial Harem,* 38, 118.

23. Zimra, "Disorienting the Subject," 161.

24. On the distinction between *hijab,* "a key visual/spatial/ethical concept," and *jilbab,* the garment covering women, see Mernissi, *The Veil and the Male Elite,* 93, 180; and Barlas, "Women's Readings of the Qur'an," 267. Both also discuss the recommendation as opposed to the prescription to wear the veil (Mernissi, *The Veil and the Male Elite,* 186–87, Barlas, "Women's Readings of the Qur'an," 267).

25. For the reference to early feminists in the Arab world, see Mernissi, *Dreams of Trespass,* 128. Margot Badran has studied "a feminist discourse and practice articulated within an Islamic paradigm," at times in convergence with secular feminism (Badran, *Feminism in Islam,* 242).

26. Chebel, *L'Imaginaire arabo-musulman,* 96.

27. About the connection, which is also a disruption, between the religious and the cultural in Djebar, see Rice, *Time Signatures,* 91. On *laïcité* or secularism in independent Algeria, see Djebar, *La Disparition de la langue française,* 163, 168.

28. Fanon, "L'Algérie se dévoile," 40.

29. Djebar, *Women of Algiers in Their Apartment,* 139.

30. Djebar, *A Sister to Scheherazade,* 31.

31. Djebar, *Women of Algiers in Their Apartment,* 140.

32. Djebar, *Fantasia*, 128.

33. Lazreg, *The Eloquence of Silence*, 128. For Lazreg, while demystifying the colonial discourse about women, Fanon also shares with the French a residue of prejudice about Algerian women's roles.

34. See Aït Sabbah, *Woman in the Muslim Unconscious*.

35. Fanon, "L'Algérie se dévoile," 23.

36. Djebar, *Women of Algiers in Their Apartment*, 139.

37. Zimra, "Disorienting the Subject," 168.

38. Djebar, *Women of Algiers in Their Apartment*, 139.

39. Fanon, "L'Algérie se dévoile," 23; Derrida, *Specters of Marx*, 7; Derrida and Stiegler, *Echographies of Television*, 121.

40. Fanon, "L'Algérie se dévoile," 25, 26.

41. Djebar, *Women of Algiers in Their Apartment*, 153. About the uses of images of the harem at the beginning of French colonization, see Grigsby, "Orients and Colonies."

42. Djebar, *Fantasia*, 127–28, 125.

43. Djebar, *Women of Algiers in Their Apartment*, 140.

44. Djebar, *Fantasia*, 124.

45. Djebar, *The Tongue's Blood Does Not Run Dry*, 34.

46. Djebar, *A Sister to Scheherazade*, 86, 145.

47. Cixous, "Sorties," 70.

48. Cixous and Derrida, *Veils*, 101.

49. Derrida, *Memoirs of the Blind*, 32.

50. Cixous, "Savoir," in Cixous and Derrida, *Veils*, 9.

51. Cixous, "Writing Blind," 139.

52. Diderot, *Letter on the Blind for the Use of Those Who Can See*, 171.

53. Cixous and Derrida, *Veils*, 3; Cixous, *Messie*, 143.

54. Cixous and Derrida, *Veils*, 9; "She saw that she was seeing the visible it was a joy a youth a marvelous lightness, and the source of new illusions, yes" (Cixous, *Messie*, 145).

55. Cixous and Derrida, *Veils*, 8.

56. Plato, *The Republic*, 193. "She had her leash. Her myopia her native fault. As the prisoner of the cave, she had never broken the membrane of credulity" (Cixous, *Messie*, 119).

57. Derrida, *Memoirs of the Blind*, 12.

58. Plato, *The Republic*, 195.

59. Heidegger, "Plato's Doctrine of Truth," 164, 165.

60. Derrida addresses the ways in which Heidegger's thought of *aletheia* remains caught within the effects of the *topos* or topic of the veil (Cixous and Derrida, *Veils*, 75). Likewise, Jean-Luc Nancy writes that with the very sense of arrival to *presence*, Heidegger's *aletheia*, "like all other types of truth, continues to operate

as presentation, placing-in-view, exhibition, and manifestation," thus still within a relation to visibility, a "placing-in-the-light on a scene," if not to vision (Nancy, *The Sense of the World,* 16).

61. Cixous, "Writing Blind," 140; Cixous and Derrida, *Veils,* 13.

62. Plato, *Republic,* 196; Heidegger, "Plato's Doctrine of Truth," 174; Derrida, *Memoirs of the Blind,* 16.

63. Cixous and Derrida, *Veils,* 9.

64. Cixous, *Messie,* 115. See also her remark that "voices touch each other" over the phone (Cixous, *First Days of the Year,* 145), so that telephony would be better understood as "teleaphony" (Cixous, *La Fiancée juive,* 87).

65. Cixous and Derrida, *Veils,* 35, 51–54, 84–85.

66. Derrida, *Paper Machine,* 144; Derrida, *On Touching,* 41.

67. Derrida, *Memoirs of the Blind,* 104; Cixous, *Portrait of Jacques Derrida,* 48.

68. Cixous, *Messie,* 143; see Cixous and Derrida, *Veils,* 11.

69. Cixous and Derrida, *Veils,* 9.

70. Cixous, "Writing Blind," 140; Cixous and Derrida, *Veils,* 9, 11.

71. Cixous and Derrida, *Veils,* 12, 13, 9.

72. Cixous, *Messie,* 121, 125.

73. Cixous and Derrida, *Veils,* 34–35. Mireille Calle-Gruber argues that "*Savoir* is not an unveiling, it makes veiling visible" ("Le fil de soie," 78).

74. Cixous, "Writing Blind," 140.

75. Cixous and Derrida, *Veils,* 85.

76. About the messianic without messianism as "the coming of the other, the absolute and unpredictable singularity of the *arrivant as justice*" and as "thinking of the other and of the event to come," see Derrida, *Specters of Marx,* 28, 59. Both Derrida and Cixous link the messianic and affirmation (Derrida, ibid., 89; Cixous's title *Messie* affirms: "Mais si!").

77. Derrida, *Memoirs of the Blind,* 127, 65.

78. Cixous, *Messie,* 118, 119.

79. Cixous and Derrida, *Veils,* 86.

80. Derrida has abundantly reflected on the margin, the *parage,* the spur and the cape, as well as the passage and the *pas,* which is relevant to the thinking of the event, for instance as the minimal question "qu'est-ce qui se *passe*?/what is going on?" (Derrida, *Psyche,* 80).

81. Mernissi, *The Veil and the Male Elite,* 94.

82. Cixous and Derrida, *Veils,* 13.

83. Nancy, "The Political and/or Politics," 6.

84. Ziarek, *An Ethics of Dissensus,* 1.

85. Calle-Gruber, *Du café à l'éternité,* 154.

86. Nancy, "The Political and/or Politics," 9.

Bibliography

Abitbol, Michel. *Les Juifs d'Afrique du Nord sous Vichy*. Paris: Maisonneuve et Larose, 1983.

Achour, Christiane Chaulet. *Ecritures algériennes. La règle du genre*. Paris: L'Harmattan, 2012.

Ahmed, Leila. "The Discourse of the Veil." In David A. Bailey and Gilane Tawadros, eds., *Veil: Veiling, Representation and Contemporary Art*, 40–55. Cambridge: MIT Press, 2003.

———. *A Quiet Revolution: The Veil's Resurgence, from the Middle East to America*. New Haven: Yale University Press, 2011.

Aït Sabbah, Fatna. *Woman in the Muslim Unconscious*. Trans. Mary Jo Lakeland. New York: Pergamon, 1984.

Algérie Littérature/Action, eds. "Entretien avec Assia Djebar." *Algérie Littérature/Action* 1 (May 1996): 183–87.

Alloula, Malek. *The Colonial Harem*. Trans. Myrna Godzich and Wlad Godzich. Minneapolis: University of Minnesota Press, 1986.

Amrane-Minne, Danièle Djamila. *Des Femmes dans la guerre d'Algérie*. Paris: Karthala, 1994.

Appiah, Anthony. "The Uncompleted Argument: Du Bois and the Illusion of Race." In Henry Louis Gates, ed., *"Race," Writing, and Difference*, 21–37. Chicago: University of Chicago Press, 1986.

Azéma, Jean-Pierre et al. "Liberté pour l'Histoire." *Libération*, December 13, 2005. Accessed July 21, 2014. http://www.liberation.fr/societe/2005/12/13/liberte-pour-l-histoire_541669.

Babayan, Liana. "La représentation de l'exil dans les oeuvres de Djebar et de Cixous: *Vaste est la prison, Nulle part dans la maison de mon père, Les Rêveries de la femme sauvage*." PhD diss., University of Georgia, 2010.

Badran, Margot. *Feminism in Islam: Secular and Religious Convergences.* Oxford: Oneworld, 2009.

Bailey, David A. and Gilane Tawadros, eds. *Veil: Veiling, Representation and Contemporary Art.* Cambridge: MIT Press, 2003.

Barclay, Fiona. *Writing Postcolonial France. Haunting, Literature, and the Maghreb.* Lanham, MD: Lexington, 2011.

Barlas, Asma. "Women's Readings of the Qur'an." In Jane Dammen McAuliffe, ed., *The Cambridge Companion to the Qur'an*, 255–71. Cambridge: Cambridge University Press, 2006.

Beauvoir, Simone de. *Force of Circumstance.* Trans. Richard Howard. New York: Putnam's, 1965.

Belarbi, Aïcha, ed. *Femmes et Islam.* Casablanca: Editions Le Fennec, 1998.

Bensmaïa, Réda. *Experimental Nations, Or, The Invention of the Maghreb.* Trans. Alyson Waters. Princeton: Princeton University Press, 2003.

———. "Multilingualism and National 'Character': On Abdelkebir Khatibi's 'bilanguage.'" In Anne-Emmanuelle Berger, ed., *Algeria in Others' Languages*, 161–83. Ithaca: Cornell University Press, 2002.

———. "*La nouba des femmes du Mont Chenoua*: Introduction to the Cinematic Fragment." *World Literature Today* 70, no. 4 (Autumn 1996): 877–85.

Bertrand, Louis. *Les Villes d'Or. Algérie et Tunisie romaines.* Paris: Arthème Fayard et Cie, 1921.

Bhabha, Homi. *The Location of Culture.* New York: Routledge, 1994.

Blanchot, Maurice. *The Book to Come.* Trans. Charlotte Mandell. Stanford: Stanford University Press, 2003.

———. *Friendship.* Trans. Elizabeth Rottenberg. Stanford: Stanford University Press, 1997.

———.*The Infinite Conversation.* Trans. Susan Hanson. Minneapolis: University of Minnesota Press, 1993.

———. *The Writing of the Disaster.* Trans. Ann Smock. Lincoln: University of Nebraska Press, 1986.

Bonn, Charles. *Le Roman algérien de langue française.* Paris: L'Harmattan, 1985.

Boudjedra, Rachid. *Lettres algériennes.* Paris: Grasset, 1995.

Bourdieu, Pierre. *The Algerians.* Trans. Alan C. M. Ross. Boston: Beacon, 1962.

Branche, Raphaëlle. *La torture et l'armée pendant la guerre d'Algérie 1954–1962.* Paris: Gallimard, 2001.

Bray, Abigail. *Hélène Cixous, Writing and Sexual Difference.* Basingstoke: Palgrave Macmillan, 2004.

Budig-Markin, Valérie. "Writing and Filming the Cries of Silence." *World Literature Today* 70, no. 4 (Autumn 1996): 893–904.

Calle-Gruber, Mireille. *Assia Djebar ou la résistance de l'écriture. Regards d'un écrivain d'Algérie.* Paris: Maisonneuve et Larose, 2001.

———. *Du café à l'éternité: Hélène Cixous à l'oeuvre*. Paris: Galilée, 2002.

———. "Le fil de soie." In Marie-Louise Mallet, ed., *L'animal autobiographique: Autour de Jacques Derrida*, 61–85. Paris: Galilée, 1999.

Camus, Albert. "Misère de la Kabylie." In *Chroniques algériennes, 1939–1958: Essais*. Paris: Gallimard, Pléiade, 1965.

———. *The Stranger*. Trans. Matthew Ward. New York: Vintage, 1989.

Caruth, Cathy. *Unclaimed Experience: Trauma, Narrative, and History*. Baltimore: Johns Hopkins University Press, 1996.

Cass, Jeffrey. "Interrogating Orientalism: Theories and Practices." In Diane Long Hoeveler and Jeffrey Cass, eds., *Interrogating Orientalism: Contextual Approaches and Pedagogical Practices*, 25–45. Columbus: Ohio State University Press, 2006.

Césaire, Aimé. *Discourse on Colonialism*. Trans. Joan Pinkham. New York: Monthly Review Press, 1972.

Chebel, Malek. *L'Imaginaire arabo-musulman*. Paris: Presses universitaires de France, 1993.

Chikhi, Beïda, ed. *Figures tutélaires, textes fondateurs: Francophonie et héritage critique*. Paris: Presses de l'Université Paris-Sorbonne, 2009.

Cixous, Hélène. *L'Ange au secret*. Paris: Des Femmes, 1991.

———. "Bare Feet." In *An Algerian Childhood*, ed. Leïla Sebbar, trans. Marjolijn de Jager, 49–59. St. Paul, MN: Ruminator, 2001.

———. "Coming to Writing." In *"Coming to Writing" and Other Essays*, 1–58. Trans. Sarah Cornell, Deborah Jenson, Ann Liddle, and Susan Sellers. Cambridge: Harvard University Press, 1991.

———. "De la scène de l'Inconscient à la scène de l'Histoire." In *Hélène Cixous, chemins d'une écriture*, ed. Françoise van Rossum-Guyon and Myriam Diaz-Diocaretz, 15–34. Saint Denis: Presses Universitaires de Vincennes; Amsterdam: Rodopi, 1990.

———. *The Day I Wasn't There*. Trans. Beverley Bie Brahic. Evanston: Northwestern University Press, 2006.

———. *La Fiancée juive: De la tentation*. Paris: Des Femmes, 1995.

———. "Fiction and Its Phantoms." In *Volleys of Humanity: Essays 1972–2009*, ed. and trans. Eric Prenowitz, 15–40. Edinburgh: Edinburgh University Press, 2011.

———. *First Days of the Year*. Trans. Catherine A. F. MacGillivray. Minneapolis: University of Minnesota Press, 1998.

———. "How Not to Speak of Algeria." In *Volleys of Humanity: Essays, 1972–2009*, 160–76. Ed. Eric Prenowitz. Edinburgh: Edinburgh University Press, 2011.

———. *L'Indiade ou L'Inde de leurs rêves*. Paris: Théâtre du Soleil, 1987.

———. *Inside*. Trans. Carol Barko. New York: Schocken, 1986.

———. "The Laugh of the Medusa." Trans. Keith Cohen and Paula Cohen. *Signs* 1, no. 4 (1976): 875–93.

———. "Letter to Zohra Drif." *Algeriad*, ed. Kostas Myrsiades and Geetha Ramanathan, trans. Eric Prenowitz. *College Literature* 30, no. 1 (Winter 2003): 82–90.

———. *Manhattan: Letters from Prehistory*. Trans. Beverley Bie Brahic. New York: Fordham University Press, 2007.

———. *Messie*. Paris: Des Femmes, 1996.

———. "My Algeriance, in Other Words: To Depart Not to Arrive from Algeria." In *Stigmata. Escaping Texts*, 153–72. Trans. Eric Prenowitz. New York: Routledge, 1998.

———. "The Names of Oran." trans. Eric Prenowitz. *Algeria in Others' Languages*. Ed. Anne-Emmanuelle Berger. Ithaca, NY: Cornell University Press, 2002.

———. *OR les lettres de mon père*. Paris: Des femmes, 1997.

———. *Osnabrück*. Paris: Des Femmes, 1999.

———. *Portrait du soleil*. Paris: Des Femmes, 1999.

———. *Portrait of Jacques Derrida as a Young Jewish Saint*. Trans. Beverley Bie Brahic. New York: Columbia University Press, 2004.

———. *Le Prénom de Dieu*. Paris: Grasset, 1967.

———. *Prénoms de personne*. Paris: Seuil, 1974.

———. *Reveries of the Wild Woman*. Trans. Beverley Bie Brahic. Evanston, IL: Northwestern University Press, 2006.

———. *So Close*. Trans. Peggy Kamuf. Cambridge: Polity Press, 2009.

———. "Sorties: Out and Out: Attacks/Ways Out/Forays." In *The Newly Born Woman*, by Hélène Cixous and Catherine Clément. Trans. Betsy Wing, 63–132. Minneapolis: University of Minnesota Press, 1986.

———. *The Third Body*. Trans. Keith Cohen. Evanston: Northwestern University Press, 1999.

———. *Three Steps on the Ladder of Writing*. Trans. Sarah Cornell and Susan Sellers. New York: Columbia University Press, 1993.

———. *Vivre l'orange/To Live the Orange. L'Heure de Clarice Lispector*. Paris: Des Femmes, 1989.

———. *Volleys of Humanity: Essays, 1972–2009*. Ed. Eric Prenowitz. Edinburgh: Edinburgh University Press, 2011.

———. "Writing Blind." In *Stigmata. Escaping Texts*, trans. Eric Prenowitz, 139–52. New York: Routledge, 1998.

Cixous, Hélène and Mireille Calle-Gruber. *Rootprints: Memory and Life Writing*. Trans. Eric. Prenowitz. New York: Routledge, 1997.

Cixous, Hélène, Mireille Calle-Gruber, and Assia Djebar. *Au théâtre au cinéma au féminin*. Paris: L'Harmattan, 2001.

Cixous, Hélène and Jacques Derrida. *Voiles*. Paris: Galilée, 1998.

———. *Veils*. Trans. Geoffrey Bennington. Stanford: Stanford University Press, 2001.

Cixous, Hélène and Frédéric-Yves Jeannet. *Rencontre terrestre*. Paris: Galilée, 2005.

Clerc, Jeanne-Marie. *Assia Djebar: Ecrire, transgresser, résister.* Paris: L'Harmattan, 1997.

Conley, Verena Andermatt. *Hélène Cixous.* Toronto: University of Toronto Press, 1992.

———. *Hélène Cixous: Writing the Feminine.* Lincoln: University of Nebraska Press, 1991.

Coquery-Vidrovitch, Catherine, Gilles Manceron, and Gérard Noiriel. "Les historiens n'ont pas le monopole de la mémoire." *Le Monde,* November 7, 2008. Accessed July 21, 2014. http://www.lemonde.fr/idees/article/2008/11/07/les-historiens-n-ont-pas-le-monopole-de-la-memoire-par-catherine-coquery-vidrovitch-gilles-manceron-et-gerard-noiriel_1116082_3232.html.

Cremonese, Laura. *Dialectique du masculine et du féminin dans l'oeuvre d'Hélène Cixous.* Fasano: Schena, 1997.

Daoud, Zakya. *Féminisme et politique au Maghreb. Soixante ans de lutte.* Paris: Maisonneuve et Larose, 1994.

De Jager, Marjolijn. "Translating Assia Djebar's *Femmes d'Alger dans leur Appartement:* Listening for the Silence." *World Literature Today* 70, no. 4 (Autumn 1996): 856–58.

Déjeux, Jean. *Assia Djebar, romancière algérienne, cinéaste arabe.* Sherbrook, Quebec: Naaman, 1984.

———. *Femmes d'Algérie. Légendes, Traditions, Histoire, Littérature.* Paris: La Boîte à Documents, 1987.

———. *La Littérature féminine de langue française au Maghreb.* Paris: Karthala, 1994.

Deldyck, Jean-Jacques. *Le Processus d'acculturation des Juifs d'Algérie.* Paris: L'Harmattan, 2000.

De Man, Paul. *The Rhetoric of Romanticism.* New York: Columbia University Press, 1984.

Derrida, Jacques. "Abraham, the Other." In Bettina Bergo, Joseph Cohen, and Raphael Zagury-Orly, eds., *Judeities,* 1–35, 239–40. Trans. Bettina Bergo and Michael B. Smith. New York: Fordham University Press, 2007.

———. *Adieu to Emmanuel Levinas.* Trans. Pascale-Anne Brault and Michael Naas. Stanford: Stanford University Press, 1999.

———. *The Animal That Therefore I Am.* Ed. Marie-Louise Mallet. Trans. David Wills. New York: Fordham University Press, 2008.

———. *Archive Fever. A Freudian Impression.* Trans. Eric Prenowitz. Chicago: University of Chicago Press, 1996.

———. *The Beast and the Sovereign II.* Trans. Geoffrey Bennington. Chicago: University of Chicago Press, 2011.

———. "Circumfession." In *Jacques Derrida.* Trans. Geoffrey Bennington. Chicago: University of Chicago Press, 1993.

———. *Demeure: Fiction and Testimony.* Trans. Elizabeth Rottenberg. Stanford: Stanford University Press, 2000.

———. *Dissemination.* Trans. Barbara Johnson. Chicago: University of Chicago Press, 1981.

———. "Force of Law: The 'Mystical Foundation of Authority." In Gil Anidjar, ed., *Acts of Religion*, 230–98. Trans. Mary Quaintance. New York: Routledge, 2002.

———. *Geneses, Genealogies, Genres, and Genius.* Trans. Beverley Bie Brahic. New York: Columbia University Press, 2003.

———. *"H.C. for Life, That Is to Say . . ."* Trans. Laurent Milesi and Stefan Herbrechter. Stanford: Stanford University Press, 2006.

———. *Margins of Philosophy.* Trans. Alan Bass. Chicago: University of Chicago Press, 1982.

———. *Memoirs of the Blind: The Self-Portrait and Other Ruins.* Trans. Pascale-Anne Brault and Michael Naas. Chicago: University of Chicago Press, 1993.

———. *Monolingualism of the Other; Or, The Prosthesis of Origin.* Trans. Patrick Mensah. Stanford: Stanford University Press, 1998.

———. *Of Grammatology.* Trans. Gayatri Chakravorty Spivak. Baltimore: Johns Hopkins University Press, 1976.

———. *Of Hospitality.* With Anne Dufourmantelle. Trans. Rachel Bowlby. Stanford: Stanford University Press, 2000.

———. *On Touching—Jean-Luc Nancy.* Trans. Christine Irizarry. Stanford: Stanford University Press, 2005.

———. *Paper Machine.* Trans. Rachel Bowlby. Stanford: Stanford University Press, 2005.

———. *Politics of Friendship.* Trans. George Collins. New York: Verso, 1997.

———. *Psyche: Inventions of the Other,* vol. 1. Ed. Peggy Kamuf and Elizabeth Rottenberg. Stanford: Stanford University Press, 2007.

———. *Specters of Marx: The State of the Debt, the Work of Mourning, and the New International.* Trans. Peggy Kamuf. New York: Routledge, 1994.

———. *A Taste for the Secret.* Trans. Giacomo Donis. Cambridge: Polity, 2001.

———. *Writing and Difference.* Trans. Alan Bass. Chicago: University of Chicago Press, 1978.

Derrida, Jacques and Elisabeth Roudinesco. *For What Tomorrow . . . A Dialogue.* Trans. Jeff Fort. Stanford: Stanford University Press, 2004.

Derrida, Jacques and Bernard Stiegler. *Echographies of Television.* Trans. Jennifer Bajorek. Cambridge: Polity, 2002.

Desbois, Evelyne. "Des images en quarantaine. Guerre d'Algérie, une mémoire amputée de ses images." In Jean-Pierre Rioux, ed., *La Guerre d'Algérie et les Français.* Paris: Fayard, 1990.

Detienne, Marcel and Jean-Pierre Vernant. *Cunning Intelligence in Greek Culture and Society.* Trans. Janet Lloyd. Chicago: University of Chicago Press, 1991.

Dib, Mohammed. "Encounters." *An Algerian Childhood*, 103–13. Ed. Leïla Sebbar. Trans. Marjolijn de Jager. St. Paul, MN: Ruminator, 2001.

Dick, Kirby and Amy Ziering Kofman, dirs. *Derrida, Screenplay and Essays on the Film*. New York: Routledge, 2005.

Diderot, Denis. *Correspondance* I (1713–1757). Ed. Georges Roth. Paris: Minuit, 1955.

———. *Letter on the Blind for the Use of Those Who Can See*. Trans. Kate E. Tunstall. In Kate E. Tunstall, *Blindness and Enlightenment: An Essay*. New York: Continuum, 2011.

Dine, Philip. *Images of the Algerian War: French Fiction and Film 1954–1992*. Oxford: Oxford University Press, 1994.

Djebar, Assia. *Algerian White*. Trans. David Kelley and Marjolijn de Jager. New York: Seven Stories, 2000.

———. *Les Alouettes naïves*. Paris: Babel, 1997.

———. *La Beauté de Joseph*. Arles: Actes Sud, 1998.

———. *Le Blanc de l'Algérie*. Paris: Albin Michel, 1995.

———. *Ces Voix qui m'assiègent*. Paris: Albin Michel, 1999.

———. *Children of the New World*. Trans. Marjolijn de Jager. New York: Feminist Press at the City University of New York, 2005.

———. *La Disparition de la langue française*. Paris: Albin Michel, 2003.

———. *Fantasia, an Algerian Cavalcade*. Trans. Dorothy S. Blair. London: Quartet, 1989.

———. *Far from Madina*. Trans. Dorothy S. Blair. London: Quartet, 1994.

———. *La Femme sans sépulture*. Paris: Albin Michel, 2002.

———. *The Nouba of the Women of Mount Chenoua*. New York: Women Make Movies, 2007.

———. *Nulle part dans la maison de mon père*. Paris: Fayard, 2007.

———. *A Sister to Scheherazade*. Trans. Dorothy S. Blair. London: Quartet, 1987.

———. *So Vast the Prison*. Trans. Betsy Wing. New York: Seven Stories, 2001.

———. *The Tongue's Blood Does Not Run Dry*. Trans. Tegan Raleigh. New York: Seven Stories, 2006.

———. "Violence de l'autobiographie." In Alfred Hornung and Ernstpeter Ruhe, eds., *Postcolonialisme et Autobiographie*, 89–96. Amsterdam: Rodopi, 1998.

———. *Women of Algiers in Their Apartment*. Trans. Marjolijn de Jager. Charlottesville: University Press of Virginia, 1992.

Donadey, Anne. "Assia Djebar's Poetics of Subversion." *L'esprit créateur* 33, no. 2 (Summer 1993): 107–17.

———. "The Multilingual Strategies of Postcolonial Literature: Assia Djebar's Algerian Palimpsest." *World Literature Today* 74, no. 1 (Winter 2000): 27–36.

———. *Recasting Postcolonialism: Women Writing Between Worlds*. Portsmouth, NH: Heinemann, 2001.

Doubrovsky, Serge. *Fils*. Paris: Galilée, 1977.

Drif, Zohra. *La Mort de mes frères*. Paris: Maspero, 1960.

Droz, Bernard and Evelyne Lever. *Histoire de la guerre d'Algérie, 1954–1962*. Paris: Seuil, 1984.

Dunwoodie, Peter. *Writing French Algeria*. Oxford: Clarendon, 1998.

Elia, Nada. *Trances, Dances, and Vociferations: Agency and Resistance in Africana Women's Narratives*. New York: Garland, 2001.

Ellison, Ralph. *Invisible Man*. New York: Vintage, 1995.

Fanon, Frantz. "L'Algérie se dévoile." In *L' An V de la révolution algérienne*, 12–49. Paris: Maspero, 1960.

———. *Black Skin, White Masks*. Trans. Charles Lam Markmann. New York: Grove, 1967.

Feraoun, Mouloud. *Journal 1955–1962: Reflections on the French-Algerian War*. Ed. James D. Le Sueur. Trans. Mary Ellen Wolf and Claude Feuillade. Lincoln: University of Nebraska Press, 2000.

———. *Jours de Kabylie*. Paris: Seuil, 1968.

Freud, Sigmund. "Femininity." In *The Standard Edition of the Complete Psychological Works*, 22:112–35. Ed. James Strachey. London: Hogarth, 1953–1974.

Fromentin, Eugène. *Une Année au Sahel*. Paris: Michel Lévy Frères, 1859.

Gabara, Rachel. *From Split to Screened Selves: French and Francophone Autobiography in the Third Person*. Stanford: Stanford University Press, 2006.

Gadant, Monique. *Le nationalisme algérien et les femmes*. Paris: L'Harmattan, 1995.

Gafaïti, Hafid. "The Blood of Writing: Assia Djebar's Unveiling of Women and History." *World Literature Today* 70, no. 4 (Autumn 1996): 813–22.

———. "The Monotheism of the Other." In *Algeria in Others' Languages*, ed. Anne-Emmanuelle Berger, 19–43. Ithaca: Cornell University Press, 2002.

Gauvin, Lise. *L'écrivain francophone à la croisée des langues: Entretiens*. Paris: Karthala, 1997.

Geesey, Patricia. "Collective Autobiography: Algerian Women and History in Assia Djebar's *L'Amour, la fantasia*." *Dalhousie French Studies*, no. 35 (1996): 153–67.

Glissant, Edouard. *Introduction à une poétique du divers*. Paris: Gallimard, 1996.

Gosnell, Jonathan R. *The Politics of Frenchness in Colonial Algeria, 1930–1954*. Rochester, NY: University of Rochester Press, 2002.

Gracki, Kathleen. "Assia Djebar et l'écriture de l'autobiographie au pluriel." *Women in French Studies*, no. 2 (Fall 1994): 55–66.

———. "Writing Violence and the Violence of Writing in Assia Djebar's Algerian Quartet." *World Literature Today* 70, no. 4 (Autumn 1996): 835–44.

Grigsby, Darcy Grimaldo. "Orients and Colonies: Delacroix's Algerian Harem." In Beth S. Wright, ed., *The Cambridge Companion to Delacroix*, 69–87. Cambridge: Cambridge University Press, 2001.

Guerin, Frances and Roger Hallas, eds. *The Image and the Witness: Trauma, Memory, and Visual Culture.* London: Wallflower, 2007.

Guillot, Anne. "Assia Djebar: Au commencement de l'aventure littéraire." In Beïda Chikhi, ed., *Figures tutélaires, textes fondateurs: Francophonie et héritage critique,* 181–95. Paris: Presses de l'Université Paris-Sorbonne, 2009.

Hale, Thomas A. *Ecrits d'Aimé Césaire: Bibliographie commentée. Etudes françaises* 14, nos. 3–4 (1978).

Hammerschlag, Sarah. *The Figural Jew: Politics and Identity in Postwar French Thought.* Chicago: University of Chicago Press, 2010.

Hannoum, Abdelmajid. "The Legend of the Kahina: A Study in Historiography and Mythmaking in North Africa." PhD diss., Princeton University, 1995.

Harbi, Mohammed. *L'Algérie et son destin. Croyants ou citoyens.* Paris: Arcantère, 1992.

———. *Le F.L.N. Mirage et réalité.* Paris: J.A., 1980.

———. *Une vie debout: Mémoires politiques,* vol. 1: *1945–1962.* Paris: Découverte, 2001.

Harbi, Mohammed and Benjamin Stora. *La Guerre d'Algérie, la fin de l'amnésie.* Paris: Robert Laffont, 2004.

Heidegger, Martin. "Plato's Doctrine of Truth." In William McNeill, ed., *Pathmarks,* 155–82. Trans. Thomas Sheehan. Cambridge: Cambridge University Press, 1998.

Hiddleston, Jane. *Assia Djebar: Out of Algeria.* Liverpool: Liverpool University Press, 2006.

———. "Feminism and the Question of 'Woman' in Assia Djebar's *Vaste est la prison.*" *Research in African Literatures* 35, no. 4 (Winter 2004): 91–104.

Hoodfar, Homa. "The Veil in Their Minds and on Our Heads." In Elizabeth Castelli, ed., *Women, Gender, Religion,* 420–46. New York: Palgrave, 2001.

Horkheimer, Max and Theodor W. Adorno. *Dialectic of Enlightenment.* Trans. John Cumming. New York: Continuum, 1997.

Humphries, Rolfe, trans. *Ovid's Metamorphoses.* Bloomington: Indiana University Press, 1955.

Huughe, Laurence. "'Ecrire comme un voile': The Problematics of the Gaze in the Work of Assia Djebar." *World Literature Today* 70, no. 4 (Autumn 1996): 867–76.

Ibn Khaldoun. *Histoire des Berbères et des dynasties musulmanes de l'Afrique septentrionale,* vol. 1. Trans. William MacGuckin. Paris: Paul Geuthner, 1968.

Kamuf, Peggy. "To Give Place: Semi-Approaches to Hélène Cixous." *Yale French Studies* 87 (1995): 66–89.

Kateb, Kamel. *Européens, "Indigènes" et Juifs en Algérie (1830–1962). Représentations et Réalités des populations.* Paris: L'Ined, 2001.

Kateb, Yacine. *Parce que c'est une femme.* Paris: Des femmes, 2004.

———. *Le Poète comme un boxeur.* Paris: Seuil, 1994.

Kemp, Anna. *Voices and Veils: Feminism and Islam in French Women's Writing and Activism*. London: Legenda, 2010.

Khatibi, Abdelkebir. "A Colonial Labyrinth." Trans. Catherine Dana. *Yale French Studies* 83, no. 2 (1993): 5–11.

———. "Diglossia." In Anne-Emmanuelle Berger, ed., *Algeria in Others' Languages*, 157–60. Ithaca: Cornell University Press, 2002.

———. *Jacques Derrida, en effet*. Paris: Al Manar, 2007.

———. *Love in Two Languages*. Trans. Richard Howard. Minneapolis: University of Minnesota Press, 1990.

Lattimore, Richmond, trans. *The Odyssey of Homer*. New York: Harper and Row, 1967.

Lazreg, Marnia. *The Eloquence of Silence: Algerian Women in Question*. New York: Routledge, 1994.

———. *Questioning the Veil: Open Letters to Muslim Women*. Princeton: Princeton University Press, 2009.

Le Clézio, Marguerite. "Assia Djebar: Écrire dans la langue adverse." *Contemporary French Civilization* 9, no. 2 (1985): 230–44.

Lejeune, Philippe. *On Autobiography*. Trans. Katherine Leary. Minneapolis: University of Minnesota Press, 1989.

Le Sueur, James D. *Between Terror and Democracy: Algeria Since 1989*. Halifax: Fernwood, 2010.

———. *Uncivil War. Intellectuals and Identity Politics During the Decolonization of Algeria*. Philadelphia: University of Pennsylvania Press, 2001.

Levinas, Emmanuel. *Difficult Freedom: Essays on Judaism*. Trans. Seán Hand. Baltimore: Johns Hopkins University Press, 1997.

———. *God, Death, and Time*. Trans. Bettina Bergo. Stanford: Stanford University Press, 2000.

———. *Otherwise Than Being or Beyond Essence*. Trans. Alphonso Lingis. The Hague: Martinus Nijhoff, 1981.

———. *Totality and Infinity*. Trans. Alphonso Lingis. Pittsburgh: Duquesne University Press, 1969.

Louis, Marie-Victoire. "Les Algériennes, la lutte." In *Algérie, espoirs et réalités, Les Temps Modernes*, nos. 432–33 (July–August 1982): 152–94.

Lyotard, Jean-François. *The Differend: Phrases in Dispute*. Trans. Georges Van Den Abbeele. Minneapolis: University of Minnesota Press, 1988.

———. *La Guerre des Algériens: Ecrits 1956–1963*. Paris: Galilée, 1989.

———. *Political Writings*. Trans. Bill Readings and Kevin Paul Geiman. Minneapolis: University of Minnesota Press, 1993.

Marder, Elissa. *The Mother in the Age of Mechanical Reproduction: Psychoanalysis, Photography, Deconstruction*. New York: Fordham University Press, 2012.

Marx-Scouras, Danielle. "Muffled Screams/Stifled Voices." *Yale French Studies* 82 (1993): 172–82.

Maschino, Maurice T. "La colonisation telle qu'on l'enseigne: L'histoire expurgée de la guerre d'Algérie." *Le Monde diplomatique* (February 2001): 8–9.

Memmi, Albert. *The Colonizer and the Colonized.* Trans. Howard Greenfeld. Boston: Beacon, 1991.

———. *The Liberation of the Jew.* Trans. Judy Hyun. New York: Orion, 1966.

———. *The Pillar of Salt.* Trans. Edouard Roditi. New York: Orion, 1962.

Mernissi, Fatima. *Beyond the Veil.* Bloomington: Indiana University Press, 1987.

———. *Dreams of Trespass: Tales of a Harem Girlhood.* Reading, MA: Addison-Wesley, 1994.

———. *The Forgotten Queens of Islam.* Trans. Mary Jo Lakeland. Minneapolis: University of Minnesota Press, 1993.

———. *The Veil and the Male Elite: A Feminist Interpretation of Women's Rights in Islam.* Trans. Mary Jo Lakeland. Reading, MA: Addison-Wesley, 1991.

———. *Women's Rebellion and Islamic Memory.* Atlantic Highlands, NJ: Zed, 1996.

Montaigne, Michel de. *The Essays.* Trans. M. A. Screech. London: Penguin, 1987.

Mooney, George W., trans. *The Alexandra of Lycophron.* New York: Arno, 1979.

Mortimer, Mildred. "Entretien avec Assia Djebar, écrivain algérien." *Research in African Literatures* 19, no. 2 (Summer 1988): 197–205.

———. "Reappropriating the Gaze in Assia Dejbar's Fiction and Film." *World Literature Today* 70, no. 4 (Autumn 1996): 859–67.

Mosteghanemi, Ahlem. *Algérie: Femme et Ecritures.* Paris: L'Harmattan, 1985.

Motard-Noar, Martine. *Les Fictions d'Hélène Cixous: Une autre langue de femme.* Lexington, KY: French Forum, 1991.

M'Rabet, Fadéla. *La femme algérienne* suivi de *Les Algériennes.* Paris: Maspero, 1979.

Msellati, Henri. *Les Juifs d'Algérie sous le régime de Vichy.* Paris: L'Harmattan, 1999.

Murdoch, H. Adlai. "Rewriting Writing: Identity, Exile and Renewal in Assia Djebar's *L'Amour la fantasia.*" *Yale French Studies* 83 (1993): 71–92.

Nancy, Jean-Luc. "The Political and/or Politics." *Oxford Literary Review* 36, no. 1 (2014): 5–17.

———. *The Sense of the World.* Trans. Jeffrey Librett. Minneapolis: University of Minnesota Press, 1997.

Negrón, Mara, ed. *Lectures de la différence sexuelle.* Paris: Des femmes, 1994.

Nora, Pierre. "The Era of Commemoration." In *Realms of Memory*, 3:609–37, 702–4. Trans. Arthur Goldhammer. New York: Columbia University Press, 1998.

———. "*L'Histoire de France* de Lavisse." In *Lieux de mémoire*, part 1, 2:317–75. Paris: Gallimard, 1986.

O'Riley, Michael. "Place, Position, and Postcolonial Haunting in Assia Djebar's *La Femme sans sépulture.*" *Research in African Literatures* 35, no. 1 (Spring 2004): 66–86.

———. *Postcolonial Haunting and Victimization: Assia Djebar's New Novels.* New York: Peter Lang, 2007.

Penrod, Lynn. "Algeriance, Exile, and Hélène Cixous." In Kostas Myrsiades and Geetha Ramanathan, eds., *Algeriad. College Literature* 30, no. 1 (Winter 2003): 135–46.

Plato. *The Republic*. Trans. Allan Bloom. New York: Basic Books, 1991.

Pontecorvo, Gillo. *The Battle of Algiers*. Santa Monica, CA: Rhino, 1993.

Rezzoug, Simone. "Ecritures féminines algériennes: Histoire et société." *Maghreb Review* 9, nos. 3–4 (May-August 1984): 86–90.

Rice, Alison. *Polygraphies: Francophone Women Writing Algeria*. Charlottesville: University of Virginia Press, 2012.

———. *Time Signatures: Contextualizing Contemporary Francophone Autobiographical Writing From the Maghreb*. Lanham, MD: Lexington, 2006.

Richter, Elke. "Sur les traces de la trace dans l'oeuvre d'Assia Djebar." In Wolfgang Asholt, Mireille Calle-Gruber, and Dominique Combe, eds., *Assia Djebar: Littérature et transmission*, 245–57. Paris: Presses Sorbonne Nouvelle, 2010.

Rocca, Anna. *Assia Djebar, Le Corps invisible: Voir sans être vue*. Paris: L'Harmattan, 2004.

Roos, Leonard R. "Colonial Culture as Francophone? The Case of Late Nineteenth-century Algeria." In Kamal Salhi, eds., *Francophone post-colonial cultures*, 17–27. Lanham, MD: Lexington, 2003.

Rousseau, Jean-Jacques. *The Confessions and Correspondence*. In *The Collected Writings of Rousseau*, vol. 5. Ed. Christopher Kelly, Roger D. Masters, and Peter G. Stillman. Trans. Christopher Kelly. Hanover, NH: University Press of New England, 1995.

Saadi-Mokrane, Djamila, "The Algerian Linguicide." In *Algeria in Others' Languages*, ed. Anne-Emmanuelle Berger, 44–59. Ithaca: Cornell University Press, 2002.

Saadi, Yacef. *La Bataille d'Alger*. 3 vols. Paris: Publisud, 2002.

Said, Edward. *Orientalism*. New York: Vintage, 1994.

Sanson, Hervé. "Mon père, cet autre: Variations autour de la figure paternelle dans l'oeuvre d'Assia Djebar." In Wolfgang Asholt, Mireille Calle-Gruber, and Dominique Combe, eds., *Assia Djebar, Littérature et transmission*, 317–30. Paris: Presses Sorbonne Nouvelle, 2010.

Sartre, Jean-Paul. "Black Orpheus." In Robert Bernasconi, ed., *Race*, 115–42. Trans. John MacCombie. Oxford: Blackwell, 2001.

Schnapper, Dominique. "Racism and the Radical Condemnation of Modernity." In Christina Howells, ed., *French Women Philosophers: A Contemporary Reader*, 369–84. New York: Routledge, 2000.

Schreier, Joshua. *Arabs of the Jewish Faith: The Civilizing Mission in Colonial Algeria*. New Brunswick, NJ: Rutgers University Press, 2010.

Segal, Charles. "Bard and Audience in Homer." In *Homer's Ancient Readers*, ed. Robert Lamberton and John J. Keaney, 3–29. Princeton: Princeton University Press, 1992.

Segarra, Marta. *Leur Pesant de poudre: Romancières francophones du Maghreb*. Paris: L'Harmattan, 1997.

Sellers, Susan. *Language and Sexual Difference: Feminist Writing in France*. London: Macmillan, 1991.

Senghor, Léopold Sedar. *Le Dialogue des cultures*. Paris: Seuil, 1993.

———. "What Is 'Negritude'?" In *The Idea of Race*, ed. Robert Bernasconi and Tommy L. Lott, 136–38. Indianapolis, IN: Hackett, 2000.

Shiach, Morag. *Hélène Cixous: A Politics of Writing*. London: Routledge, 1991.

Soueif, Ahdaf. "The Language of the Veil." In *Veil: Veiling, Representation and Contemporary Art*, ed. David A. Bailey and Gilane Tawadros, 108–19. Cambridge: MIT Press, 2003.

Stanton, Domna C. "Difference on Trial: A Critique of the Maternal Metaphor in Cixous, Irigaray and Kristeva." In *The Poetics of Gender*, ed. Nancy K. Miller, 157–82. New York: Columbia University Press, 1986.

Stevens, Christa. *L'Ecriture solaire d'Hélène Cixous*. Amsterdam: Rodopi, 1999.

Stora, Benjamin. *La gangrène et l'oubli: la mémoire de la guerre d'Algérie*. Paris: Découverte, 1991.

———. *Histoire de l'Algérie coloniale (1830–1954)*. Paris: Découverte, 1991.

———. *Histoire de l'Algérie depuis l'indépendance*. Paris: Découverte, 1994.

———. *Histoire de la guerre d'Algérie (1954–1962)*. Paris: Découverte, 1995.

———. *Les Trois exils: Juifs d'Algérie*. Paris: Hachette, 2008.

Strand, Dana. "Assia Djebar's *La Femme sans sépulture* as Postcolonial Primer." *Contemporary French and Francophone Studies* 13, no. 3 (June 2009): 339–47.

Taïeb, Jacques. *Etre juif au Maghreb à la veille de la colonisation*. Paris: Albin Michel, 1994.

Tillion, Germaine. *The Republic of Cousins*. Trans. Quintin Hoare. London: Al Saqi, 1983.

Turk, Nada. "*L'Amour la fantasia* d'Assia Djebar: Chronique de guerre, voix des femmes." *CELFAN Review* 7, nos. 1–2 (1987–88): 25–29.

Valensi, Lucette. "The Scheherazade Syndrome: Literature and Politics in Postcolonial Algeria." In Anne-Emmanuelle Berger, ed., *Algeria in Others' Languages*, 139–53. Ithaca, NY: Cornell University Press, 2002.

Varda, Agnès. *Documenteur*. Paris: MK2/Diffusion, 1985.

Weber, Elisabeth. *Questioning Judaism*. Trans. Rachel Bowlby. Stanford: Stanford University Press, 2004.

Weitz, Margaret Collins. "As I Was Then: Women in the French Resistance." *Contemporary French Civilization* 10, no. 1 (Fall/Winter 1986): 1–19.

Ziarek, Ewa Plonowska. *An Ethics of Dissensus: Postmodernity, Feminism, and the Politics of Radical Democracy*. Stanford: Stanford University Press, 2001.

Zimra, Clarisse. "Disorienting the Subject in Djebar's *L'Amour la Fantasia*." *Yale French Studies* 87 (1995): 149–70.

———. "Writing Woman: The Novels of Assia Djebar." *SubStance* 21, no. 3, 69 (1992): 68–84.

Zytnicki, Colette. "Un épisode de la vie politique de la Révolution nationale: l'exclusion des enfants juifs des écoles publiques." In Jean-Jacques Jordi and Guy Pervillé, eds., *Alger 1940–1962: Une ville en guerres*, 62–69. Paris: Autrement, 1999.

Index